The Mind
of
Black Africa

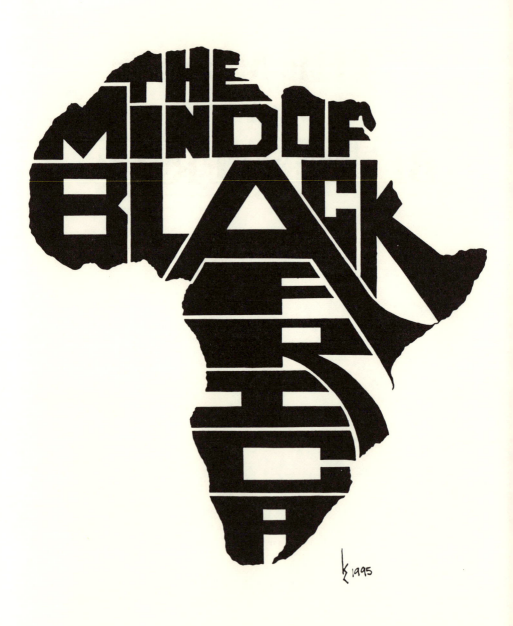

THE MIND
OF
BLACK AFRICA

DICKSON A. MUNGAZI

 PRAEGER

Westport, Connecticut
London

Library of Congress Cataloging-in-Publication Data

Mungazi, Dickson A.
    The mind of Black Africa / Dickson A. Mungazi.
       p. cm.
    Includes bibliographical references and index.
    ISBN 0–275–95260–6 (alk. paper). — ISBN 0–275–95429–3 (pbk. :
alk. paper)
      1. Decolonization—Africa, Sub-Saharan. 2. Africa, Sub-Saharan—
Civilization. 3. Self-perception—Africa, Sub-Saharan. I. Title.
  DT30.5.M86   1996
  960.3—dc20   95–34094

British Library Cataloguing in Publication Data is available.

Library of Congress Catalog Card Number: 95–34094
ISBN: 0–275–95260–6
     0–275–95429–3 (pbk.)

First published in 1996

Praeger Publishers, 88 Post Road West, Westport, CT 06881
An imprint of Greenwood Publishing Group, Inc.

Printed in the United States of America

♾™

The paper used in this book complies with the
Permanent Paper Standard issued by the National
Information Standards Organization (Z39.48–1984).

10 9 8 7 6 5 4 3 2 1

To the memory of my uncle, Rindai Elias Chimonyo,
whose pride in the accomplishments of his
children was inspirational

One of the great tragedies of colonialism in Africa is that the white man never came to know the mind of the African.

An elderly African, August 14, 1989

A mind all logic is like a knife all blade. It makes the hand bleed that uses it.

Rabindranath Tagore, 1916

Contents

Preface

The colonization of Africa by European nations in the nineteenth century had a profoundly negative impact on the lives of Africans. One form of this impact was the violent manner in which European nations subjected Africa to colonial rule. The colonization of Africa was a result of the negative perceptions that Enlightenment Europe formed about the intellect of the Africans. As colonization was imposed, the colonial systems sought to control the African mind in order to control African behavior.

A critical issue in this study is the serious cultural conflict between the European perceptions of the African mind and the African perceptions of it. This cultural conflict led to political conflict in the twentieth century. In this study, the terms *the African mind, the mind of black Africa*, and *the African* carry the same general meaning. That the African perceptions of the African mind and the European perceptions of it could not be reconciled was mainly a result of differences in culture. It was also a manifestation of the so-called scientific enthusiasm of the Enlightenment.

ORGANIZATION OF THE STUDY: PHASES IN THE DRAMA OF THE AFRICAN MIND

Beginning with the Enlightenment, four phases marked the drama of the African mind. During the first phase, leading figures in the Enlightenment formed unsubstantiated opinions and conclusions about the lack of intellectual potential among Africans. The conclusion that the cranial cavity of the Africans was smaller than that of Europeans led to the corresponding conclusion that their intellectual capacity was also less than that of Europeans. This latter conclusion led to a further assumption that the only way the Africans could improve their intellectual potential was to submit to European influence.

In the second phase, the opinions that Europeans formed about the so-called lack of intellectual potential among the Africans became the basis for justifying the colonization of Africa upon the adjournment of the Berlin Conference in February 1885. The need for raw materials among Europeans required the formulation of colonial policies that led to inevitable conflict between the Africans and the colonial governments. The belief that colonial systems would last at least a thousand years "justified" atrocities and political violence against the Africans. The discontent sown in the African mind by this violence quickly took root following the inception of the colonial systems.

While the colonial governments designed strategies for controlling the African mind to serve their own political and economic interests, the Africans themselves formulated an effective strategy to ensure their survival. This strategy allowed them to initiate a process for restoring their mind. This period witnessed the development of a phenomenon that theoreticians call "the culture of poverty," or "the culture of ignorance," among Europeans. This phenomenon was heavily influenced by the erroneous belief that, because the Africans lacked intellect, they did not have anything positive to contribute to human interactions.

In this setting, Europeans lost an opportunity to know the mind of the Africans. This culture of ignorance had its origins in the Enlightenment itself. This period, also known as the Age of Reason, became the age of ignorance among Europeans. Recognizing that the colonial governments were victims of the culture of ignorance, the Africans discerned that they were vulnerable to a concerted effort to bring about an end to colonization. By the time the colonial governments acknowledged the error of their perceptions about the African mind, it was too late. The Africans had gained an upper hand in the struggle for the restoration of their own minds.

This leads to the third phase, the rise of the African mind and the struggle for political independence following the end of the Second World War. Tragic as it was, the war gave the Africans a new opportunity to study the mind of the white man in relationship to his thought process and behavior toward them. To their amazement the Africans discovered that, indeed, while the whites had many positive attributes, they also had serious shortcomings.

The Africans concluded that contrary to what the colonial system would have the Africans believe, the whites were not perfect. They saw for themselves the misery and the suffering that the vast majority of people in Europe endured. They also concluded that the Industrial Revolution of the nineteenth century had helped improve conditions for some people, but had left many more in the dark shadows of a social utopia and economic millennium dreamed about but never realized.

Above all else, the Africans realized that the character of European social institutions was dictated by the summative political behavior of individuals, with no single individual possessing all knowledge about human conditions and political realities. Winston Churchill, Clement Attlee, Charles de Gaulle, and Antonio Salazar were not Edmund Burke, Julius Caesar, Thomas Hobbes, and Machiavelli reincarnate. They were human beings who exhibited simple, ordinary, and somewhat questionable political astuteness and personal character.

Yet, these were the leaders of European nations that had vast colonial empires in Africa. What was the basis of their claim that the white man's intellect was superior to that of the African if they themselves manifested questionable political savvy? What was the justification of their conclusion that the Africans would benefit from colonialism if the social institutions they led in Europe were marred by gross social malaise and decay? What was the origin of their belief that the African culture was primitive if their own societies were riddled with crime, squalor, and poverty?

If the political philosophy and cultural values of these European leaders were adopted as a new *modus vivendi*, where would they lead Africa? Clear answers to these questions began to emerge out of the reality that the African mind now encountered. It was time for the African intellect to restore itself and assume its legitimate place in a world in which human conflict and want could be mitigated by a concerted effort to create conditions better than those created by colonialism.

The Africans' conclusion about the limitations of the colonial society transformed itself into action that stemmed from high-order cognitive processes that were uniquely African. This the colonial governments could not understand and control. The African mind was now aware that, in terms of political thought process and action, it was capable of competing with the colonists. In this context the cards were on the table.

The colonial mind and the African mind were not ready to engage in a game of wills until after the Second World War when the stakes became much higher than they had been in the past. The wind of change formed a breeze that turned into a nationalistic storm; this storm helped the African mind chart a new course toward self-determination and independence. It also defeated the ill-conceived game plan of the colonial officials. The days of colonial domination over the African mind were numbered; the dawn of its awareness heralded the daybreak of a new order.

POLITICAL INDEPENDENCE AND BETRAYAL OF THE AFRICAN MIND

Ghana's independence in 1957 represented that daybreak, and the African mind would never be the same again as it now entered a new phase. By 1968, when most colonies in Africa had achieved political independence, the African mind would look to the future with great expectations, totally unaware of its own impending betrayal. This development suggests the fourth phase in the drama of the African mind. This phase started out as the best of times, full of hope and renewal. It quite possibly could end as one of the worst chapters in the history of Africa and become known as the "era of betrayal of the African mind."

Caught in the midst of the great excitement for independence and the call to demonstrate national manhood, African politicians and military establishments were led into deadly combat. This struggle for power to impose their own will on the people emerged out of the conditions created by the colonial governments. African leaders completely discarded the basis of their original dynamic and vibrant society, and failed to uphold democratic values. The role of the people in shaping the character of their new society was ignored. One by one, the newly independent countries of Africa fell victims to the actions of new African elite groups as they instituted new forms of dictatorship that were even more offensive and oppressive than the colonial systems they had replaced.

The attainment of political independence never gave the African mind a chance to envisage itself, to demonstrate its capability to revive the dying aspirations of people struggling for development. Africa's brightest hope and star—Kwame Nkrumah—fell victim to the power that he possessed. By resorting to dictatorial methods, Nkrumah turned the hopes and dreams of his people into an abyss of despair. The conflict between practices of the past and values of the present was cast in the shadows of a milieu that paralyzed the hopes of the people for a better future. The days of S. T. von Soemmering and Charles White, of Cecil John Rhodes and Godfrey Huggins, and of Walter Coutts and Philip Mitchell were being revisited in painful ways.

The fourth phase of this tragic dramatic development was the continent's virulent one-party and one-man rule, which began to corrode the great potential of the people. As soon as their countries achieved political independence, these African elite groups moved quickly to assert themselves as the new order.

Kwame Nkrumah, Kamuzu Hastings Banda, Kenneth Kaunda, Jean-Bedel Bokassa, Mobutu Sese Seko, Milton Obote, Idi Amin Dada—all became ruthless dictators in an era of great expectations. The opportunity for the African mind to shape new directions for itself by democratic means for national and continental development was lost. The African nationalist heroes who had championed the cause of their own people now turned to oppress them—a sad irony, a sinister turn of events, and the ultimate betrayal of the African mind.

THE MIND OF BLACK AFRICA AND THE FUTURE: CONCLUSION

What, then, does the future hold for the African mind? The avalanche of demand in 1990 for the end of corruption, which has gone hand in hand with African one-party rule and dictatorships, suggests that Africa's salvation lies in the action of the people themselves. Unless the people take it upon themselves to restore their rights, which have been so flagrantly violated by the self-seeking elitists, those in positions of power will continue to plunder their nations. They will rob the people of the most valued national resources they possess—their minds. Without these minds, which are urgently needed to place their countries on the road to development as an outcome of restoring the mind of the Africans, the destiny of Africa is questionable.

The defeat of Kenneth Kaunda of Zambia in the presidential elections in 1991 and of Hastings Banda of Malawi in 1994 was the best thing that happened to those countries since independence in October 1964. The outcry of the people for democratic rule in 1990 forced Kaunda to face the music and to agree to hold free elections under a multiparty system. The extent of the atrocities committed by Hastings Banda from 1964 to 1994 came to light at the end of 1994 when a commission of inquiry reported that four men who had opposed Banda were killed in cold blood in May 1983 by Banda's orders. For Banda to be brought to trial was a cold comfort to the nation that he left in disarray following mismanagement of thirty years.

These developments indicate that the Africans are determined to restore democracy. Today Zambia and Malawi have an opportunity to reinstitute true democracy and shape their social institutions accordingly. Indeed, the greatest recent event in Africa took place in South Africa in April 1994 when Nelson Mandela was elected president. Under these conditions, the mind of black Africa is poised for a new era of greatness.

The people of Zambia, Malawi, and South Africa, and, indeed, all of Africa, must never allow dictatorship to appear again. The Africans must now demonstrate their unwillingness to compromise with principles that erode the quality of their minds. Their mission is to restore the mind of black Africa. The challenge is great, but it must be met, for failure in this mission will mean continental disaster.

Acknowledgments

In the process of writing a book that covers a period of turbulent history in a troubled continent and the problems of its people one becomes indebted to many individuals and organizations. The author wishes to express his profound gratitude to the various African embassies in the United States and the various ministries in Africa for responding to his request for materials and furnishing responses to his questionnaires.

The author also wishes to thank his colleagues at Northern Arizona University: John W. Bloom, Robert E. Holloway, L. Kay Walker, David Williams, and Neil Kunze for encouragement and support. L. Kay Walker spent some years in Africa as a Peace Corps volunteer and so came to know Africans well. The frontispiece that appears in this book was her inspiration. The study began to take form as a result of informal discussions the author held with John W. Bloom, Robert E. Holloway, and L. Kay Walker, who, in advising African students over a period of time, have gained some valuable insights into the mind of black Africa. L. Kay Walker, Robert E. Holloway, and the author share common interests in the influence of culture and history on society. The author also wishes to thank many individuals who participated in the interview process during the two research trips he made to Africa in 1994.

In addition, the author wishes to thank members of the National Social Science Association and Association of Third World Studies for their interest in the study and for the valuable criticism offered while he was presenting papers at professional conferences in the United States from 1989 to 1995. His special appreciation goes to Debrah K. Hawthorne of the

Office of Research and Development in the Center for Excellence in Education at Northern Arizona University for typing parts of the manuscript; and to Jeannette Weatherby, supervisor in the Faculty Service Office, for her assistance in producing the manuscript.

Special gratitude is extended to Betty Russell and Ed Bulinski, both of the Personnel Office in the Center for Excellence in Education, for their programming assistance; to the National Library of Jamaica for sending valuable information on Edward Long; and to Linda Gregonis, indexer and proofreader.

Introduction

THE HUMAN MIND IN PERSPECTIVE

Reading Wilbur Joseph Cash's *The Mind of the South* (1941) and Allister Sparks's *The Mind of South Africa* (1990) led directly to this author's interest in the mind of black Africa. Similarities in their treatment of the general subject of the human mind and the author's own approach are interesting when viewed from two perspectives. The first is that the study of the human mind is a fascinating subject when considered from the standpoint of the action emanating from human cognition. The second perspective is that to study the human mind is to study both the character and behavior of the human species.

These two perspectives help to pose a fundamental question: What is the basis of human cognition? Although psychologists have wrestled with this question, there has not been a definitive explanation of why people behave differently under similar circumstances. Why, for example, do twin brothers, coming from the same environment, develop totally different personalities, with one becoming a model citizen and the other a criminal?

This study, however, is not an attempt to write a book on the psychology of the African. Rather, it is an effort to discuss the various implications of the mind of black Africa within the context of European and African perceptions based on historical and contemporary settings. Cash, Sparks, and the author have one thing in common: we seek to place human cognition within the confines of human behavior. But while Cash and Sparks focus on the dynamics of political ideology and survival strategies in a rapidly changing social environment, in this study the author attempts to go beyond their level of analysis.

From the time that Swedish sociologist Gunnar Myrdal published *An American Dilemma* in 1940 to the time that the Nationalist government of South Africa introduced the notorious racial policy of apartheid (a time simultaneous with the publication of Alan Paton's *Cry the Beloved Country* in 1948), the minds of black America and of black Africa went through a period of crisis. In both the United States and South Africa, the cognitive capacity of the black people was a subject for contempt and derision.

In this regard, *The Mind of the South* and *The Mind of South Africa* cover tragic social systems whose designers regarded some people as superior human beings and others as inferior or less than human. The social stigma that both countries applied would not be eliminated for years, although in various ways, since Emancipation, the United States has tried to correct the social problems created by racist thinking.

When Myrdal discussed the American dilemma as arising from the conflict between idealism and practice, he was recognizing the cruelty of the struggle between the white mind and the black mind. The white mind and the black mind perceived the structure of the American society from two opposing points of view. This suggests the elusiveness of the human mind itself. This conflict of perception translated into social conflict of major proportions, posing fundamental questions as to what organized society should be about. Both the United States and South Africa have experienced social conflict in a way that has threatened to disintegrate both nations.

This is why in 1990 the government of South Africa and the African National Congress led by Nelson Mandela made a gallant effort to search their own minds to put their society back on track. Both perspectives recognized that apartheid was destroying the country's most valued re-sources and thereby threatening not only its survival, but also its progress. This study traces the agony that apartheid has created for all the people of South Africa and how it inhibited the mind of its people from thinking rationally. When a solution was at last found in the elections held in April 1994, a fascinating facet of the study of the human mind, especially of the African mind, was presented.

PHASES OF THE DRAMA OF THE AFRICAN MIND

In discussing the drama of the African mind, we must seek answers to the following questions: Why was the mind of black Africa a subject of study by Europeans of the Enlightenment? When did interest among Euro-peans in studying the mind of black Africa begin? What factors influenced this interest? Exactly what did the studies conducted by Europeans reveal as to the character of the African mind? Who were some of the leading European individuals who tried to understand the mind of black Africa? What methods did these individuals utilize to conduct their studies? What influence did the conclusions reached by these studies have on human relationships?

In order to provide adequate answers to these questions, this study is divided into four basic phases that form the drama of the African mind: (1) The Influence of the Enlightenment, (2) The Colonization of the African Mind, (3) The Rise of the African Mind and the Struggle for Self, and (4) Independence and the Betrayal of the African Mind.

THE FIRST PHASE: THE INFLUENCE OF
THE ENLIGHTENMENT

This study focuses on the drama of the African mind during these four phases, and in order to do so it is necessary to review events that began in the eighteenth century, the so-called Age of Reason, or the Enlightenment. During the Enlightenment Europeans discarded traditions that had influenced daily life for hundreds of years. The influence of the church and religion was slowly being replaced by the emergence of new practices that suggested that man was now the master of his own destiny and that, while religion played an important role in the life of the people, the application of logic and reason brought social institutions and human cognition to the fore. Nothing was greater than the thought that human reason and logic, when properly applied, could resolve problems of human existence and lead to the ultimate salvation of the human race.

One major component of the Enlightenment was the emphasis placed on the idea of the scientific approach to human and social problems. The human mind possessed an untapped potential that could lead to greatness. Leading figures of the Enlightenment advocated the promotion of education in order to elevate the human mind to a new and higher level so that its utilization could be the basis of the advancement of society. Education was necessary because the advancement of society could not be ensured without the advancement of the individual.

In seeking education to promote the progression of society, and by ensuring the development of the individual, the leading figures of the Enlightenment placed their confidence in human intellectual potential. Their basic assumption was that every human being was born with intellectual potential that must be refined through education for the benefit of society. This line of thinking, however, was not shared by all leading figures of the Enlightenment, and this study presents the reasons why.

As the people of the Enlightenment began to place their confidence in human intellectual potential instead of in religious values and practices, two groups of thinkers began to exert new influence on the question of human intellectual potential. The first group consisted of individuals like Thomas Jefferson (1743–1826), Jean-Jacques Rousseau (1712–1778), Johann Pestalozzi (1746–1827), Friedrich Froebel (1782–1852), and Johan Herbert (1776–1841). These individuals shared three philosophical beliefs: (1) that the human mind, in its universal definition, is capable of reaching its highest potential when certain conditions are present, such as a nurturing environment, culture, and support systems; (2) that the best way to develop that mind is through education and interactions between people that are based on mutual trust; and (3) that because the environment is crucial to the development of the human mind, society has a responsibility to seek its improvement as a necessary condition for its own progression.

These three philosophical beliefs led to three conclusions. The first was that because society was the ultimate beneficiary of the human mind, educational opportunity must be available to all people on the basis of equality. Jefferson so strongly believed in this line of thinking that he argued, "Enlighten the people and the tyranny and oppression of body and mind will vanish like evil spirits at the dawn of day. I know of no safe depository of the ultimate powers of the society but the people themselves, and if we think them not enlightened enough to exercise their control with a wholesome discretion, the remedy is not to take it from them but to inform their discretion."[1]

The second conclusion was that the best interests of society could be served only if discriminatory practices, prejudice, and bias were eliminated in all areas of human relationships and endeavor. The third was that since the environment played a critical role in the development of the human mind, society had a duty to provide a good environment so that development of the human mind could take place in order to promote the enhancement of society. It was acknowledged that without utilizing every aspect of human intellect, society would continue to endure the agony of underdevelopment, both in the collective and individual realms.

The second group of thinkers consisted of individuals that included S. T. von Soemmering of Prussia and Charles White of Britain. Both men—and the increasing number of their disciples and supporters—promoted the belief that some people possessed more intellectual potential than others depending on their hereditary traits. The individuals in this group concluded that people are born either with intellectual ability or without it and that environmental factors have nothing to do with its development. The individuals who subscribed to this school of thought concluded that intellectual ability was determined by race. Both von Soemmering and White argued that of the four major human races—white, yellow, brown, and black—the white race possessed the most intellectual ability and the black race the least.

According to von Soemmering and White, the black race was perpetually condemned, as descendants of the son of Ham, by its heredity. There was nothing that its members could do to improve its mind to reach a level of ability equal to that of the white race. The best that the black race could do, according to von Soemmering and White, was to accept its destiny and live within a social environment that designated for it a position inferior to that of other races.

Von Soemmering and White concluded that the other two races, the yellow and brown, possessed more intellectual ability than the black race but were still far inferior to the white. One does not have to do much reading to realize that, although this controversy about human intellectual potential and race was articulated over two hundred years ago, it still remains an emotionally charged subject to debate among researchers to this very day.

In an effort to substantiate their theory of the intellectual inferiority of the black race, both von Soemmering and White decided to conduct what later proved to be a pseudoscientific investigation. In 1785 von Soemmering published an essay that made him an instant celebrity because he concluded from the study of a single Egyptian skull that the cranial capacity of Africans was smaller than that of Europeans, surmising that the Africans in general possessed less intellectual capacity as well.

Ten years later, when Charles White reached the same conclusion, Enlightenment research enthusiasts were quick to conclude that the Africans were decidedly inferior to the white man intellectually. By the end of the eighteenth century, a popular belief gathered momentum, became a myth, and was rapidly accepted as fact. Both von Soemmering and White had a profound influence on the formation of attitudes and perceptions among Europeans toward the intellectual potential of the Africans.

But if von Soemmering and White thought they had a legitimate claim to exclusive knowledge about the intellectual potential of the Africans, they soon learned that not all Enlightenment research enthusiasts shared their perceptions. In 1803 Thomas Winterbottom, a British medical missionary who had spent more time among the Africans than any other researcher of his time, published an essay, *An Account of the Native Africans*, in which he disputed von Soemmering's and White's conclusions about the intellectual capability of the Africans.

Winterbottom concluded that there was no difference between the intellectual capacity of Europeans and Africans, and he thereby set in motion a dispute that continues today. Winterbottom was most convincing when he argued that von Soemmering and White fabricated evidence in their investigation in order to support their prejudice against the black race. He also noted that the environment in which the Africans lived was below the standard of the Europeans.

This study examines in some detail the various implications of the von Soemmering–White school of thought—as opposed to that of Winterbottom and his supporters—on the mind of black Africa. As the Enlightenment gave way to the nineteenth century, two questions had not been resolved. Do the Africans possess an intellectual prowess equal to that of Europeans? Does the environment play a role in the development of human intellect? That no definitive answers were forthcoming compounded the problems of human interactions when European nations colonized Africa.

THE SECOND PHASE: THE COLONIZATION OF THE AFRICAN MIND

The difference of perception between von Soemmering, White and their followers, and Winterbottom and his supporters regarding the intellectual potential of the Africans took a strange and dramatic twist by the mid-nineteenth century. During this time, the promotion of European economic interests in Africa was motivated by the Industrial Revolution. The knowledge that Africa contained large quantities of raw materials needed to improve the standard of living in Europe influenced the thinking of social enthusiasts. The support for the Winterbottom position waned as the von Soemmering–White view became the predominant one. The interest of European nations in colonizing Africa strengthened the myth that had started during the Enlightenment.

The reality generated by this situation is that the mind of black Africa was subjected to a new form of degradation by European colonial enthusiasts. The publication in 1859 of Charles Darwin's *Origin of Species* and of Charles Dickens's *A Tale of Two Cities* provided new ammunition for the von Soemmering–White forces as they now braced themselves for the battle to subjugate the African mind. Dickens's concept of the best of times and Darwin's view of the survival of the fittest were utilized to strengthen the belief among colonial enthusiasts that Europeans had never had it so good regarding their strategy for dominance of the presumed intellectually weak African mind.

When Darwin published his *The Descent of Man* in 1871, colonial enthusiasts hailed it as a blueprint of their opinion that the people of the "Dark Continent" lacked intellectual potential. It did not worry these colonial enthusiasts that they were reading into Darwin's ideas and meaning that he never intended. What was important was the effect. They were exploiting his ideas to promote their own political agenda. It was open season for European nations in Africa.

By the time the Berlin Conference was convened at the end of 1884 to map out the colonization of Africa, the African mind had been reduced to a level where European nations could manipulate it in a way that served their own political and economic purposes. The brutality and the lack of concern for the Africans' welfare became the behavioral norm of colonial entrepreneurs. The closing of the African mind was now under way. The contest of the survival of the intellectually fittest began in earnest. It was a deadly form of combat between two paradigms, that of the oppressor and that of the oppressed.

For European colonial adventurers the best of times were here, and nothing would be allowed to stand between them and the goals they had set. To them it was to know that the vast resources in Africa, including its people, were at their disposal. The African mind was presumed to be unaware of what was happening. This miscalculation would later cost the colonial governments dearly.

As the colonization of Africa became an accomplished fact, the colonial systems designed policies to govern their African empires in accordance with the specifications of the Berlin Conference and their own colonial principles and policies. By the beginning of the First World War, only three countries were politically independent. The first of these was Liberia, which was founded in 1817 by the American Colonization Society as a haven for freed slaves from the United States. It is ironic that in 1990 Liberia subjected itself to a brutal betrayal of the African mind in the form of a cruel civil war that left it devastated.

The second independent African country in 1914 was Ethiopia, which claimed its independence from biblical times. It is equally a tragic fact that in 1974 Ethiopia endured the agony of the betrayal of its own mind by deposing Emperor Haile Selassie and installing a Marxist regime led by Mariam Mangisto who was so oppressive that he was turned out of office in 1990. The civil war that had been raging for years over Eritrea's claim of independence from Ethiopia reached a decisive stage when the Mangisto regime was removed from power. But the end of the civil war did not result in the restoration of the African mind, and an all too familiar pattern in Africa was being strengthened.

The third politically independent country in Africa by 1914 was South Africa, the land of the infamous policy of apartheid. South Africa had gained independence in 1910 following a bitter war with Britain in which the Boers were slaughtered. The introduction of apartheid was intended to ensure full control of the African mind. But, again in 1990, South Africa paid the price of trying to sustain a political and social system that left a trail of racial bitterness unparalleled by that of any other country of Africa. Chapter 5 of this study begins with a discussion of some theoretical considerations that may help us understand apartheid as a principal cause of the agony of South Africa. However, the international community refused to admit South Africa to the inner circle of the international order until after the elections held in April 1994.

The three countries that gained independence in Africa prior to 1914 illustrate that the gaining of political independence set the stage for the betrayal of the African mind regardless of whether independence was achieved by a white-ruled or an African-ruled government. That African countries used the attainment of independence to betray the mind of their own people is a great tragedy and forms a large part of this study.

During the height of the colonial systems, from 1885 to 1914 and from 1919 to 1939, the colonial governments formulated policies that can best be understood in the context of their effort to control the thinking and behavior of the indigenous people of Africa. For example, Germany formulated the policy of *Deutsche Kolonialbund*, France and Belgium introduced the policy of *evalue*, Britain developed a policy known as *indirect rule*, and Portugal had a policy known as *Estado Novo*. The Boers had a policy known as *apartheid*. In addition to seeking full control of African behavior through control of the African mind, these policies had two other components in common.

The first component was to instill in the African mind an attitude or self-concept that it was inferior to the white mind. The myth that had been fabricated during the days of von Soemmering and White was being relived in the African psyche in painful ways. But for the colonial governments it was "happy days are here again." The second component was that at no time would the African mind ever be able to achieve equal status with the white mind.

During this time, new spokesmen for the myth of the superiority of the white race began to exert new influences in a new social order in which the African mind was reduced to the level of bare existence. These included James Hunt, president of the London Anthropological Society; Wynwood Read, a popular and influential member of the society known better for his emotional support of the myth of black intellectual inferiority than for any claim to scholarly ability; Cecil John Rhodes, Read's protégé; and Godfrey Huggins, Rhodes's disciple. All came forward to strengthen a myth that had its origins during the Enlightenment. It is the thinking of these men that the colonial adventure rested on and formed a foundation on which to build the best of times for the white mind.

To strengthen their hold on their African empires, the colonial governments enacted laws that left no room for doubt as to the place of the African mind in the colonial society. As Ethel Tawse Jollie, one of the first women to sit in a colonial legislature, put it bluntly in 1927, the purpose of colonial policy was to strengthen the position of whites and weaken that of the Africans. Nothing else mattered. Severe penalties were meted out to those Africans who dared question the subjection of the African mind. Thus began a period that theoreticians have appropriately called "the colonial culture of violence."

The Africans provided the labor to produce the materials that would enhance the standard of living in Europe—and labor was the only function. The control of the African mind was now complete, and the colonial establishments looked to the future as a social utopia with great expectations. Once the control of the African mind was fully established, the colonial governments did not worry about African behavior. They believed it had been broken and tamed like a horse and was controlled by the bridle of psychological conditioning. This is what Huggins had in mind when he argued in 1954 that the policy of his government in colonial Zimbabwe was designed to promote partnership between the Africans and the whites, the kind of partnership Huggins said exists between the horse and the rider.

THE THIRD PHASE: THE RISE OF THE AFRICAN MIND AND THE STRUGGLE FOR SELF

In 1939 the hope that the colonial governments had expressed at their inception following the conclusion of the Berlin Conference in 1885—that they would last at least a millennium—was revived. But this hope was shattered by events in Europe, not in Africa. The outbreak of the war in September 1939 permanently altered the course of events in Africa, as well as the rest of the world, and changed the relationships that the colonial governments had established with the Africans. The rise of Adolf Hitler and his Third Reich was a phenomenon whose impact was profoundly felt on the African continent in ways far more serious than the European nations could imagine.

Having invaded Poland and paralyzed France and the Lowlands in rapid succession, Nazi forces launched a relentless blitz on Britain in an effort to force it to sue for peace on Hitler's terms. By 1941 the Nazi forces were within striking distance of bringing Britain to its knees. This was the second stage of Hitler's objective of bringing the entire world under his rule. Winston Churchill, the beleaguered British leader who had succeeded Prime Minister Neville Chamberlain, who died suddenly in 1940, felt that Britain was fighting the battle for democracy alone and requested the support of the United States in the war against the Axis powers.

On August 14, 1941, still feeling the pressure to do something dramatic to turn the war around in favor of the Allies, Churchill and President Franklin Roosevelt met secretly and issued the famous Atlantic Charter. This human rights proclamation stated that their governments respected the right of all people to choose the form of government under which they would live and that they wished to see sovereign rights and self-determination restored to those who had been forcibly deprived of them.

With this statement the Allied nations that had colonies in Africa began a vigorous campaign to recruit Africans into the ranks of their armed forces, promising improved conditions of life as a reward for their effort to defeat the Axis powers. The Africans could not believe what they were hearing in both the Atlantic Charter and the recruitment campaign. They regarded both as a solemn vow of self-determination. Although the war was not of their making, the Africans responded enthusiastically. Some joined the colonial armies out of a desire to see Europe; others did so from curiosity.

Then, there were those who did so to gain for themselves the respect of the white man. The Africans' decision to join the colonial forces against the Axis powers raised a profound question: Did the colonial governments now think that the Africans had a mind that could be utilized to eliminate the threat of Nazi domination? There was no point in the Africans trying to find an answer to the question in the climate of the war, but as soon as the conflict was over in 1945, the colonial governments could no longer avoid the question because it was foremost in the mind of the Africans.

As soon as the war was over and the threat of Nazi domination was eliminated, the Africans turned their attention to the restoration of their mind in accordance with the pledge made in the Atlantic Charter and the promise of improved living conditions made by the colonial governments. The days of S. T. von Soemmering and Charles White were gone forever and could not be relived (until, that is, after the Africans had gained independence and their own leaders resurrected oppression). The African mind had at last come of age; the genie was out of the bottle and could not be put back in.

While in war service, the Africans learned as much as they could about life in Europe and came to two basic conclusions. The first was that the white man had both positive attributes and negative features, and the second was that contrary to his claim of intellectual superiority, the white man had nothing more than a political strategy to subject Africans to oppressive conditions.

The African mind needed to regain its self-respect. Meeting in London to design a strategy for action to restore their mind, Africans realized that the war had impacted on their thinking in ways that the colonial governments could not expect to understand. Once they put that strategy in place, the Africans were determined to put it into effect and expected to see the results they had anticipated. First, they demanded an improvement in the conditions of their lives as promised by the Atlantic Charter.

When the colonial governments declined to initiate that improvement, the Africans decided to adopt the next phase of that strategy and to demand political independence. They knew that they risked imprisonment and death in adopting a strategy of confrontation with the colonial governments. The colonial culture of violence now found both expression and a target in the Africans' demand for social change and justice.

Twelve years following the end of the war, the Africans scored a resounding victory in their struggle against the colonial governments. The strategy of survival they had learned during the height of colonization and during the war now found an appropriate forum in confronting the colonial powers. Ghana's attainment of independence in 1957 signaled a spiraling series of events that finally led to the restoration of the African mind. Kwame Nkrumah, Jomo Kenyatta, Milton Margai, Albert Luthuli, Joshua Nkomo, Patrice Lumumba, Eduardo Mondlane, and so on, became undisputed leaders in a new phenomenon of the rising African mind. Indeed, Ghana's independence triggered developments that led to the untimely collapse of the colonial empires in Africa, well short of the thousand years that some colonial enthusiasts, such as Cecil John Rhodes and others, had predicted as their minimum duration.

In 1991 the Africans knew that only the Afrikaners of South Africa were still trying to mislead the African mind. This was why an intense struggle arose between them and their colonizers. By 1994 the Afrikaners were well advised to listen to the voice of reason and to realize that they were fighting a losing battle. Previously, they had failed to realize that no colonial power, no matter how oppressive and brutal, could win a struggle against the mind of the colonized once it had decided to restore itself. It is not surprising that with the independence of Namibia in 1990, following seventy years of brutal rule by the Afrikaners, South Africa now stood alone as the only colonial power on the continent. The elections held in April 1994 finally put an end to this political grandstand.

THE FOURTH PHASE: POLITICAL INDEPENDENCE
AND BETRAYAL OF THE AFRICAN MIND

Without question, the achievement of political independence in Africa epitomizes the highest level to date of the prowess of the African mind. Nowhere in human history did colonialism last so short a time as it did in Africa. This was not because of the goodwill of the colonial governments, but because of the Africans' determination to reclaim its rightful place. But the euphoria with which the Africans celebrated independence quickly gave way to the Tower of Babel phenomenon. The unity of purpose that had brought the Africans together to struggle for independence quickly ended in an intense struggle for personal power. The interests of countries were replaced by the interests of politicians.

This betrayal of the African mind has been one of the great tragedies in human history. This tragedy is evident in two forms. The first is that the African politicians have denied their people an opportunity to participate in the events of their countries in meaningful ways because they have reinstituted either one-man dictatorship or one-party regimes that care little for the welfare of their people. One after another, the African leaders have turned their backs on the people whom they serve. On assuming office, the African leaders have quickly instituted ruthless forms of one-man dictator-ships that have robbed their people of their legitimate right to a democratic system of government and raped them of the self-determination for which they struggled.

The second form of the betrayal of the African mind has been the violent military coups that have swept across the continent with impunity. More vicious and more brutal than colonial regimes, the military regimes show neither sensitivity to the needs of the people nor any ability to restore their countries' political stability and democracy. Jerry Rawlings, Idi Amin Dada, Mobutu Sese Seko, Ibrahim Babangida, Olusegun Obasanjo—all have reduced their countries to a state of desperation. No military leader in Africa has risen to a position of benevolent dictator, envisaging the well-being of the people and the country. Instead, they loot their countries, deposit their immoral take in Swiss banks, and callously leave their suffering people to languish in abject poverty, their countries in economic ruin.

The problems Africans are facing as a result of the betrayal by their politicians and military warlords go far beyond the phrase "Dark Conti-nent." As a consequence, Africa lacks an effective voice in international matters and holds no credibility in the emerging global economy. In addition Africa will remain in a state of underdevelopment. Africa remains in a weak position to promote the development of its people and is the subject of ridicule by other countries because its nations cannot effectively run their own affairs. Poverty, mass starvation, and political conflict have remained the hallmark of a continent in trouble.

Some individuals in the West do not appear to understand the seriousness of Africa's situation. For example, Davidson Nicol of the International Studies Department at Cambridge University argued in the *Los Angeles Times* in October 1991 that Africa could play an important role in international affairs. While this is true, Nicol and like individuals seem to ignore a crucial fact about Africa: that is, no leader of any nation can play an important role in international affairs unless he can play an effective role in the affairs of his own country.

Besides Nelson Mandela, who is new to the political leadership of the continent and whose influence has not yet been tested, no leader in Africa at the present time can play such a role because most of these leaders impose their will on the people. Mandela is still too preoccupied with the problems of South Africa to devote much attention to the problems of the continent.

The ruling Zimbabwe African National Union's (ZANU) announcement in Zimbabwe in June 1994 that it would initiate a door-to-door campaign to recruit new members triggered a wave of protest and criticism throughout Zimbabwe because of past abuses. Although President Robert Mugabe reportedly possesses the integrity required for national leadership, some members of his party and government in their enthusiasm to promote the political interests of their party have failed to recognize the basic principles of democracy. This has had the obvious effect of tarnishing Mugabe himself.

The betrayal of the African mind by the politicians and the military will not end any time soon unless the people themselves demand it. It is hoped, however, that the end of apartheid in South Africa and the beginning of democracy in 1994 will set an example that other countries of Africa will follow.

CONCLUSION: A CALL TO ACTION

The reader should keep these four phases in mind throughout the study. In this way, the reader will discover that the African mind has moved from being a victim of perceptions of the Age of Reason and subsequent colonization to being a victim of its own betrayal following the attainment of political independence. In order to avoid any misunderstanding, two points should be made clear.

The first point is not that political independence was a bad thing for Africa. On the contrary, political independence was a necessary condition for human advancement and national development. However, the attainment of political independence should never have been used to betray the African mind by replacing one form of dictatorship, colonial, with another, African.

The second point is that Africans must summon their willpower to unite and end the betrayal of their mind once and for all. The social malaise, the economic ruin their countries have endured, the political grandstanding by the African politicians, and the callous behavior of military regimes have all combined to form a continental cancer that has been destroying the vital tissue of the people. The author strongly believes in the collective wisdom of the African people, and in the last chapter of the study some strategies for healing the African mind are put forth.

The African mind would be well to take the advice of Thomas Jefferson, that the survival of a nation rests squarely on the eternal vigilance of the citizens. The elections in Malawi and South Africa in 1994 would appear to support the need to exercise this vigilance. Unless the Africans act in a manner that will restore their rights, their nations will continue to disintegrate at the hands of corrupt politicians and military regimes. The author hopes that the reader will gain from these pages an understanding of the mind of black Africa.

NOTE

1. John Bartlett, *Familiar Quotations*, 4th ed. (Boston: Little, Brown and Co. 1968), p. 473.

The Mind
of
Black Africa

European Perceptions of the African Mind

> The Natives (of Africa) are like children. They have human mind, but they are like children.
>
> *Cecil John Rhodes, 1891*
>
> God has divided His gifts fairly evenly among His various children of all races so that in the end there is no overall superiority or inferiority.
>
> *Ralph Dodge, 1964*

THE BEGINNING

Writing in 1975 about Western perceptions of the Africans, Charles Lyons observed, "English fascination with black skin was not confined to litera-ture. Philosophers, churchmen, and scientists became keenly interested in the causes and significance of the black complexion. It is important to note that such interest came about at a time when England was experiencing something of a classical revival."[1]

From the time that William Shakespeare (1564–1616) was writing his plays to the time the great colonial adventure began in Africa in the nineteenth century, European preoccupation with skin pigmentation was the primary basis used for interaction and social relationships between people. Nothing else seemed to matter. To Europeans of that time skin color was an important criterion used to determine a person's place in society.[2] This criterion was used to its fullest extent during the period of colonial rule in Africa.

The literature that came out during this time persistently argues that, because of the color of their skin, the Africans possessed a mind less capable than that of white people. The literature argued that Africans were less intelligent because of their skin. The implicit hope was that they would eventually evolve and improve the potential of their minds by living in a temperate climate and adopting the white man's cultural practices.[3] The thinking among Europeans was that this change would also help improve the physical appearance of the African skin, making the Africans more like human beings.

It was clear from the Elizabethan European perception that, as long as the African complexion remained what it was, the African intellect would remain severely handicapped and would never be able to reach the full human potential associated with that of Europeans. It became a fashionable and an accepted practice among Europeans to blame both the black color of their skin and the physical environment in which the Africans lived for their presumed inferior mind. This is the reason why, for example, the Moor in Shakespeare's *The Merchant of Venice* attempted to explain that his dark skin was the result of "the shadowed livery of the burnished sun to whom I am neighbor and bred."[4] In his famous play, *Othello*, Shakespeare employs graphic racial themes to portray some characters and develop a plot whose tragic outcome seems determined by the pigmentation of those characters.

THE CONCEPT OF BLACKNESS, THE DARK
CONTINENT, AND WESTERN PERCEPTIONS
OF THE AFRICANS

The Europeans' repulsion by the physical appearance of the Africans inevitably influenced their attitudes and behavior toward them. To Europeans blackness symbolized everything that was negative. For example, during a visit to the coast of Guinea in 1566, Walter Wren was totally surprised to see that "Although the people were black and naked, they were civil."[5] It is clear that Wren did not expect the people of Guinea to have any cultural refinements because they were black. From the moment Europeans came into contact with black people, they formed prejudicial opinions of them based purely on the color of their skin. When Martin Luther King, Jr. (1929–1968) argued in 1963, "I hope that some day my four little children will be judged not by the color of their skin, but by the content of their character,"[6] he was fully aware of the impact of this prejudice. Indeed, race and color were the only criteria that the U.S. Supreme Court used to rule in the infamous *Dred Scott v. Sanford* case in 1857. The ruling legally affirmed the view that Negroes had no rights that the white man would respect because they were black and thus inferior. A fundamental philosophical and constitutional consideration of the American system of social justice, "All men are created equal," did not apply to black people simply because they were black. Out of this line of thinking came the *Plessy* decision of 1896 establishing the doctrine of "separate but equal," which was finally reversed by the *Brown* decision of 1954. It is not surprising that the United States has experienced enormous problems with race.

Two conclusions arise from King's observation. The first is that race and color, as two criteria used to determine a person's place in society, are not a remote aspect of history. Rather, they are features of human behavior that have found their way into present twentieth-century thinking. The second conclusion is that the southern states have, until recently, used color as a basis for treating people differently and this explains the powerful influence of this form of prejudice. As Shakespeare would deduce, under the weight of this prejudice the black people "had seen better days."[7] The whole civil rights movement of the 1960's in the United States reflected the reality of the thinking that some dramatic action was needed to erase racial prejudice as a criterion for treating people differently in society. Today affirmative action takes a similar line of thinking because the United States has not been able to get rid of race as a consideration in human interactions. In 1990 South Africa finally acknowledged an awareness of the enormous problems created by apartheid in their society.

The obvious outcome of associating blackness with inferior intellect is the reason why Africa has been known as the "Dark Continent." It is important to remember that, in portraying the Africans as lacking in civilization and culture, Europeans were implying that the white man was willing and able to offer his assistance in the process of the transformation they believed was needed to initiate the Africans' acquisition of basic elements of Western culture. It was not possible for Europeans to recognize the viability of the African culture. When the colonization process began in the nineteenth century, it was based on the assumption that it was advantageous for the Africans because it would salvage them from the condemnation of their primitive culture. The extent to which this notion influenced the relationships between the Africans and the colonial governments will be addressed in this study. It is a tragic truth that the colonial governments did not conceive of the idea of cultural diversity as an avenue of human enrichment on which national programs would be built for the benefit of all.

An examination of history reveals a disturbing truth about how Westerners have associated the color black with everything that is negative. Here are only a few examples. In the history of the United States, Black Friday of 1869 and 1873 represented an economic collapse caused by the sudden and rapid decline in the price of gold. In the Northern Hemisphere black is the color for the month of January because the bitter cold season comes during that month. The everyday English language is filled with expressions using black in a negative way: blackmail, black armband, black magic, black looks, black holes, black despair. The infamous Black Death of the Dark[8] Ages was the bubonic plague that killed 25 percent of the European population. The black cat is associated with misfortune. Black clothing is worn at funerals to signify mourning. The black hat is worn by villains in westerns. A personification of evil, witches, are portrayed as wearing black clothing. The Romans originally named the Black Sea Pontus Euximus which meant "Friendly Sea." The Europeans renamed it the Black Sea because heavy fog made navigation dangerous during certain times of the year.

There are yet more examples of how Europeans throughout history have used the color black in a negative sense. In 1921 members of Benito Mussolini's Fascist party were known as the Black Shirts because of the brutality and callousness with which they treated political opponents. The black widow is one of the most dangerous spiders in the United States. The black tupelo is a tree with a bitter fruit. In 1756 Indian troops captured British soldiers and imprisoned them in a small room where many died for lack of sufficient fresh air. The room has become notoriously known to history as the Black Hole of Calcutta. And I recall a television commercial in the 1970s featuring a housewife who desperately tried to exterminate house ants and roaches using a house broom. Finally, she reached for her Black Flag, a chemical insecticide, and gleefully coddled the can and showed her happiness to the viewer.

When he arrived in Cairo on July 28, 1980, to attend the funeral of the exiled shah of Iran who died July 27, former U.S. President Richard Nixon characterized the failure of the U.S. government to send an official delegation to the funeral as a black page in the history of U.S. foreign policy. In February 1981, as British Prime Minister Margaret Thatcher, elegantly dressed in a black dress, walked into the British Parliament to participate in a crucial debate on rising unemployment, the worst since the days of the Great Depression, a Labour Member of Parliament asked if she was dressed in black because she was mourning the death of the economy. The next day Mrs. Thatcher came to Parliament dressed in a gray dress. The stock market tremor that caused a ripple on Wall Street on Tuesday, November 19, 1991, immediately earned the name "Black Tuesday." It cast a shadow on the hoped-for economic recovery in a period of recession as Americans seemed to wonder whether the Black Tuesday of 1929, which signified the start of the "Great Depression," was returning.

The important thing to remember in these examples is that the color black has negative connotations and that when such expressions are used in reference to black people, they take on additional powerful racial dimensions. Until the advent of the twentieth century, Europeans failed to recognize the Africans' intellectual potential because they associated their belief in their inferiority with the color of their skin. The entire character and structure of the colonial society was built on the foundation of this very basic assumption. What did this mean to both the colonial governments and the Africans? This study will provide an answer to the question.

THE AGE OF EXPLORATION AND THE UNVEILING OF THE AFRICAN MIND

The collapse of the Roman Empire ushered in a new period of intense struggle among loosely structured groups of nation-states in Europe for influence and power to control trade and commerce. The known world of the Roman Empire had been dominated by an almost omnipotent Rome since the days of the Caesars. There was no influence comparable to that which the Roman Empire exerted on the political, commercial, and social conditions of human life. Now that centuries of Roman power had come to an end, we can understand the obsession for new power. Indeed, European nation-states approached their mission of seeking control in the belief that, once in place, their influence and power would last longer than the Roman Empire. It was from this perspective that the Germanic tribes and the Vikings ventured forth to extend their newfound power and influence. Their quest for territorial expansion ignited the age of exploration.

Although the Crusades failed in their initial objective of restoring the Holy Land to Christianity, they expanded man's horizons of knowledge about the existing world. Trade with the East resumed at a pace never known before. A wealthy merchant from Venice, Nicolo Polo, who might have been the subject of Shakespeare's famous play, wondered whether he could purchase precious goods from China and India directly, instead of dealing through the Arab trade agents who controlled the existing system of trade for their own gain. Soon the Portuguese, the British, the Spaniards, and the Italians joined in the hunt for wealth and influence through exploration of distant lands. Their strategy was straightforward—any nation that controlled the lucrative trade with distant lands would rule Europe itself. With this attitude and strategy as a catalyst, the political landscape of Europe and the existing world was about to be reshaped as nations vied for positions of power.

Unwilling to submit to the Arabs' trade tricks and wishing to initiate a new trade venture independently, Nicolo Polo and his brother, Maffeo, set out from a port at the eastern end of the Black Sea on one of the monumental voyages of exploration. When the Polo brothers came into contact with a powerful oriental chieftain, Kublai Khan, both their fortune and the course of world history were inextricably and forever transformed. In their ten-year stay in China, the Polo brothers amassed a huge fortune that attracted the greedy interests and attention of other European entrepreneurs. Two years after returning to Europe the Polo brothers set out again, this time with Nicolo's son Marco (1254–1324), who became one of Kublai Khan's most trusted confidants. In the course of his duties, Marco traveled the entire length of Khan's empire. On his return to Venice, Marco published an impressive account of his travels entitled *The Adventure of Marco Polo*, which had an enormous influence on later voyages of exploration.

The descriptions that Marco Polo made in this book provided a blueprint that European adventurers followed in their pursuit of fortune and fame. This seven-hundred-year quest for economic gain and political power eventually led to Africa. Nineteenth-century colonial imperial adventurers set their sights on Africa and began the plunder of its people and raw resources.

Taken prisoner in 1289 in a sea battle between Venice and Genoa, Marco Polo dictated fascinating stories to a French friend about his travels, contacts with people whose cultural practices were strange, the enormous wealth that these distant and strange people possessed, and how it could be obtained to improve the standard of living in Europe. He told of the wars that Kublai Khan fought against barbaric and uncivilized neighboring people. This was the pattern of activity that would be replicated by colonial entrepreneurs in Africa in the nineteenth century.

The influence and popularity of Marco Polo's books are demonstrated by their translation into many European languages. They inspired later explorers who read them with great interest and intensity. Among these were Christopher Columbus, whose own adventure on the high seas and in the New World has made him a major historical figure to this day. Although Marco Polo was a keen observer of the events he saw, he tended to exaggerate, especially when he discussed the strange culture of the people with whom he interacted. This suggests that Marco Polo's travels and book had a greater impact on European perceptions of people in distant lands than on matters relating to trade.

Indeed, the sudden upsurge of interest in exploration among Europeans can be attributed to a man who never undertook a voyage of exploration further than North Africa, Henry the Navigator (1394–1460), the brother of the king of Portugal. From the earliest days of exploration, the Portuguese took an early lead in establishing themselves as superior in knowledge about navigation and exploration to people of any other nation in Europe. However, because they were unable to overcome the adverse conditions caused by winds and the tides, they were not able to go beyond the shores of Portugal. That position would soon change as Henry the Navigator felt that more enduring voyages could be successfully undertaken with stronger ships and better navigational instruments. In order to accomplish these critical objectives, he established a naval school at Sagres in 1416. He invited people from all over Europe and the Arab world to come to Sagres to learn and share knowledge about navigation, geography, and what they knew about people in distant lands. His sole intent was to ensure better understanding among the peoples of the world.

By the time Henry died in 1460 the Europeans' interest in acquiring knowledge about the world had increased considerably. Within a short period of time, a new phenomenon was rapidly developing—the shift in interest from gaining knowledge about the world to an understanding about the people in distant lands, especially their skin, culture, behavior, and cognitive abilities. Within a short period of time, the major focus of European interest in human cognition was directed toward the Africans. The paramount consideration was the question of whether the Africans, because of the color of their skin, possessed an intellectual potential comparable to that of Europeans. It is accurate to state that the interest in acquiring knowledge about the mind of the Africans greatly intensified the interest in African exploration. This is why the Portuguese dramatically increased their exploratory efforts on this continent. The desire to gain access to the lucrative trade in spices from the Indian subcontinent combined with their efforts to scale the mind of the Africans in ways that had not been accomplished in the past.

In 1488, when a Portuguese sailor named Bartholomew Diaz (1457–1500), who was commissioned by King John II, arrived at the southern tip of Africa in search of a sea passage to India, the African mind was subjected to a new form of human adventure. This contact permanently introduced a new phase in the nature of human relationships.[9] The adventure that began with the desire to discover the world and learn more about it now turned into an expedition to formulate opinions about the African mind. This was seen as a necessity so that it would be controlled for the benefit of European entrepreneurs. Diaz's journey provided such valuable information about Africans that ten years later, in 1498, Manuel I, who succeeded John, commissioned Vasco da Gama (1469–1524) to complete the expedition that Diaz had started. Diaz had encountered two problems that da Gama had to overcome in order to succeed in his expedition. They were the hostility of the Africans and the violent storms that raged on at the southern tip of the continent of Africa.

While da Gama succeeded in overcoming the threat of the storms, he had no such luck in overcoming the hostility of the Africans. For this reason, the Cape of Storms, which eventually was named the Cape of Good Hope, remained relatively free of European occupation until 1652 when the Dutch made a fateful decision to establish a settlement there, causing problems that have defied solution to this day because of the contempt they showed toward the Africans. However, da Gama's success manifested the hope that both Henry the Navigator and Manuel had of reaching India. Utilizing the knowledge that the naval school at Sagres had yielded, Portuguese explorers followed Diaz and da Gama managed to bring the elements, especially the violent storms at the southern tip of the continent, under control. Diaz's Cape of Storms was renamed the Cape of Good Hope—to signify the hope that soon both Africa and India would come under Portuguese control. It was a new day for the Portuguese who now began to lay grandiose plans to bring both the people and the wealth of India and Africa under their domain.

When the Arabs knew that da Gama's success would give the Portuguese an advantage in the lucrative spice trade, they managed to incite the Hindus against Portuguese explorers, putting them and their adventure in harm's way. At the Cape of Good Hope the increasing navigational activity created a climate that turned the Africans against the Portuguese, causing da Gama to recommend that Portugal establish a permanent military presence at the Cape to protect its sailors and trade. It never occurred to the Portuguese that a better course of action would have been to demonstrate respect toward the Africans, their culture, and their highly structured institutions. This would have translated into respect for the African way of thinking. Violence, both political and military, was the type of relationship that the Portuguese established with the Africans. This position continued up until the crisis that led to the war of independence in the Portuguese African colonies beginning in 1960.

The rivalry between the Portuguese and other European explorers, combined with periodic violent storms at sea and the hostility of the Africans, forced the Portuguese to suspend their trade dominance objective. This allowed the Dutch a perilous window of opportunity to establish their own permanent station at the Cape. The killing of Francisco d'Almeda by the Hottentots in 1510 convinced the Portuguese that efforts to establish a permanent station at the Cape involved dangers that they could easily deal with. The Portuguese entrepreneurs concluded, however, that the only way to solve the problem of security for their sailors was to initiate a hard-line policy toward the Africans. This meant that military force had to be used. Once this strategy was adopted, it became a new *modus operandi*.

Questions of brutality against the Africans never arose because the notion that the end justifies the means became an accepted justification for military intervention. In this manner a dangerous precedent was set as other European explorers adopted similar tactics that would create a climate of permanent conflict between the Europeans and the Africans. Nothing else seemed to matter. Dialogue and diplomacy were aspects of human interaction that were never given a chance. Wealth, territory, and conquest by the European explorers were far more important objectives than seeking to establish human relationships based on mutual respect. In this way, the Portuguese set a precedent that they utilized in their efforts not only to establish colonies in Africa but also to institute colonial violence as a means of maintaining their stranglehold on the populace they enslaved.

The Portuguese use of force in seeking to dominate the Africans and the realization that violence was the only way to control them, combined with Portugal's annexation by Spain in 1580, weakened Portugal's trade with India. This gave the Dutch an opportunity to establish themselves in Africa.[10] However, the failure of the Portuguese to establish a permanent station at the Cape did not imply the demise of their adventure and their efforts to control the African mind. Rather, it meant that when conditions were right, they would direct those efforts elsewhere in Africa. The adventure to India and the competition in the spice trade were too important to European countries to subject them to a secondary purpose. In effect, in 1575, seventy-seven years before the Dutch established a permanent station at the Cape, the Portuguese claimed Angola on the west coast and Mozambique on the east coast of southern Africa as their colonial possessions.[11]

With this development, efforts made by Europeans to control the African mind led to an uncharted course in the voyage of human relationships. The instruments of navigation were the military force at their disposal, and the ultimate end was to control the African mind in ways it had not been controlled in the past. The bitterness and hostility that characterized the response of the Africans were no match for the brutality used to subdue and repress them. It never occurred to the Portuguese that they had not fully understood the mind of the Africans. This failure would later prove to be the ultimate demise of the mind of the Europeans themselves.

Having contained the Africans' opposition to the invasion of their culture and society, the Portuguese introduced the next step in their strategy to control the African way of life. In 1680 they demanded trade concessions from the Africans, including the shipment of large numbers of slaves, ivory, and copper to Portugal.[12] When King Afonzo of Angola declined to yield to these demands, the relationship between him and the Portuguese deteriorated rapidly. Following Afonzo's death, the Portuguese coerced his inexperienced successor into accepting their ever increasing demands. This march toward oppression was accomplished through the threat of military action against the Africans. Once set, the objective of seeking total control of the African mind would not be abandoned. But in designing their strategy to control the African mind in the way they did, the Portuguese, and other European nations that followed them, became masters of gross miscalculations about the state of the African mind. This would later prove to be their ultimate deception, a deception perpetrated on the Europeans by themselves.

Portuguese efforts to violate the African mind reached a new level of intensity in 1560 when Paulo Dias de Novais unceremoniously occupied Luanda after scouting reports convinced him that the African resistance could be crushed and the Africans could psychologically be conditioned to accept Portuguese colonization and domination.[13] To his surprise, de Novais discovered that the Africans had a strategy of their own to resolve the problems arising out of the Portuguese desire to control him. They united under the leadership of several vassals and joined forces to resist Portuguese invasion. Following colonization in 1575, heavy fighting ensued until 1858. This imperiled the purpose that the Portuguese pursued in their endeavor to control the African mind and hence the African land and resources in relation to their desire to discover new avenues of trade and commerce. By resorting to military force to subject the Africans to colonial rule, the Portuguese lost forever an opportunity to learn the real character of the African mind.

The Portuguese believed that the colonization of Angola and Mozambique manifested their efforts to subdue the African mind and that it could be used as an instrument for meeting their larger national objectives. They regarded colonization as the quintessential proof of their power to control the subcontinent, as well as a demonstration of their resolve to bring the Africans under their dominance forever. However, the Africans themselves knew that at some point in time they would rise to the occasion, seize their sense of self, and rid their land of colonization and all that it represented. This is precisely how the Portuguese miscalculated the African mind.

In recognizing the Portuguese efforts to control both African cognition and the raw materials they arrogantly believed rightly belonged to them, we must acknowledge three basic premises underlying their action. The first is that they believed that the African mind was of such little quality that it could easily be utilized to promote national objectives. They believed that the Africans lacked a depth of intellectual power and that anything they did represented the action of a group of primitive people. The second belief was that the Portuguese explorers, from Diaz to de Novais, regarded Africa's abundance of raw materials as an act of divine providence, placed at the disposal of the European. Portugal had been cast by divine fate into a position from which it had the duty to exercise appropriate power and influence so that all of Europe would benefit.

This belief was one of the reasons why Prince Henry the Navigator felt he had a mission not only to elevate Portugal to a position of absolute power and influence in Europe, but also as a prerogative and exclusive right to chart a new course in all of human endeavor. Indeed, Portuguese nationals believed that this right was ordained by divine providence and that it could not be challenged in Europe or anywhere else in the world. They thought that the days of the Caesars were over and that the days of Portuguese omnipotence were here to stay. The third conclusion was that the belief in the inferiority of the African mind led the Portuguese to assume that they had a mission of great Christian importance to salvage the Africans from the condemnation of their primitive culture. Their way of thinking and behaving stood in the way of their efforts to see things beyond the immediate present. Whether or not the Africans wanted it, they must unconditionally accept Portuguese civilization, culture, and plans for their future.

The Portuguese also concluded that for the Africans to resist this act of divine grace constituted an act of rebellion against properly sanctioned authority. For all practical purposes, the Portuguese concluded that the Africans must never be allowed to do that. Throughout their entire duration, colonial systems in Africa operated under this dangerous notion, setting the two cultural groups on a perilous and unavoidable course of confrontation. When Antonio Salazar assumed power in Portugal in 1932, he operated under these aforementioned basic premises. These conclusions played out in the drama of human interactions in profound ways. In their study *Southern Africa Since 1800*, Donald Denoon and Balam Nyeko conclude that in this act the Portuguese were carrying out a dangerous experiment in human relations. They go on to observe, "Not all experiments are successful: sometimes the material circumstances simply do not permit improvements in production, and sometimes experiments make life worse than it was."[14] This is exactly what happened under the Portuguese programs of that time.

THE AGE OF REASON AND THE EMERGENCE OF SCIENTIFIC RACIAL BIAS

That the Portuguese establishment of colonies in Angola and Mozambique was not followed immediately by colonization of other parts of Africa by other European nations until the nineteenth century seems reason enough to substantiate the Portuguese claim to the wisdom that they assumed was their exclusive possession. Afraid to challenge the Portuguese in an area in which they had an advantage, other European nations decided to follow a better part of valor, positioning themselves to scale the African mind in their own way in a manner that was consistent with their understanding of the African intellectual potential. By the time the Portuguese developed an active interest in founding colonies in Africa, their intent, as well as that of other European nations, had shifted away from the original goal set by Henry the Navigator in seeking to expand knowledge about navigation and the world in general to focusing exclusively on the benefits of colonizing distant lands. Even so, European nations quickly realized that colonization was not possible without seeking first to control the African mind, a task they recognized was monumental.

To know why Europeans substituted the importance of establishing colonies for that of ensuring the spices trade in India, we need to understand the character of human institutions and relationships that emerged in the roughly six-hundred-year period called the Renaissance (A.D. 1000 to 1600). When the Renaissance began, Europe was divided into feudal states owned and operated by wealthy noblemen. Most people were mere serfs who worked on the land for their landlords.[15] Religion played a major role in the life of the people, for almost all activity reflected religious practices. That the Catholic Church exercised more power over both the social life and religious practice of the people suggests its undisputed influence on national institutions. The loosely structured governments that existed in the form of what was known as city-states were subordinated to the authority of the church, because no political leader wanted to risk excommunication by challenging the authority of the church leaders. As the Renaissance progressed, kings and princes assumed more power and control of governments and social institutions. Feudal lords structured stronger systems of socioeconomic institutions that placed the serfs at a great disadvantage. European society was on its way to fundamental change. It was the strength of these new secular institutions that led to colonial adventure in distant lands.

The people who lived during the Renaissance regarded the Middle Ages as a period when life and institutions were dominated mainly by religious and superstitious practices. This is why one of the earliest achievements of the Renaissance was scholarship and the arts. It was a period of the rebirth of human thinking, a reawakening of the human mind in its universal meaning. For Europeans this was a new day; it heralded the dawn of a new era and the emergence of the new level of human cognition replacing the external locus of control mindset with an internal locus of control. Man had control over what would happen to both himself and his society. The study of ancient civilizations generated new interest in human intelligence. Scholars found and translated ancient literature that had no meaning to life in the Middle Ages. The study of past accomplishments, neglected during the Middle Ages, now formed the thrust for new endeavors to chart a fresh course for the future. In the Renaissance the study of man, rather than of God alone, became the major focus of investigation for scholars and their students. The knowledge that theology must be supplemented by sociology ushered in a new era in the cognitive schemes of those who saw the study of the universal man as a mission to initiate fundamental improvement in the conditions that controlled human life.

But as exciting and innovative as they made the Renaissance in terms of seeking to understand human experience in order to fashion a more meaningful future, the scholars of the Renaissance left a legacy of bias and inadequacy in their efforts to study people outside Europe, especially Africans. Scholars of the Renaissance became fascinated with the study of the universal man, his culture, and the conditions that controlled life and social institutions. They carried out scientific studies to examine these areas. They were quite ignorant, however, of people in distant lands. This was largely due to an error in their object of study. They equated the universal man with themselves; Europeans were synonymous with the universal man.

Although emphasis on the study of man formed a philosophy known as humanism, the concept of humanity excluded the Africans until studies were conducted to determine whether they were actually human. The plays of William Shakespeare provided the basis of unsubstantiated opinions about the mind of the Africans and its role in human interactions. Any effort to determine the quality of that mind, or a lack of it, would help Europeans decide whether or not the Africans had a mind that made them human. The advent of the Enlightenment gave Europeans an opportunity to study the African mind to ascertain whether they had any intellectual potential at all. The descriptions contained in Shakespeare's plays about the mind of the Africans had to give way to actual studies—at least that is what some European researchers of this period thought. The question posed was: How accurate would these studies be?

What one sees as a legacy of the Renaissance is that fundamental change was taking place in both lifestyle and cognition among people. In many respects, the Enlightenment was an extension of the Renaissance: it stressed the application of human reason and rationale through critical thinking, rather than utilizing religious dogma and ritual alone to address human issues. The change in application from depending on religious beliefs to find solutions to human problems to utilizing human reason suggested a scientific or logical method for dealing with human situations.[16] As the Enlightenment slowly gave way to the era of the Industrial Revolution in the nineteenth century, those who were interested in promoting scientific methods of seeking knowledge glamorized the search for it by trying to unravel the mysteries of all aspects of human life. They approached their newly found interest and task with a religious zeal for their mission. For the scholars of this time, nothing was more important than the feeling and belief that it was within their grasp to transform social institutions in ways that translated into a higher order of existence for humankind. The reality that man was capable of shaping the future posed implications far beyond the realm of their wildest dreams and imagination.

The study of the social, physical, anthropological, and intellectual attributes of man now formed the thrust, the major focus, and, indeed, the preoccupation of the social scientists of the Victorian period. Thus it was that Charles Dickens (1812–1870) and Charles Darwin (1809–1882) became instant literary and scientific celebrities when they respectively published in 1859 *A Tale of Two Cities* and *Origin of Species*. Dickens became famous for his ability to relate to his readers the actual human condition in his novels. His unhappy childhood, caused mainly by his father's financial difficulties, provided the social background for his books. For example, in *Oliver Twist*, Dickens exposed the abuses of children in the workhouse system and the slums. His portrait of the insensitive Schoolmaster Squires in *Nicholas Nickleby* is too vicious to be real but too graphic and convincing not to be taken for real. It was the unveiling of the cruel conditions of life in the Victorian period that made Dickens a social reformer. But a critical dimension of Dickens's works is that those who read them supposed a parallel between conditions of life in Europe and conditions of life in distant lands.

When the Europeans refused to accept the reality that the Industrial Revolution was not a panacea for all social evils, an aggressive attitude was adopted in formulating opinions about the way of life of people in less developed areas of the world. This denigration justified the effort to control the thinking of those people whose resources they sought to exploit in order to end the social ills that the nations of Europe were experiencing. Dickens's perceptions of his own society provided an appropriate forum in which Europeans saw the Africans as people at their disposal who could be used to improve conditions of life in Europe. The institution of slavery would be relied on, relived, and realized all over again for what it really is–the malevolent side of humanity. Europeans were convinced that the African mind could not and would not comprehend the meaning of affluence and material comfort in the way the Industrial Revolution afforded them. This thinking contributed significantly to the opinion that Africa must be colonized in order to bring its people and the raw materials it contained under the control of Europeans. By all calculations these conditions, when fully implemented, implied nothing less than slavery.

Darwin did in natural science what Dickens did in social science. Before the publication of *Origin of Species*, several natural scientists, including Darwin's grandfather, Erasmus Darwin, had espoused theories of evolution in a logical manner. Darwin's publication of *The Descent of Man* (1871), in which he speculated that man might have come from the same species that included the chimpanzee and was the beginning of a new period in the process of seeking knowledge and forming attitudes and perceptions about man in general and Africans in particular. The adventure that began with the objective of discovering new routes to distant lands now shifted to focus on studying the African mind in order to design appropriate strategies for controlling it. This new direction attracted researchers of both the Enlightenment and the Victorian period. Although they did not deliberately set out to distort the quality of the African mind by engaging in biased study, it still remains that the effect of their action, though with the best of intention, was to grossly misunderstand it in a way that damaged the relationships between the people of these two cultural groups.

Although Darwin based his books on scientific speculation, rather than on data obtained from actual scientific inquiry and empirical investigation, science enthusiasts of the Victorian period "hailed them as a touchstone of promoting their own ideas and ambitions in an area that was attracting the interest and attention of the members of the scientific community."[17] The shift of interest from voyages of discovery to the study of conditions affecting human cognition and environmental adaption was a phenomenon that had a profound impact on the attitudes of European researchers toward people in less developed areas of the world, especially Africans. The questions these researchers considered in the realm of scientific investigation included: Is there a relationship between the color of skin and intellectual potential? Does climate affect the quality of the human mind? Does the size of the skull or cranial cavity have any relationship to the level of intellectual potential? Ignored and neglected were questions such as: How does the environment affect human intellectual performance? How does cultural variation impact that intellect? This omission would prove to be a crucial factor in the colonial setting of the twentieth century.

Within a relatively short period of time, efforts to supply answers to these questions constituted what was considered scientific inquiry. For this reason, comparative studies of different racial and ethnic groups became an immensely popular area of scientific study. Any individual who sought to make a name for himself endeavored to spend time gathering some form of data on some aspect of life of people in distant lands. The study of human cognition in those lands became the major focus of their purported investigation. But the fact that their methods of inquiry were as seriously flawed as the instruments they used was not important. This error of procedure proved to be the basis for the ultimate distortion of the African mind. In this kind of setting, the findings they obtained and the conclusions they reached were variegated with gross inaccuracies. The fascination of Victorian scientific researchers with the intellect of people in distant lands and with the belief that they were engaging in an endeavor of great importance negated the inadequacy of both the instruments they used and the data they collected. It is not hard to see that in making interpretations from their data the researchers did not come close to comprehending the cognitive prowess of the African mind.

Charles Lyons concludes that European perceptions of the African mind were strengthened by accounts of some publications that earlier researchers claimed to have gathered from Africa.[18] In order to understand why the Victorian researchers formed perceptions about the African mind, we need to understand those who were part of forming them during the era of the Enlightenment. As they began to generate a new level of interest in the conditions that shaped the African mind, Victorian researchers initiated a practice of arriving at conclusions based on speculative studies. This practice relied on a series of studies conducted during the Enlightenment. For example, in 1785 a German researcher, S. T. von Soemmering, published an essay that made him an instant literary celebrity. He ventured in his speculation much further than anyone had done before: he presented an unproved theoretical assumption that because the cranial capacity of the Africans was much smaller than that of the Europeans, their intellectual potential must also be smaller.[19] That von Soemmering reached this conclusion after studying only one skull of an Egyptian and one of a European suggests his flawed methods of investigation. Nonetheless, it set a precedent that other researchers utilized to shocking lengths.

Out of this precedent came a belief among researchers of both the Enlightenment and the Victorian period that human intelligence was a direct product of the size of the cranial cavity. The speculation was that the larger the cranial capacity, the more intelligence one possessed. It was on this basis that von Soemmering concluded that because the Africans' cranial cavity was smaller they possessed less intelligence than Europeans. Von Soemmering's speculation was immediately taken for a statement of fact on which to base future studies: this indicates the serious nature of the problems researchers of that time faced. The researchers of that period also concluded that the smallness of the cranial capacity of people in warm areas of the world, meaning Africans, was due to the fact that they had a thicker skull to protect their brain from the excessive heat of the sun, and that the thicker the skull, the smaller the cranial capacity, and hence the less intelligence.[20] Size was everything to them; it dictated cognitive ability. The bigger the brain, the smarter the person.

These researchers' inevitable conclusion was that the reverse was true of people in temperate climates, meaning Europeans. Because they did not need a thick skull to protect their brain from excessive heat by the sun, their cranial capacity was larger, and, thus, so was their intelligence. This speculative thinking among researchers can be traced to Shakespeare's time. For example, the Moor in *The Merchant of Venice* tried to gain the sympathy of his listeners by attempting to explain that his skin was dark because of the excessive heat of the sun. This is also the reason why the Moor, and other black characters portrayed in Shakespearean plays, were considered to have less intelligence than people of light skin.

Two elements of Shakespeare's portrayal of black characters are critical here. The first is that the black characters were made to believe that they were intellectually inferior to the white man purely on the basis of the color of their skin. No other factor was considered more fundamental to human intellect and achievement than skin color. This is exactly what the policy of apartheid has done to the black people of South Africa. The second element is that they were made to feel guilty for being black, and forced to accept the culpability of their inferiority because it was a result of their own nature. This made their situation both inevitable and inescapable, and added to their subjection to the white man because they resigned themselves to the limitations forced upon them by the supposed inadequacy of their blackness and accepted the dictates that this fate delegated them. The only way they could hope to improve themselves was to imitate the white man. Psychological conditioning was the name of the game being played on the mind of black Africa. This is the tragedy of some of Shakespeare's plays.

In 1795, ten years after von Soemmering had published his speculative study, a British medical doctor, Charles White, supported his conclusion and went even further. White speculated that of the four races of the human being—black, yellow, red, and white—the black race was the least intelligent and the white race the most intelligent.[21] If Charles White were here today, how would he explain the fact that some students from Asia have demonstrated an intellectual capacity that is unmatched by that of white students? However, during the next seven years researchers regarded the search for knowledge into the character of the African mind as an open season, with both von Soemmering and White enjoying an unprecedented wave of popularity in a new area of study in which they had established themselves as undisputed authorities. No researcher had the courage to question the basis of an ever increasing popular trend that was rapidly gaining support in the direction of pseudoscientific speculation, which they failed to recognize as slowly but steadily becoming an equally popular myth.

Regardless of the popularity of von Soemmering's and White's conclusions, not all researchers of the Enlightenment jumped on the bandwagon of this scientific speculation and myth. For example, in 1803 a British medical researcher, Thomas Winterbottom, who had spent more time than any other researcher conducting studies on the relationships between the size of the cranial cavity and intellectual potential among Africans, published the findings of his investigation in *An Account of the Native Africans* in which he disputed von Soemmering and White's conclusions and questioned their methods. Winterbottom argued that what von Soemmering and White considered research was nothing more than mere speculation and that the faulty instruments they used led to inaccurate data. Winterbottom then went on to argue that his own studies convinced him that there was no difference between the physical structure and cranial capacity of the African skulls and those of Europeans.[22]

Naturally, the disciples of von Soemmering and White were not pleased to have the reputation of their mentors impugned. They would rather lose confidence in Santa Claus than lose the trust they had placed in two men who had embarked on what they considered a pious crusade in the course of human enterprise. But the care, detail, and method that Winterbottom had utilized to reach his conclusions left no room for doubt as to the accuracy of his studies. It was unusual for an Enlightenment researcher to employ logical analysis, and in this endeavor Winterbottom set the pattern that future researchers should follow. Winterbottom's findings and conclusions were so accurate that no researcher tried to dispute either his method of gathering the data or his conclusions. One would have thought that from that point on Enlightenment researchers would approach their task with an added dimension of objectivity and sensitivity to make sure that cultural and racial prejudice did not influence their studies and the conclusions they reached. But cultural and racial sensitivity and objectivity were not the hallmark of Enlightenment researchers, and this helps to explain the serious nature of the problems they faced in their claim to know the African mind.

It is for this reason that the Victorian researchers elected to neglect Winterbottom's findings and conclusions because it was not popular to suggest that there were no fundamental differences in both the physical structure of the African skulls and in intellectual potential. To accept the thinking that the Africans possessed a cognitive potential equal to that of Europeans would imply that the people of the two cultures must be treated equally. If this line of thinking were accepted, how would Europeans justify colonization of Africa? It was inconceivable to the Victorian researchers that intellectual potential was, in effect, a relative quality of the human mind greatly influenced by the kind of environment in which one lived, and that it had absolutely nothing to do with the size of the skull or cranial cavity. Winterbottom argued that the differences in culture and environmental factors did not remotely indicate that Europeans were more intelligent than Africans. His view, however, did not appear to have any influence on the efforts of the Victorian researchers to understand the African mind from a perspective rooted in accurate scientific inquiry.

By the mid-nineteenth century Winterbottom's conclusions had added a new dimension to an area of human endeavor that was becoming increasingly controversial as the African mind was subjected to a self-serving debate among European intellectuals. Darwin's speculation that man in general might have originated from the ape was now altered to suit a new line of thinking among those who argued that the Africans were the first-generation cousins of apes. Thus, as early as 1863 James Hunt, president of the London Anthropological Society, speaking at the annual meeting of the society, fully supported the von Soemmering–White conclusion about the intellectual potential of the Africans. Hunt also attempted to influence the society to accept the resolution that because the Africans had a smaller cranial capacity than Europeans, they had less intelligence.[23] Melvin Tumin, a noted American sociologist, describes the importance of environment to human intellectual potential: "Race in human thinking is a very minor concept. There is possibly no mammalia species in which the environment has a larger and more direct effect than on man. Studies show that a weak environment may be devastating to the development of the individual."[24]

To this point of view, Methodist Bishop Ralph Dodge,[25] who went to Africa as a missionary in 1936, adds, "God has divided His gifts fairly evenly among His various children of all races so that in the end there is no overall superiority or inferiority. Achievement and failure are both known to all."[26] But Dodge's reasoning ran against the wall of traditionally negative views espoused by the colonial officials. As a result, in 1964 he was deported from colonial Zimbabwe by the government of Ian Smith. Colonial governments, including that of Ian Smith, could not tolerate the idea that Africans possessed an intellect equal to that of the Caucasian. By minimizing the worth of Africans, they could justify their own thinking and behavior.

At the height of the Victorian perceptions of human intellectual potential, many enthusiasts subscribed to the belief that the Africans were decidedly inferior to Europeans because they had minimal intellect. Among the strongest supporters of this point of view was Wynwood Read, an influential and popular man who became better known for his nationalistic feeling, patriotic stance, and emotional support of British imperial and colonial adventure in Africa than for his intellectual depth. Read had neither time nor patience for those who seemed to suggest that the Africans possessed a cognitive potential equal to that of Europeans. It was therefore not by coincidence that Read had a young and devoted admirer in Cecil John Rhodes (1853–1902).

Rhodes's regard of Read as his hero and mentor, the high priest of British superiority complex, cast a long shadow on the horizon of the quest for unbiased knowledge of the mind of black Africa. This malevolent side of human history victimized both the European researchers and the people in distant lands whom European governments later came into contact with in the course of their colonial and imperial adventures. As the ancient Chinese philosophy might put it, the journey of a thousand miles to colonial supremacy began with a single step of forming perceptions about the mind of the Africans. In this trek, the colonial enthusiasts were never quite able to predict the outcome of their thinking and resulting consequences.

Perhaps this is what Albert Einstein (1879–1955) had in mind when he observed in August 1945, following the dropping of the atomic bomb over Hiroshima and Nagasaki, that the development of weapons of massive destruction did not produce a rational human mind, but, instead, they poised man on the brink of self-destruction brought on by his own mind. This is why Einstein declined an invitation to become president of Israel. It is reasonable to conclude that great as he was, Einstein did as much disservice to humankind with his self-claimed ignorance of the human mind as he did with his knowledge of science. In many respects Einstein was Alfred Nobel (1833–1896) reincarnate. Nobel discovered a method of producing explosives as a way of ensuring world peace. But toward the end of his life Nobel regretted the fact that the destructive nature of explosives controlled human thought. This guilt led him to try to see the positive side of his invention by creating the now famous Nobel Peace Prize. Was it possible that in their overwhelmingly negative perceptions of the African mind Victorian researchers would regret their approach to the dangerous journey that they had initiated in human relationships? It remained to be seen.

Indeed, Read, without stopping to think about the implications of his action, decided to assume the leadership of a movement that wanted to adopt as the official position of the London Anthropological Society the belief that adult Africans and their American descendants had a mind no more developed than that of a child and that it was unable to develop further after reaching the age of sixteen.[27] Fortunately, the pattern of Read's erratic behavior took a toll on his desires and goals; his ambitions were no substitute for rational thinking. His lack of intellectual depth stood in the way of his efforts. It is not surprising that his protégé, the equally ambitious Cecil John Rhodes, utilized Read's attitudes and beliefs as his *modus operandi*. There is no question that the target of Read's action was the black race, the descendants of Edward Long (1734–1813), a black man born in Britain whose father moved to Jamaica—people whom Read wanted to believe were intellectually inferior to Europeans. After hearing the view that the black race was inferior for so long, Long, a well-educated man, began to doubt his own intellectual ability, reinforcing a myth that was accepted as fact in the eighteenth century. When this myth was applied to Africa in the context of the colonial setting, it had a profound impact on the potential of the African mind.

The sad truth about the perceptions of both the eighteenth- and nineteenth-century figures is that they ignored some solid accomplishments by Long. In a letter dated January 30, 1992 addressed to the author, Eppie D. Edwards, the director of the National Library of Jamaica, stated:

Edward Long became a law student at Gray's Inn in 1752 and distinguished himself as a student. After his studies Long returned to Jamaica where he became private secretary to Sir Henry Moore, the governor who was married to his sister, Catherine Maria. Always of literary inclination, Long wrote several articles and light tales. His *History of Jamaica*, published in 1774 in three volumes, was his greatest work. While on the island he became judge of the vice-Admiralty court. Later he left Jamaica and lived in England where he devoted himself to his literary works, especially completing his *History of Jamaica*. Besides the *History of Jamaica*, Long published various other works particularly the *Reflection on the Sugar Cane,* 1772, *The Sugar Trade,* 1782."[28]

These are not the accomplishments of an individual who had no mind. Where did the Europeans get the notion that Long and his descendants lacked intellect simply because they were black?

Two things stand out as landmarks in the perceptions of Europeans in the Age of Reason with reference to the mind of black Africa. The first is that the concept of research was utilized to generate a set of ideas that simply could not be substantiated. The era of the Renaissance, when man was expected to rejuvenate his mental capacity to see things in ways that had not been done in the past, slowly witnessed man's inability to be objective. Regardless of the efforts they made to see things as they were, the researchers of the Age of Reason were still victims of that old form of human emotion, prejudice. From this period to the time of the colonization of Africa, prejudice and racial bias played a major role in shaping the attitudes and actions of colonial officials. One can understand why prejudice and bias became a principal factor of European enterprise: that is, the Africans looked very different from Europeans. The color black was the major factor Europeans used to conclude that the Africans were inferior in every conceivable way.

The second thing that one notices about the legacy of the Age of Reason is that these researchers did not think that any human behavior could mitigate the conditions that restructured human cognition. Environmental influences, much in discussion today, were considered to have absolutely no bearing on efforts to improve human thinking. Once it was decided that the Africans lacked intellect, there was nothing that they could be expected to do to improve it. Therefore, the logical conclusion that one reaches is that since these researchers deduced that the mind of black Africa could not be improved, they argued that the only meaningful role that the Africans could play was to function as laborers. Prejudice and racial bias had come full circle to reenslave the African mind through a set of negative attitudes and actions designed to condition them to accept their prescribed inferior position as an act of divine providence. These elements combined to cast the African mind in a mold from which there was no escape. In this context, the legacy of the Age of Reason was felt throughout the colonial period. Indeed the researchers of the Age of Reason applied no reason at all in forming perceptions about the mind of black Africa.

THE COLONIZATION OF THE AFRICAN MIND

From the time that James Bruce of Scotland explored the interior of Ethiopia and the Nile River in 1770 to the time that the Berlin Conference was convened in 1884, European interest in Africa was based on the perceptions that researchers had espoused since the Enlightenment. Since the days of the Portuguese exploration for sea routes to India, Bruce's expedition represented a new European adventure into the interior of Africa in an effort to scale the vast resources of the continent and to unveil the African way of life and the secrets it possessed. By 1852 a number of European explorers ventured into the interior of Africa. Their journeys yielded valuable information that was later utilized to facilitate colonization. Among these explorers were Richard Burton and John Hanning Speke, two British explorers who traveled across the eastern part of Africa and discovered Lake Victoria.

Among the more famous British explorers was David Livingstone (1813–1873), who went to Africa in 1841 in the service of the London Missionary Society, which had sent Robert Moffat (1796–1883) to Africa in 1825. In 1866 Livingstone began an expedition to find the source of the Nile River. This mysterious and sacred river symbolized the mysteries of the African mind itself. In his endeavor to locate its source, Livingstone was, in essence, trying to discover the mind of black Africa. But it was his disclosure of the Victoria Falls and the Zambezi River between Zambia and Zimbabwe in 1855 that made him famous. Livingstone, and other European explorers, were never quite able to discover the true nature of the African mind; this played a crucial role in shaping relationships between the Africans and the colonial adventurers. All the European explorers and colonial entrepreneurs could do was to speculate on its character, just as S. T. von Soemmering and Charles White had done during the Enlightenment.

The Europeans who have written the history of nineteenth-century Africa have portrayed Livingstone as a dedicated Christian missionary who had a vision of the continent, its people, and their lives, who radically and permanently transformed its culture through the introduction of Christianity and European values. These writers, however, seem to neglect a very important aspect of his work in Africa, and that is his great impact on the African mind. With the advent of the Industrial Revolution, the message that Livingstone and other Western missionaries tried to persuade the Africans to accept, that of conversion to Christianity, seems to have been lost in the confusion and conflict that emerged between their pursuit of new religious values for Africans and the embrace of the secular doctrine known as materialism. The Christian message had become a victim of the search for material comfort and commercial entrepreneurial endeavors that even the most enthusiastic missionaries found difficult to resist, including Livingstone himself.

This reality is precisely why, speaking at Oxford University in 1864, Livingstone went to great lengths to explain why he and other Western missionaries were reversing their goal from seeking the conversion of the Africans to Christianity to ensuring the success of commercial enterprise. Livingstone went on to argue:

Sending the Gospel to the heathens of Africa must include more than is implied in the usual practice of a missionary, namely, a man going about with a Bible under his arms. The promotion of commerce ought to be specially attended to as this, more than anything else, makes the heathen tribes depend on commercial intercourse among civilized nations. I go back to Africa to open a new path to commerce, do you carry on the work I have started?[29]

Without doubt, Livingstone and other missionaries had failed to understand the African mind and that its response to their Christian message had been negative. This is not because the Africans did not grasp its meaning, but because it was camouflaged in efforts to exploit them and the resources of their land for the benefit of the Christian European. For Livingstone and his missionary colleagues to expect the African mind to understand that the white man himself was a victim of his own conflicting values was unrealistic. Besides, the enthusiasm among Western missionaries for material comfort was not limited to this group of Europeans. It was shared by colonial enthusiasts who now began to believe that Africa must be settled in order to bring its vast wealth under their control because Europe lacked such raw materials.

The Western missionaries' change of objectives from the pursuit of establishing Christianity in Africa to that of promoting Western commercial enterprise was a development that had a profoundly negative influence on the Africans' response to the message the missionaries were trying to get them to accept. Thus, in 1882 Robert Moffat expressed total disappointment with his failure to persuade the Africans to accept Christianity: "A few individuals may have been influenced for good, but there is no organic result. There does not seem to be two people of the tribe who recognize each other as Christians. There is no indication that life in the tribe is in any way touched by the Gospel."[30] This suggests the conclusion that in all their enthusiasm to promote Christianity as a new way of life in Africa, Western missionaries failed to fathom the real cause of African negative response, the contradiction in the behavior of the missionaries and that of the colonial entrepreneurs. The only way the African mind could be receptive to the missionary's message was for the white man himself to resolve this conflict. One can see that while the African mind was subjected to pressure to accept the values of the white man, its ability to retain its distinct character placed the white man in a difficult situation. This ability would prove crucial to the survival of the Africans and to retaining their sense of self when the colonial systems were fully established.

By 1875 interest among the nations of Europe in various aspects of Africa was slowly turning into intense competition and creating an environment of conflict. Otto von Bismarck (1815–1898), the disciple of S. T. von Soemmering and the charismatic chancellor of Germany following the Franco-Prussian War of 1870–1871, realizing that Germany was not ready for a major conflict over Africa, decided to play his political cards carefully. He persuaded other European nations to go slow in their desire to establish spheres of influence and control in order to secure the raw materials they needed to improve the standard of living in Europe. Bismarck concluded that a major conflict in Europe over resources in Africa would undermine the very purpose of the Industrial Revolution as well as the objectives they were trying to accomplish toward the "Dark Continent." Bismarck then concluded that there was a better course of action to follow relative to the need among European nations to have total access to the raw materials and human resources of Africa.

In 1884, utilizing his newly acquired influence and power following the defeat of France in the Franco-Prussian War, Bismarck convened a conference at Berlin to be attended by major European nations that were interested in launching a colonial adventure in Africa. By that time, the knowledge among European nations that they needed colonies as a source of raw materials and as markets for their products accentuated the need for the conference in order to avoid conflict. The need for such a conference was also enhanced in 1875 when Benjamin Disraeli (1804–1881), British prime minister, ensured British control of the Suez Canal, which was completed in 1869 by buying shares from the Khedive of Egypt.[31] That Bismarck and other leaders of European nations saw this action as threatening larger European security and economic interests highlighted the sense of urgency and the importance of holding such a conference so that they would coordinate their activities in Africa.

The success of the conference is seen in two specific decisions. First, its participants recognized that the success of the colonizing enterprise lay in a collective action in accordance with the principles they agreed on in order to avoid conflict. The second is that they established what they called spheres of influence demarcated on the map of Africa. They created boundary lines that paid no regard to African ethnic and tribal groupings.[32] The participants of the Berlin Conference concluded that seeking to sustain their colonial and commercial interests was a far more important objective than trying to preserve the ethnic and cultural integrity of the Africans. They hoped that in this action they would control the African mind far more effectively than in any other way. Divide and conquer was the name of the game.

To give further effect to their intent, European nations tried to manipulate the thinking of the African chiefs by having them sign treaties, whose terms and implications they thought they did not fully understand.[33] To their surprise, the colonial governments soon discovered that the African mind could not so easily be misled. However, the efforts of European nations to control the African mind reflect their obsession with converting the resources of the continent into a means of sustaining their own political and socioeconomic purposes in Europe. The success of the Berlin Conference could also be measured in terms of how European nations managed to subdue the African way of life and convert it into an instrument of fulfilling their grand scheme of expanding the notion that in order for them to survive, the Africans had to function under new conditions. In this basal element of colonial thinking, the perils of their adventure had now been put in place. The European nations' use of raw and brutal force to subject the Africans to colonial rule would play a critical role after 1945 when the African mind sought to liberate itself.

The conclusion of the Berlin Conference in February 1885 signaled the beginning of a new and decisive phase in the European adventure to subjugate the African mind in order to control the resources of the continent. The machinery of that control was now in place. After narrowly averting conflict among themselves over colonial possessions in Africa, European nations now began in earnest the process of colonization. It was open season for them and anything that moved was fair game. While this phase represented the best of times for European nations, it ushered in the worst of times for the African way of life. The resources of the continent and the Africans themselves were now at the mercy of European fortune hunters. For them the season of hope was here, but for the Africans it was a season of despair. Their future, mired in the dark cloud of colonial exploitation, could only be salvaged by their own ability to utilize internal resources, their resilient willpower and sense of self.

In their determination to bring the African mind under colonial control so as to exploit the resources of the continent, European entrepreneurs were as callous as they were brutal in their treatment of the Africans. This is what led Kenneth Knorr to the conclusion that European colonial governments systematically sought to reduce the Africans to a position where they were forced to become "raw material to be employed in the service of the white man. The Africans were not allowed to decide for themselves because they were considered incapable of doing so. It was therefore decided for them, to serve the white man as his master."[34] In this basic colonial philosophy, the conclusions reached by S. T. von Soemmering and Charles White now found an appropriate form of application as the African mind was being forced to become an instrument with which European colonial masters sought to fulfill their own grandiose objectives. Indeed, the African mind was also forced to revisit in painful ways the days of the myth that came out of the Enlightenment and those of the period of Edward Long.

The principal architect of the new era of colonization was none other than Cecil John Rhodes, the faithful and devoted disciple of the histrionic Wynwood Read. On arriving in South Africa in 1870, Rhodes quickly sought to pave his way to the top rung of the political ladder by seeking to control the African mind in ways that had not been done in the past. He played a psychological game that he had learned to perfection. In the process, he formulated a racial philosophy that he used as a basis for his action. Its principal component was that because the Africans were uncivilized and possessed less intellectual potential than Europeans, they must be afforded a treatment less than that given to the whites. In 1891 Rhodes was quite candid in arguing his support of the von Soemmering–White school of thought that as adults Africans had the mind of children. Rhodes was quickly recognized as the new spokesman of the knowledge that the whites claimed to possess about the African mind. He was immediately elevated to new political pronouncements when he said in that year, "I say that the Natives are like children. They are just emerging from barbarism. They have human mind, but they are like children, and we ought to do something to develop that mind."[35]

Rhodes regarded his racial philosophy as the ultimate evidence that, for European colonial entrepreneurs, the best of times were here and now. Therefore, during his life, and after his death, Rhodes's influence on white perceptions and attitudes toward Africans became larger than life. He became the undisputed authority and spokesman, the deity and the un-crowned guardian angel of European efforts to control the African mind and to condition it to accept what the whites claimed to be their exclusive cultural refinements. These self-purported saviors of the evolutionary stunted Africans pushed this view because they saw the Africans as lacking any positive attributes of the human species.

In 1896, speaking during a debate on the position of the Africans in Parliament in Cape Town, Rhodes received an extended standing ovation when he argued that the only function the Africans could fulfill was to accept the reality that because they possessed less intellectual ability they must serve as servants for the whites. Fully conscious of the impact of what he was about to say, Rhodes deliberately chose his words as he went on to argue, "We have got to treat the Natives where they are, in a state of barbarism. We are to be lords over them. We will continue to treat them as a subject race as long as they continue to be in the state of barbarism."[36] With Rhodes's pronouncements, the mission among European colonial entrepreneurs to control the African mind now acquired powerful new dimensions. Rhodes, like his mentor Wynwood Read, was never quite able to comprehend the character of the African mind and the richness of the African culture. This failure raises some doubt concerning his own intellect.[37]

It is indeed a tragic fact that Rhodes never came to know the mind of George Washington Carver (1864–1943), a major twentieth-century black scientist who invented more than three hundred products from peanuts. As a baby, Carver and his mother were stolen and sold during the waning days of slavery in the United States. This experience did not in any way diminish the quality of his mind. Nor did Rhodes ever come to know the mind of Albert Luthuli (1898–1967), who was awarded the Nobel Peace Prize in 1961 for arousing the conscience of the international community about the slavery of apartheid in South Africa. Nor that of Stanlake Samkange (1923–1988), a distinguished historian, freelance journalist, and social critic who, through his works, posed fundamental questions about the oppressive colonial conditions in Africa. But that reality is beside the point. The issue is that Rhodes, devoted to the views of his mentor, placed the African mind at a level that was totally unrealistic. By 1896, the year that Rhodes made his indelible imprint on European perceptions of the African mind, the colonial systems were fully operational. A new era of white supremacy had just begun.

SUMMARY AND CONCLUSION

This chapter discusses how European perceptions of the African mind translated into a set of actions to colonize Africa and bring its raw materials under the control of European nations. By the beginning of the Victorian period, the voyages of exploration that the Portuguese sailors initiated to discover new lands to enhance trade had turned into a mission for forming perceptions about the African mind as the first step in seeking to establish colonial empires in Africa. The reality of these developments is that Victorian European colonial enthusiasts concluded that by seeking to control the African way of life they would not care about the action of the Africans. This was how they would have access to the raw materials they needed to enhance the standard of living in Europe. The behavior of colonial governments in Africa was quite consistent with colonial behavior elsewhere—that is, they justified both their policy and action on the assumption that the colonized are inferior to the colonizers.

By the time the colonial governments were fully established in Africa by the end of the nineteenth century, European perceptions of the African mind, overwhelmingly negative as they were, had not improved at all since they were first formulated during the Enlightenment some years before. The Europeans made no effort to appreciate the fact that the African way of life was a product of an environment that was totally different from that in Europe, and that the Africans had positive attributes that could be utilized to improve human conditions. Instead, during the height of colonial conquests, Europeans sought to accentuate the myth that had been fabricated in the past. They used the basic premises of this myth to strengthen their real lack of understanding about the African mind in order to initiate the process of colonization. This is why Cecil Rhodes used a new but questionable psychological game of brainwashing to elevate himself to a position of political power.

Whereas Rhodes argued that Africans had intellectual potential, he did not hold out any real hope for their advancement because he concluded that they lacked the developmental potential of their mind. The tragic part of Rhodes's views is that he did not see colonial conditions as the ultimate form of oppression of the African mind. That this myth of intellectual arrest was the basis of colonial policy in Africa is not in doubt. It is an equally sad irony that Rhodes, like Adolf Hitler after him, believed that his influence would last a thousand years in the process of building a British super race.

Rhodes's protégé, Godfrey Huggins (1883–1971), served as prime minister of colonial Zimbabwe from 1933 to 1952 and fully adopted Rhodes's philosophy and policies. Speaking during a political campaign in 1952, Huggins echoed the voice from the past:

We must reject permanently the notion that democracy can consist of mere counting of heads. We must unhesitatingly accept the doctrine that our superiority over the Natives rests on the color of our skin, civilization, and heredity. We must appreciate that we have a paramount monopoly of these qualities and that the Natives have been denied them by their primitive culture. You can call me an imperialist of the old school. True imperialism entails paternal government. It would be outrageous to give the Native a so-called political partnership when he is likely to ruin himself as a result.[38]

Huggins's own protégé, Ian Smith, was the last prime minister of colonial Zimbabwe (1964–1979), and launched his own fateful crusade to place the white race in Africa at the pinnacle of absolute political power over the Africans. That Smith used the theme of a thousand years as the standard criterion of his political philosophy suggests the powerful influence of the perceptions that had been formed in the past. In 1966, when his administration was charged with converting colonial Zimbabwe into a police state, Smith defended the action of his government saying, "When you have a primitive people such as the Africans of this country are, it would be completely irresponsible of the government not to have done so."[39]

Smith's justification of his own government policy toward the Africans by arguing that they were not intelligent enough to understand the importance of education shows how his own mind was controlled by the past. During an interview in 1983 Smith stated: "Before World War II the Africans did not believe in education because they thought it was something that belonged to the white man."[40] It is little surprise that both Hitler and Smith placed humanity on a course of unprecedented conflict. There is no doubt that Rhodes, Huggins, Smith, and the host of other colonial officials based their national policy and action on the assumptions and perceptions that emerged during the Enlightenment about the African mind. Did these assumptions and perceptions lead to policies and actions that ensured the longevity of the colonial governments, or was it the beginning of a new phase that led to major cultural conflict?

NOTES

1. Charles H. Lyons, *To Wash an Aethiop White: British Ideas about Black African Educability, 1530–1960* (New York: Teachers College Press, 1975), p. 9.

2. Today, in contemporary South Africa, preoccupation with the color of the skin has been used as the sole criterion to determine a person's place in society. The inauguration of apartheid in 1948 was based on this line of thinking until its end in 1994.

3. Lyons, *To Wash an Aethiop White*, p. 11.

4. Shakespeare, *The Merchant of Venice*, II, 2–3.

5. Ibid., p. 7.

6. Martin Luther King, Jr., Speech delivered during the March on Washington, August 28, 1963.

7. William Shakespeare, *As You Like It*, II, 7, 120.

8. The adjective *Dark* in the expression *Dark Ages* denotes blackness. It is quite surprising that the period of the Dark Ages was not officially called the *Black Ages*.

9. Dickson A. Mungazi, *The Struggle for Social Change in Southern Africa: Visions of Liberty*. (New York: Taylor and Francis, 1989), p. 17.

10. Ibid., p. 18.

11. Dickson A. Mungazi, *To Honor the Sacred Trust of Civilization: History, Politics and Education in Southern Africa* (Cambridge, Mass.: Schenkman Publishers, 1983), p. 23.

12. Kevin Shillington, *History of Southern Africa* (Essex, England: Longman, 1987), p. 19.

13. Mungazi, *To Honor the Sacred Trust of Civilization*, p. 24.

14. Donald Denoon and Balam Nyeko, *Southern Africa Since 1800* (London: Longman, 1984), p. 1.

15. The contemporary term *landlord* derives from these conditions.

16. Dickson A. Mungazi, *Colonial Policy and Conflict in Zimbabwe: A Study of Cultures in Collision, 1890–1979* (New York: Taylor and Francis, 1991), p. 2.

17. Ibid., p. 2.

18. Lyons, *To Wash an Aethiop White*, p. 68.

19. Vincent Battle and Charles Lyons, *Essay in the History of African Education* (New York: Teacher College Press, 1970), p. 2.

20. Ibid., p. 4.

21. Charles White, "The Gradation of Man, 1795" in Philip D. Curtin, *The Images of Africa: British Ideas and Action, 1780–1850* (Madison: University of Wisconsin Press, 1964), p. 45.

22. Thomas Winterbottom, *An Account of the Native Africans*, 2 vols. (London: Richard Brooks, 1803).

23. Battle and Lyons, *Essays in African Education*, p. 3.

24. Melvin Tumin (ed.), *Race and Intelligence: A Scientific Evaluation* (New York: Anti-Defamation League of B'nai B'rith, 1963), p. 54.

25. For a detailed discussion of Bishop Dodge's work in Africa, see, for example, Dickson A. Mungazi, *The Honored Crusade: Ralph Dodge's Theology of Liberation and Initiative for Social Change in Zimbabwe* (Gweru, Zimbabwe: Mambo Press, 1991).

26. Ralph E. Dodge, *The Unpopular Missionary* (Westwood, N.J.: H. Revell, 1964), p. 86.

27. Battle and Lyons, *Essays in the History of African Education*, p. 9.

28. Eppie D. Edwards, Director, National Library of Jamaica, a letter dated January 30, 1992, addressed to the author.

29. David Livingstone, "Missionary Trends in Southern Africa, 1857–1870." Zimbabwe National Archives.

30. G. C. Grove, "The Planting of Christianity in Africa" (London: Murray, 1954), Vol. II

31. George Kimble, *Emerging Africa* (New York: Scholastic Books, 1960), p. 6.

32. Leo Marquard, *The Peoples and Policies of South Africa* (London: Oxford University Press, 1960), p. 15.

33. For a detailed discussion of how European colonial governments put this strategy into operation, see, for example, Dickson A. Mungazi, *Colonial Policy and Conflict in Zimbabwe: A Study of Cultures in Collision, 1890–1979* (New York: Taylor and Francis, 1992), pp. 9, 143.

34. Kenneth Knorr, *British Colonial Theories* (Toronto: University of Toronto Press, 1974), p. 375.

35. British South Africa Company Records. Ref. AV/1–01. Zimbabwe National Archives.

36. Ibid.

37. Some people have questioned Rhodes's own intelligence. Some say that he dropped out of Oxford University because of poor grades. Others say that he was asked to leave because his work fell below the minimum requirement. History seems to indicate that he was given an honorary degree by Oxford University after making a sizable donation. He was also admitted to Oriel College at Oxford in 1873 but did not graduate until 1881. (See *Parade, The Arizona Republic*, August 11, 1991, for details.)

38. Godfrey Huggins, "Partnership in Building a Country," a political speech, 1952, Zimbabwe National Archives. Two years later in 1954, Huggins addressed the Southern Rhodesia Christian Conference held at Goromonzi, August 25, 1954, entitled "Taking Stock of African Education," in which he reiterated his views of the Africans. For the complete text of the address, see Dickson A. Mungazi, *Colonial Policy and Conflict in Zimbabwe*, p. 167.

39. G. Sparrow, *Rhodesian Rebellion* (London: Brighton, 1966), p. 25.

40. Ian Smith during an interview with the author in Parliament Building, Harare, Zimbabwe, July 20, 1983. For the full text of the interview, see Mungazi, *The Struggle for Social Change in Southern Africa,* p. 120, or Dickson A. Mungazi, *The Challenge of Educational Innovation and National Development in Southern Africa* (New York: Peter Lang Publishing, 1991), p. 165.

2

African Perceptions of the
African Mind

> The African mind is quite teachable and capable of learning. The
> African can understand and undertake responsible work after training.
> *Colonial official in Zimbabwe, 1930*
>
> The student in traditional African setting manifested a high level of
> intellect showing the innate capability of the African mind.
> *An elderly African in Zimbabwe, 1974*

THE EFFECT OF COLONIZATION ON THE
AFRICAN MIND

The colonization of Africa could not be effected without first colonizing the
African mind, but European nations failed to realize that the colonization
of the African way of life did not substantiate the myth of its cultural
inferiority. Rather, it meant the application of European criteria of intellectual potential cast into African settings. Whatever Europeans defined as a
lack of intellect of the African mind, they failed to recognize that it was not
the same thing as intellect among themselves because they neglected to
realize that the environment in which Europeans grew and lived was totally
different from the one in which the Africans resided. The only accurate way
to determine the level of intellect among the Africans was to study it under
African environmental conditions, including cultural. Researchers in both
the Age of Reason and the Victorian period negated the effect of culture and
environment, thereby demonstrating the powerful influence of the racial
bias with which they approached their assigned task.[1]

The reality of the methods Europeans have adopted to determine the level of cognition among Africans leads to the inevitable conclusion that if measured by the criteria that would assess African intelligence that accounted for their specific environmental conditions, the European mind would be found to be inadequate.[2] The tables would be reversed. One must deduce that the colonization of Africa was founded on the myth of the inferiority of the African mind. This chapter has two objectives. The first is to show that Cecil John Rhodes, the mastermind of British colonial adventure in Africa, came face to face with the high level of African cognition in a way that he never expected. This prowess created a situation that forced Rhodes to adopt deceptive methods in his dealings with the Africans because he and his associates could not manipulate the logic exhibited by the African mind. The second objective is to discuss the nature of the African mind, as it shaped the character of African society, based on certain philosophical constructs. It will demonstrate that contrary to popular European myth, African society was highly organized and functioned effectively to serve the needs of all people.

The delusion of the inferiority of the African way of life also suggests that there was nothing in the Victorians' so-called scientific study of the African mind to indicate that the colonization process was an outcome of humanitarian considerations for the African people. Therefore, European colonization of the African way of life was motivated by the desire to exploit it in order to bring the raw materials of the continent under the socioeconomic control of Europeans. As long as European colonial governments were able to sustain the myth of the Africans' intellectual inferiority, they utilized it to psychologically condition them to accept the whites' presumed superiority. This is how the exploitation of raw materials could also be sustained. In basing the entire colonization process on this myth, the colonial governments were instituting a definite form of violence against the Africans—mental, cultural, and economic rape.

RHODES AND THE AFRICAN MIND COLLIDE

The delusion that the African mind was inferior to that of Europeans became the basis of the colonization of Africa following the conclusion of the Berlin Conference in February 1885. As a result, European colonial governments ignored the Africans' objections to the intrusion of their society and culture. The Africans were also believed incapable of forming opinions and defining positions consistent with human logic on critical issues.[3] Since the Age of Reason, the application of logic to problems has demanded a demonstration of a fully developed intellect. Within the British grand colonial design, Cecil Rhodes exerted greater influence than any other single individual in perpetuating the belief that the Africans were incapable of exercising logic. Indeed, Rhodes became the vehicle by which the British government, including Queen Victoria herself (1837–1901), sought to accomplish their objective of bringing all of Africa under their colonial control.

But in his insatiable appetite for raw materials and his uncompromising desire to achieve British colonial objectives, as well as his self-appointed mission to salvage the African mind from its presumed condemnation by its equally presumed primitive culture, Rhodes paved the way for a deadly collision with the African mind. His attitude, policy, and behavior toward the Africans showed a callousness that was consistent with the views of S. T. von Soemmering and Charles White. This is how Rhodes became the spokesman of the British colonial adventure in Africa. In his dealing with the Africans, he had neither the sensitivity nor the diplomacy that Europeans, especially the British, always claimed as among their more distinctive cultural attributes. Why did Rhodes abandon these traits in his dealings with the Africans? How could he convince the Africans that European culture was superior to African culture when his own behavior showed an absence of cultural attractiveness? Could Rhodes really expect the Africans to accept this contradiction in the behavior of the Christian European?

The specific event that reveals Rhodes as the mastermind of Britain's gross miscalculations of the African mind and the British objective of seeking total control of it came in October 1888 when he sought to fulfill his schemes in Africa on behalf of the British government. Convinced of his political power and financially secure, Rhodes embarked on a mission that he believed would eventually transform the continent of Africa into a massive British empire unchallenged by any other power, an empire that he thought would surpass even that of the Romans. Rhodes believed that he was the man of the hour; he held all the political cards in his hands as the game of colonization began.

Under these conditions, he commissioned a party of men led by Charles Rudd (1844–1916) to prove the accuracy of his theory of the inferiority of the African mind by holding bogus negotiations with King Khumalo Lobengula (1836–1894) of modern western Zimbabwe. The stated purpose was to allow British fortune hunters to prospect for minerals in his land for a limited period of time. The casualness and low regard of the African mind with which the Rudd team approached its assigned mission proved to be the first episode in the demise of the myth of the superiority of the European mind. King Lobengula, who had ascended the Ndebele throne in 1870, the year Rhodes arrived in South Africa, following the death of King Mzilikazi

(1792–1868), proved that the Africans possessed a high-level intellect that surprised not just Rhodes, but whites generally.

This mission and the negotiations, false as they were, proved a milestone in the interactions between the African and European minds. Never before had the people of the two cultures come together to engage in dialogue. The Rudd team, on Rhodes's behalf, felt that this was an opportunity of a lifetime to make a permanent imprint on the Africans' inferior mind. In addition to Rudd,who was a partner of Rhodes in the diamond diggings at Kimberly, the party included Rochfort Maguire (1855–1925), a leading advocate of British colonial adventure in Africa; Robert Thompson (1857–1927), who was once secretary to Rhodes; and Reverend Charles Helm (1834–1915), who was born in South Africa and came to Lobengula's country in 1875 in the service of the London Missionary Society, of which both Robert Moffat and David Livingstone were members. Helm had studied aspects of African culture, including language, well enough for the colonial entrepreneurs to recognize him as an expert on African culture. Helm gave Lobengula the impression that because he was a churchman, he had no interest in promoting the objectives of the Rudd team. But events would prove otherwise.

Given the circumstances of the time and the impact that the Christian missionaries were trying to make on the life on the Africans, King Lobengula thought that Reverend Helm was a good and honest Christian gentleman who would not mislead or deceive him in any way, or allow the members of the Rudd team and the whites in general to take advantage of him. It is important to remember that Lobengula did not place his total confidence in Reverend Helm out of a lack of intelligence or because he made irrational decisions. Rather, he was a victim of placing trust and confidence in a deceptive individual. King Lobengula did not know that the members of the Rudd team, including Reverend Helm, were not honest. Was it fair for the Rudd team to place the king in a situation in which he had to second-guess his negotiating partners?

King Lobengula, to his bitter disappointment, would discover that Reverend Helm, the so-called Christian gentleman in whom he had placed his total trust, was actually secretly paid by Rhodes to provide information that he could later use to facilitate the colonization of Zimbabwe in accordance with the provisions of the Royal Charter that Rhodes had received from Queen Victoria in 1889.[4] The dishonesty of the members of the Rudd team, both individually and as a group, suggests that circumstances forced King Lobengula and his counselors to face insurmountable odds from the Rudd team, not because they lacked the intellect to measure up, but because the white man employed deception.

As soon as the so-called negotiations between the two sides began, members of the Rudd party, including Helm, were astonished to discover that Lobengula was a shrewd politician and a highly intelligent man who fully comprehended the deliberations. His ability to articulate positions and to understand the significance of the discussions brought the views of S. T. von Soemmering, Charles White, Wynwood Read, and Cecil John Rhodes to shame. The Victorian delusion that had influenced the whites' attitude and behavior toward the Africans—that the African mind was inferior because it was the product of a subordinate culture—produced a shocking revelation for them. Peter Gibbs discusses the extent to which Lobengula demonstrated great intellectual prowess as a negotiator, saying, "Hour after hour, week after week, month after month, the king argued with remarkable success with the Cambridge men. He tore to shreds their thesis on the advantage of granting Rhodes a concession. The pillars of learning made so little headway that Rhodes felt compelled to force the issue."[5]

Rudd himself later admitted that he was greatly surprised by Lobengula's great intelligence, adding, "He was as sharp as a needle and remembered everything. If you contradicted yourself, he was on you at once."[6] But even more devastating to the Rudd party, and the Europeans in general, was the fact that the whites had grossly misunderstood and that they were basing both their attitudes and behavior on an illusion that had persisted since the Enlightenment.

Although the colonial entrepreneurs did not admit it, this realization created an entirely new climate. However, instead of seeking to reevaluate both that attitude and policy to suit the conditions created by the demonstration of the competent African mind, the Rudd party and the other Europeans denied that this intelligence was real and acted as they had in the past. In this manner, they charted a new but dangerous course in human interaction. For Rhodes to discover the reality that the entire colonial systems were based on myth was as devastating as it was revealing about a new age of reality.

For Rhodes to discover that myth had dictated both his attitude and his behavior toward the Africans, that it was an illusion, must have been a shattering experience. This paradigm shift forced him to turn his low regard of Lobengula's mind into anger, and his anger turned into a desire to eliminate him quickly. His ambitions and grand plan could not be thwarted by the intellectual power of an African he considered to be a member of a primitive culture. Instead of pausing to reflect on the truth that confronted him, Rhodes wanted to put an immediate end to it. His mental and emotional denial eventually became transformed into physical violence in the conflict between the two racial groups.

Indeed, there was a serious dimension to this dramatic and tragic turn of events. Lobengula's demonstration of a high intellect placed Rhodes and the Rudd party on the horns of a dilemma. If they failed to manipulate the king, then Rhodes's pursuit of his grand plan of building a vast British colonial empire in Africa would suffer a severe setback. If he forced the issue, then he would risk the danger of a serious military confrontation with Lobengula's army, which was estimated at 6,000 strong. Rhodes therefore instructed Rudd to ensure that by fair means or foul, the king must be pressured to sign a piece of paper that, in effect, seemed to carry the appearance of a properly drafted legal contract.[7] Rhodes was so pleased with the terms of the agreement that he remarked, "Our concession is so gigantic that it is like giving a man the whole of Australia."[8] But the fact that the entire relationship between the two sides was sealed in deception, mistrust, and conflict marked a new stage of conflict between them.

Rhodes's desire not to be the first high-level colonial official to admit that he was wrong in basing official policy toward the Africans on myth proved to be a tragic error. This error also eroded the whites' valuable opportunity to restructure human relationships on the foundations of mutual respect. Lobengula and his people had proved ready to embark on new human interactions provided the whites proved to be honest in all their dealings.

Unable to manipulate Lobengula, Rhodes turned to Helm, the man in whom Lobengula had placed his trust and confidence, and secretly paid him to spy on the king and supply him with information that he would later use in planning the colonization of Zimbabwe as the first step of implementing his grand plan of bringing all of Africa under British rule.[9] Inevitably, Rhodes's action and Helm's betrayal of Lobengula's trust produced a collision between Rhodes and the African way of life that was so forceful that it shattered any chance of designing more solid cultural relationships. Once that opportunity was lost, it would not be found again. In this setting, the colonial systems were doomed before they were established. The tragic part of all this is that neither Rhodes nor Helm fully understood the enormous impact of their action. As a result of this deception, there was nothing that the white man in general could do in the future to regain the Africans' trust and confidence. Instead, the African and the colonial mind were set on a path that led to deadly confrontation.

On October 30, 1888, taking the advice he received from Helm into consideration, Lobengula signed a piece of paper known as the *Rudd Concession*,[10] which in effect gave Rhodes exclusive rights to dig for minerals for a limited period of time. Instead, Rhodes himself used it to colonize Zimbabwe as the first leg of his *safari* to bring all of African under

British colonial rule. Soon after learning that Helm had misled him, Lobengula remarked to him, "Did you ever see a chameleon catch a fly? He gets behind the fly and remains motionless for some time. Then he advances slowly, and when well within reach, he darts his tongue and the fly disappears. Britain is the chameleon and I am the fly."[11] Obviously, Helm had no response. From this moment Lobengula's fate, as well as that of his people and land, were sealed as Rhodes secretly dispatched an occupation force in September 1890 to colonize the country.

Throughout the entire period of colonial rule in Africa, colonial government officials failed to understand a simple principle relative to human interaction. As Bertrand Russell, a twentieth-century British social critic put it, Europeans failed to show "the kind of tolerance that springs from an endeavor to understand those who are different from ourselves."[12] This cultural intolerance became the root cause of conflict between the African mind and the colonial establishments following the end of World War II.

In 1893 Lobengula was eliminated, leading to a bitter war between the forces of occupation and Lobengula's army that began in 1896. Nearly 10 percent of the white population was killed, but bows and arrows were no match for guns. Therefore, the Africans were defeated, but the colonization of the African mind came at a great price. The bitterness lingered on until the outbreak of new fighting in April 1966. Finally, in December 1979, the African mind prevailed in putting an end to colonization. Once this bitterness became the principal factor in the relationships between the colonial governments and the Africans, neither side was able to do anything to resolve it in an amicable and mutually respectable manner. This became the only form of interaction between the two cultures.

THE QUALITY OF THE AFRICAN MIND: SOME PHILOSOPHICAL CONCEPTS

Without doubt the colonization of the African mind was based on the mistaken notion of the African's intellectual inferiority. As Courtland Cox concludes, European colonial policy and action were based on the belief in the African's inferiority, and everything that was done to structure human relationships reflected this basic assumption. Cox adds: "At the base of the assumption underlying this line of thinking was the absolute belief in the inferiority of the African people and the certainty of political chaos if their subjection was eased in the slightest."[13] Both the failure to understand the quality of the African mind and deliberate efforts to distort its true character had enormous consequences. Efforts to distort the character of the African mind resulted from the failure to appreciate the viability of African culture and society. To appreciate that viability, colonial entrepreneurs had to respect the African way of life as it was related to certain philosophical concepts. This task was too complex for Victorian Europeans to undertake, but should have been undertaken.

To understand the African philosophical concepts is to appreciate the character of the African society itself. The illusion shared by Victorian Europeans that African society lacked structure was also a result of what David Hapgood identifies as a mythology of imperialism. This mythology led Westerners to believe that African culture and society were void of values and ideas. Hapgood concludes that once caught in this mythology, Westerners were unable to appreciate the quality of the African mind and the philosophy it uses to create a viable society. A compelling aspect of Cox's argument augments this view when cast in the cultural mold of the Age of Reason; it was not an easy task for Westerners to perceive the African culture as making a contribution to improving the universal human condition. By the time colonization began, Victorian colonial enthusiasts chose to ignore the viability of the African mind in order to justify colonization.[14] This justification lent legitimacy to the mythology of imperialism, but it did not take away the fact that the African society was a highly structured one.

A study of the structure of the traditional African society supports Cox's conclusion and refutes the myth that the African mind and society were disintegrated and disjointed and did not contribute to a cohesive and integrated social system. The truth is that African philosophy addressed all the inclusive elements of society. Its central component was the conviction that all members of society must play different roles to make it complete and to meet the needs of all its members. Today it is referred to as systems theory.

Society must therefore be inclusive; that is, no distinction must be made regarding the individual's position in society on account of his station in life. Class consciousness, a dominant characteristic feature of Western society, was considered detrimental to the larger interests of society and was discouraged. A person's place in society was determined more by his contribution to its well-being than by his birth or role in life. This underlying principle was the basis of a genuine practice in equality. This line of thinking showed that the character of society was determined by the role each member played in it. To enable the individual to fulfill this role, the individual had to be trained to remain sensitive to the needs of society as a whole and others as individuals.

Placide Temples, a Belgian missionary to twentieth-century Africa, states that Africans place great value on relating philosophy to their world. Temples also maintains that the Africans demonstrated an understanding of the universe such that Westerners did not have, which made it possible for Africans to relate life to other important aspects of their culture in a manner that had direct application to human conditions.[15] Michael Gelfand (1911–1985), a medical practitioner who lived most of his life in Africa, adds that the endurance of the African society reflected the strength of African philosophy as it related to the individual's position in society and his understanding of the universe.[16] Both Gelfand and Temples argue that seeking to understand the universe entailed critical elements of understanding the environment, weather conditions, and seasonal change in order to create harmony between the Africans and their ecosystem. Ability to predict weather conditions and seasonal change enabled the Africans to plan agricultural activity and other annual events.

An even more important aspect of the Africans' understanding of the universe was their seeking to understand man. Understanding man and the universe could not be separated. According to African philosophy, the attempt to comprehend the universe was a critical element of the effort to acknowledge man as the ultimate object of creation. Nature was what it was because man played a critical role in seeking a balance between the two. Both Temples and Gelfand also state that the strength of society reflected the values of its members. This required that the cognitive process in turn reflect all essential aspects of life, such as religion, commerce, weather, agriculture, law, medicine, and human interaction.

In short, understanding the universe as an important part of understanding man was a product of the application of a philosophy uniquely African. In order to understand the broader meaning of philosophy, the Africans considered the development of the mental processes as a critical dimension. Thus, logic and rationale were applied to human situations in order to sustain a life full of meaning and to seek solutions to human problems. The mere fact that this philosophy was different from Western philosophy compelled the Victorian Europeans to conclude that it was primitive.

Kwanisi Wirendu, a leading African scholar of African philosophy, concludes that the completeness of the African society was in essence a measure of the high level of intellect that the Africans manifested in their philosophy as seen in their daily activities. Wirendu submits that this completeness was synonymous with a complete knowledge of the world.[17] He proposes that the application of African philosophy to human situations had three basic elements in common with Western philosophy: (1) It demanded a demonstration of the strength of the human mind to articulate positions on critical issues; (2) it created a climate in which people viewed their society from the perspective of the dynamics that retained its integrity; and (3) it provided a wide base on which to design relationships between the individual and society itself.[18]

Respecting the individual, preserving his rights, and accentuating the collective values were all components that ensured the development of society as determined by the role of the individual.

Wirendu also maintains that the inclusiveness of African society demanded the application of reason and thinking in continually seeking ways to improve the effectiveness of society based on a complete understanding of its values. This enabled its members to live a full life of meaning for both themselves and their society. It also required an absolute acceptance of basic principles of human behavior that distinguishes man from other living species, such as embracing moral values, developing a sense of justice and fairness, integrity, faithfulness, and respect and preserving the general good of society. For this reason, Africans scorned anyone whose behavior lacked these values and an understanding of the principal components that strengthened social institutions. The Africans taught their children at an early age to understand that they held a valued place in their society.

The Africans emphasized the essential qualities and integrity of their society because they operated under a social and philosophical creed and principle that they must at all times be honest, faithful, and trustful in both business transactions and personal relationships.[19] This was the basic reason why King Lobengula acted the way he did toward members of the Rudd party. The moral demands of his culture demanded that he be honest in dealing with other people so as to preserve the integrity of his society. That Rudd and his associates did not appreciate the wholeness of the African way of life shows the malevolent side of colonialism. To understand why Lobengula depended entirely on his ability to articulate positions on issues, we need to appreciate the guiding light in African human relationships. This is their belief that any person who fails to operate by the principle of honesty lacks the essence of what is required to be a human being.

African philosophy also addressed another important universal dimension of human experience: that is, to be a human being, one must accept the responsibility of maintaining norms and values that have application to society as a whole. The Africans therefore stressed the importance of cooperation rather than competition; dialogue rather than dictatorial action; consultation rather than arbitrary behavior; understanding rather than imposition; and persuasion rather than manipulation. When these elements are put together, we can see that the Africans also operated under the principle that maintaining the integrity of society was more important than achieving individual or personal gain and that preserving collective security was more valued than maintaining the position of any one individual. African philosophy covered every aspect of individual and societal life. The evolution of a social system, stressing the importance of justice, fairness, and cooperation, all demand a full comprehension of what society is all about. Once this understanding has been accomplished, social institutions can be structured with defined purposes: how the Victorian Europeans concluded that this was a product of a primitive culture is beyond comprehension.

THE AFRICAN MIND AND THE STRUCTURE OF SOCIETY

In addition to philosophical concepts, the high level of the African mind is also evident in the hierarchy of African society itself. That society was organized to meet the needs of its members, as is evident in the components of that organization. Three levels of organizational structure show how well the African society was designed: the chief, the ward head, and the village head. At the head of society was the chief,[20] who "symbolized the unity of the whole society and was not identified with any specific segment of it,"[21] but represented and protected its wholeness. Like the system of monarchies in Western society, the African chief was a hereditary leader and was not elected because members of the society knew who was next in line of succession. The chief was also responsible for the general welfare of all the people, ensuring justice, equality, and fairness. These principles were considered so important that they were not compromised. He "ruled by consent of his subjects and therefore enjoyed popular loyalty born of genuine patriotism."[22]

The legal system shows the African mind at its best. The system was so organized as to be highly sensitive to the need to sustain justice. Unlike the case in Western societies, a person did not have to be wealthy to obtain the services of the best lawyer available. In African traditional jurisprudence, justice was not for sale. The underlying principle was that, regardless of a person's position in society, justice must serve the interests of society by serving those of the individual. The courts were required to operate under conditions that were established to sustain a balance between the needs of the individual and those of society, between the rights of the accused and those of the public, between the presumption of innocence and the preponderance of evidence against the accused. There was no death penalty because the Africans considered it cruel and unusual punishment; this shows the extent to which the African legal system respected human life.

The jury of one's peers consisted of individuals, who served as counselors to the legal system. All cases were heard in open court. The litigants in a legal process were allowed equal opportunity to express their side of the case. In addition to the regular members of the jury and the chief, independent assessors made a determination about the merits and demerits of the arguments. Although their opinions were only advisory, the official jury took them into consideration in determining the guilt or innocence of the accused. Indeed, the African legal system went to amazing lengths to ensure that justice in all situations was served on an equal basis. No one was above the law, not even the king. How does this legal system compare with that of Western countries as a reflection of the human mind? It is an easy conclusion to arrive at.

The organizational structure of African society (see Figure 1) also showcases the African mind. Society was divided into districts called wards (the equivalent of a county in the United States). The ward head was responsible for all the people in his ward. The services offered were coordinated with the chief. Below the ward was the village which was under the village head. The village head was expected to make regular reports about the village to the ward head, and the ward head in turn made regular reports to the chief. The village head had responsibility for assigning arable land to the families in the village. He distributed this land in an equitable manner to avoid conflict and disputes. The village head referred any matter he and his committee were unable to resolve to the ward head and his committee. If the ward head and his committee were unable to resolve the issues, they were required to refer it to the chief and his councillors. One can see that this organizational structure is very similar to the court appellate system that operates in Western societies. There is no doubt that the African society was well organized and structured. For the colonial governments to suddenly demand that its institutional functions be abolished without first persuading the Africans to see the claimed values for demanding change was to show utter disrespect to their culture.

Figure 1
The Structure of African Society

The King (Chief)

1. Preserves social systems
2. Ensures justice for all
3. Provides service to all the people

Ward Head

1. Ensures welfare of the district
2. Consults district council
3. Hears petitions from the people

Village Head

1. Allocates land
2. Ensures welfare of the village
3. Makes reports to ward head

The high quality of the African mind was also evident in the Africans' perceptions of the values of their culture and society. For example, if a member of a village repeatedly misbehaved, the village head would summon his committee to discuss the issues and to take appropriate disciplinary action in accordance with the provisions of tribal law. The village head and his committee would act only within the limits of the law in taking any action against the man. In doing so, they weighed the interests of the man and his family against those of the village. This was the fundamental element of justice and fairness in the traditional African culture. Before any action was taken, the man was given an opportunity to make his case. Due process, both procedural and substantive, was strictly observed. If the accused was not satisfied with the action of the village head and his committee, he was at liberty to appeal to the ward head and his committee. If he or she was still not satisfied with the action at that level, he or she was permitted to appeal to the chief and his councillors. Thus, for the colonial governments to claim that the African society had no recognized legal system was to be blind to the actual facts.

If someone from another village wished to settle in a new village, the village head and his committee first determined to see if that person was acceptable as a member. A quick background check was often initiated to make that determination. If the village head and his committee were satisfied, they made a decision to accept him. If he was not accepted, then he was invited to hear the reasons for the rejection and to advance his own reasons or rebuttal to the reasons. This procedure was designed to ensure justice and fairness for all concerned. Any action taken by the village head and his committee was relayed to the ward head and his committee. This was done to make sure that all levels of the administrative system were fully informed. As in the Western system of jurisprudence, neither the ward head nor the chief's council would take action on any issue that did not originate with the village.[23] In a similar fashion, if a member of the village repeatedly misbehaved, the village head and his committee initiated a procedure to expel him by following due process procedures. This practice was designed to ensure that all levels of the administrative system did not act out of malice or prejudice and to ensure that a balance existed between the rights of the individual and those of the community.[24]

The underlying principle of all African cultural and traditional practices was to protect the integrity of society. But to do so the rights of the individual had to be protected first. This practice preserved the democratic characteristics of society so that it continued to serve the functions for which it was instituted. This is why social operations remained open. This practice also ensured that all levels of the administrative system were required to follow closely outlined and accepted procedures to ensure justice and fairness for all.

The Africans considered justice and equality before the law an absolute value that society must endeavor to sustain at all costs and that must never be compromised. While the Africans utilized legal experts in cases as needed, this was done more to seek harmony within the existing system than to manipulate the legal system to benefit an individual, as often happens in Western legal systems. As children grew up, they were taught to understand that social values were an indispensable component of the structure of society itself and that they had an obligation to learn to live and operate by them.

The Africans also understood the value of differences of opinion on critical issues. In this context, it was a rash individual who decided to resort to dictatorial behavior. The major restraints on the abuse of power were the bonds of customs and the knowledge of what was right and fair in interactions among people. Those in positions of responsibility were reminded that they had obligations to their people and that if they failed to honor them the people were at liberty to require their removal from office. This form of electoral recall was designed to protect the interests and wholeness of the community. This practice protected social values and principles against the personal ambitions of an individual who tried to manipulate the system or the public trust placed in him by the people for his own personal gain.

Although the village head and his committee, the ward head and his committee, and the chief were not elected, they did not rule as despots. They consulted representatives of the people through various channels, and their expressed wishes were taken into account.[25] W. Raynor states that the failure of the European nations to understand this basic principle eventually led to the conflict that ended in the African demand for political independence. This conflict arose when the Africans realized that, while the colonial administrations claimed that Western systems were superior to those of their own, they did not practice any form of democracy in their dealings with them.[26]

A double standard was in effect which was totally alien to the African way of life. By the end of the Second World War, the Africans had come to recognize that the inadequate European systems of social justice were not a reasonable substitute for Africa's traditional systems. African nationalism swept the continent once the awareness of these inadequacies and the feasibility of African traditions became widespread.

The Africans continually desired to improve the institutional functions of their society and so asked the best minds to serve their society. The Africans also understood that the development of a single human being cast in an array of factors that promoted his mental capacities was critical to ensuring a society that would benefit all. The Africans assumed that every single member of society had an important contribution to make to that society and that his other mental capacities must constantly be encouraged. Diversity and variation of interests, occupation, and career combined to create an environment that enabled new directions and innovative ideas to emerge. The African mind considered these elements essential to the welfare of the society.

THE FAMILY AND THE ROLE OF CHILDREN

The virtue of the African mind was also evident in the structure and functions of the family. The traditional African family operated along clearly defined lines. The oldest member, usually the paternal grandfather, was the head of the family. He determined the standards of behavior or code of ethics consistent with the general expectations of the community as a whole. Children occupied a very important place within the family and the community; everything of importance was structured to ensure the welfare of children. They were taught at an early age how to recognize these standards and to abide by them at all times. There was a clear consensus among the community that a family that lived by accepted social and community values provided the fiber for the entire society. Therefore, the family was considered essential to the formation of the society as a whole.

As an example of fairness and equality in dispensing social egalitarianism, the amount of land distributed to a family was determined by the needs of that family. The use of land was considered to be a collective responsibility. Everyone was expected to use it properly in order to sustain human needs. As was the practice among Native Americans, land was held on a communal basis; the idea of selling or buying land was totally rejected because it was considered crucial to the survival of the entire society. Land was readily available for use by all members of the community as needed.[27] The colonial government's introduction of the system of buying land was both offensive and insulting to the Africans. It was a totally alien concept that ran afoul of the African sense of fair play and equality. This Western practice became a major cause of conflict between the Africans and colonial governments when the colonial governments forced the Africans to move to desolate land to make room for the white landowners. Many European landowners did not live in Africa. How could colonial governments fail to see that this practice was unacceptable to the Africans?

In the traditional African culture, the young were carefully instructed in the proper use of land and the exercise of stewardship over it. The family played an important role in this instruction. Any form of abuse of land resulted in action against those concerned. Land was important to Africans because of its value to future generations. Mining activity, a central component of colonization in the nineteenth century, was an affront to the African concept of proper land use. This was one reason why the Africans and the colonial officials experienced serious conflicts over the use of land.[28] The colonial governments disregarded as superstition concern among the Africans that mining activity would ruin the land formation. The truth of the matter is that mining activity on a large scale did upset the balance in the delicate African environment. Since the colonial governments always considered themselves temporary residents in Africa for purposes of exploiting the raw materials, they did not seem to care much about the condition of the land for future generations.

Relationships among members of the family also demonstrated the high caliber of the African way of life. A man's wealth was measured in terms of the number of livestock he had. It was generally accepted that before he disposed of any part of his chattel, a man consulted his wife to ensure that her opinion was reflected in the decision-making process. In the same way, his wife would consult with her husband before she decided to dispose of any of her possessions, such as grain and personal effects. Thus, both husband and wife enjoyed a high degree of freedom and independence of action within the institution of marriage. Moreover, their mutual respect for each other was consistent with the social values that sustained the interests of the community.

Children were taught to understand that the decisions of their parents, both individually and together, had to be respected in order to serve the interests of the family as a unit. Differences of opinion between a man and his wife were not grounds for divorce as they are in Western society. In traditional African society, differences of opinion between a man and his wife simply meant that spouses had the freedom to sustain the principle of individuality. The Western notion of irreconcilable differences did not exist because the Africans recognized that the institution of marriage was vitally important to the integrity of society and that it had to be sustained at all costs. Once a marriage was performed, it was expected to last a lifetime, "until death us do part," as the saying goes.

When a man died, his brothers or his eldest son automatically assumed responsibility for maintaining his family. As soon as a man thought that his eldest son was able to understand, he taught him the important aspects of life and society.[29] The concept of hard work was instilled in the minds of the young people at an early age and laziness was recognized as a disgrace. The lazy person was likely to become a burden to society and to become jealous of others' achievements. The young man or woman known to be lazy even found it difficult to get a spouse.[30] Indeed, the Africans believed that success in life depended on the kind of thinking that went into preparing for a vocation or career. An ability to articulate definite plans for the future and to work toward their fulfillment were considered essential pillars of success in life and a manifestation of the type of character that the individual carved for him or herself. The African perception of the character of an individual became the basis of perception about society itself.

The Africans also taught their children to recognize that the family's interests were paramount and had to be placed above those of the individual. The development of the individual's intellect was considered essential to the creative process, just as the development of internal human resources was needed to sustain a collective identity made up of individualized persons. Family members had to have an understanding of family relationships in their proper sense. Brothers, sisters, half-brothers, half-sisters, and cousins were regarded as belonging to one and the same family. Both polygamous and monogamous marriages were accepted forms of family systems and had the respect and support of the community. Polygamy had important political and socioeconomic implications. Members of polygamous families were expected to show good examples of family cooperation and of working together for the good of every member of the family. C. K. Omari of Tanzania explains the cultural imperatives of the African mind with reference to the African understanding of polygamy:

The African understanding of the meaning of the family is very different from Western understanding. The extended family is a concept understood by Africans as the family. This may be based on either a polygamous or monogamous marriage. It may involve members of the same family living in the same unit up to three generations including uncles, aunts, cousins. Both polygamous and monogamous families had the blessing of society and were accepted as forms of the concept of the family.[31]

An elderly African in Zimbabwe seemed to understand the consequences of the limitations of the Western mind when it came to understanding the meaning of the family.

There is a higher rate of divorce among monogamous marriages than among polygamous marriages. Members of monogamous families, as is the case in Western societies, drifted as they depended on themselves losing the relationships they must have with other members of the family. Because they put their own interests before those of the family, they lose the values that must bind them together. When they get married they have no tolerance of anything that is different. But members of polygamous families, as is the case in Africa, had closer relationships because they learned to depend on their cooperation to ensure self-reliance and economic independence.[32]

This African perception of the family suggests that the Africans declined to accept Western cultural values because they posed a threat to some of the most important aspects of their own culture. Western thinking was dramatically different from that of Africans. Because of all the negative features of Western society, Europeans could not convince the Africans to discard their own culture in favor of Western culture. To accept Western culture would mean rejecting the viability of their own mind.

THE AFRICAN MIND AND THE MEANING OF RELIGIOUS PRACTICES

Europeans had always argued that the Africans' religious practices were nothing more than superstition. To the contrary, the Africans utilized orderly and logical theological concepts that gave an important dimension to their lives. The Africans, like Westerners, believed in a supernatural being who had influence on how the world functioned. They also believed that natural phenomena, such as day and night, summer and winter, and the entire form of the universe, were the result of specific acts of creation.

The American saying "In God We Trust" is not entirely an original expression of religious faith in the supernatural being, but had its origins in African theological doctrine developed during the height of the infamous slave trade to reinforce the slaves' willpower to survive in an extremely hostile environment. During the height of the civil rights struggle in the United States, a number of religious leaders that included Martin Luther King, Jr., Jesse Jackson, and Andrew Young, exerted appropriate leadership during a time of great national crisis. During periods of crisis, American national leaders traditionally encourage their people, especially the military, by concluding, "May God bless you!" While the expression may raise questions about whether or not it is a prayer or an expression of political feeling, the fact still remains that the practice had its origins in Africa. The slaves brought it with them to America.[33]

With regard to their practice of religion, the Africans utilized a diviner who gave instructions on how to perform certain rituals. The diviner was charged with ensuring the security and well-being of his people by properly fulfilling his religious rites. Members of the Rudd party, including Reverend Helm, exploited this practice to take advantage of King Lobengula. The use of a diviner to predict events or to offer advice was not limited to the Africans. It was widely reported that President Ronald Reagan, through his wife Nancy, regularly consulted an astrologer before events were scheduled, especially following the assassination attempt on Reagan in 1981.[34] Astrology is a method of gaining greater understanding about or predicting the outcome of future events based on established beliefs about the fixed meaning of the influence of stars and planets upon people and events. In this respect the consultation of an astrologer is not unlike that of an African leader who seeks the advice of a diviner.

National leaders commonly consult with religious leaders. Reverend Billy Graham of the United States, for example, has had close relationships with several U.S. presidents. During the Watergate scandal of 1972, President Richard Nixon consulted Reverend Graham closely about appropriate courses of action to take. With escalating waves of violence in Western societies, national leaders and those who surround them want to take every precaution to ensure their safety, and the practice of religion, in one form or another, becomes a principal means of assuring a sense of well-being. How, then, did Europeans conclude that the African practice of religion was nothing more than dabbling in superstition? Quite the contrary, what this discussion has shown is that the practice of religion among the Africans follows a logical system of thought process that is very similar to that adhered to in Western societies.

THE AFRICAN MIND AND THE EDUCATIONAL SYSTEM

Although Africa's educational process was informal, it helped prepare students for an effective role in their society. From the time he began to walk, an African boy was taught to behave more like his father and brothers and less like his mother and sisters. Although his mother fed him and made sure that his other basic needs were met, she never failed to teach him that his lifestyle would be quite different from that of his sisters.

By the time he was six years old, the African boy played with his brothers and modeled his behavior on theirs. Soon he would engage in various forms of training provided by the male members of his family. By the time he was ten years old, he was taught the more advanced aspects of hunting, fishing, and other important elements of life such as art.[35] The application of logic and rationality became the thread that sewed together the features of his education. This was done to ensure that emotion and irrationality did not influence his behavior as an adult.

As he grew older, the African child was taught how to function in his political and socioeconomic environment. He was also taught to recognize the fact that, as an adult, he would not be able to get everything he might desire. So he learned to conserve what was available and to do without many things. This is why the Africans did not allow their children to eat meat until they reached the age of five.

Because hunting and similar occupations were considered dangerous, the Africans taught the boys safety devices and techniques. Bravery, courage, proper judgment, and the assessment of the situation all received special instructional attention. Nothing was left to chance or taken for granted.

While the education of the African boy was taking place, that of the girl was also in progress. She was taught how to work in the garden, how to raise crops and vegetables, and how to care for chickens, so that she would know how to provide a balanced diet and proper nutrition for her family when she became a parent. When the girl reached the age of fourteen, her mother would assign her the care of her younger brothers and sisters while she made short trips. The mother would go, leaving her family in the daughter's care, confident that she would be able to do well in her absence.

At an early age, little girls were taught to understand that they had an important role to play in society and that they should play that role well. How well the girls internalized their socially ascribed roles largely determined their level of motivation in learning how to perform them. First, they had to learn that as adult women, they were expected to fulfill certain obligations, such as to focus on the welfare of their families. They were taught to accept the notion that the success or failure of their families and that of their community depended to a large extent on how well they discharged their responsibilities.

Industrial and commercial education was also wide and diverse.The young apprentices were taught all kinds of trades. The art of blacksmithing was important. Industrial and commercial instruments were in the possession of many family units all over Africa. Today these are still found in many parts of the continent. Indeed, both the Arab traders and the Portuguese explorers of the fifteenth century obtained some of their trade techniques from the Africans. Michael Gelfand describes the complicated procedure apprentices were expected to grasp in their training as blacksmiths:

The father makes a circular hole in the ground and places in it some charcoal. Heading to this pit he digs a narrow furrow into a funnel or tube. Air is forced down through this funnel into the hole through an opening or nozzle. The charcoal in the hole is lit with the help of lighted sticks and air is fed through the funnel from two bellows to raise the lighted ambers to high temperature. When the fire is burning vigorously the son places the iron with which he is working. When the iron in the fire turns red from the intense heat he takes a source-shaped implement made from a thick branch and with it grips the top of the iron and takes it out of the fire. He holds it firmly and places the molten end on a piece of smooth metal fixed in a hole or depression. The father hits this with a special hammer to fashion the molten iron into a desired object.[36]

One high-ranking colonial official in Zimbabwe admitted in 1930 that, indeed, the Africans possessed an intellectual capacity equal to that of Europeans. He went on to add, "It is now felt that the Native has demonstrated a considerable intellectual capacity and the African mind in general is quite teachable and capable of learning in a similar fashion as the European mind. The African mind can understand and undertake responsible work after training."[37]

By 1930, after the colonial governments had been fully established and the African mind had been fully controlled, the colonial governments felt it expedient to admit what they had always rejected, the fact that the Africans had a mind equal to that of Europeans. If von Soemmering and White had adopted this idea when they were conducting their purported study of the African intellect, the agony that the colonial governments experienced in the wake of the rise of the African consciousness would have been avoided and an entirely new relationship would have emerged between the two peoples.

In addition to crafts, the students in traditional African society also learned a variety of occupations necessary to give their society a balanced service so as to sustain its social and cultural integrity. Law, politics, medicine, and social development became leading components of an educational process that was quite complete. Public debates on critical issues and problems facing society provided an appropriate setting that produced experts in various areas of African life.

Freedom of speech and self-expression were recognized as a right that belonged equally to all. In 1974 an African revealed during an interview:

By the time a young African was expected to take his place in society the entire community knew that he was ready to participate in its affairs. There were no examinations in the sense of your examinations today. But each community had a system of determining the progress of the learner measured against what he was capable of achieving. When cast in an ideal environment the student in the traditional African setting manifested a high level of intellect showing the innate capability of the African mind. Unfortunately European colonial governments either neglected or belittled this great human potential putting into peril the very essence of ideal human relationships.[38]

Another African added in August 1989:

One of the great tragedies of colonialism in Africa is that the white man never understood the potential of the African mind because European nations were preoccupied with justifying the reasons for colonizing the continent. It was not until 1930 that we heard some of the colonial officials admitting that, indeed, we possessed the same intellectual potential as the Europeans. What an admission when they knew that colonial systems were fully established!

We knew that our day will come because we were fully conscious of the fact that while the colonial governments colonized our land, we did not allow them to colonize our minds as well. This realization helped us to maintain our sense of self and proved to be our ultimate salvation. Although the colonial systems denied us freedom of self-expression, our minds remained as sharp as ever, learning as much as we could the techniques of adjustment so we could survive in a hostile environment.[39]

These two men suggest that when it had no option but to operate in a controlled setting, the African mind proved capable of surviving and retaining its distinctive quality in an oppressive and dehumanizing situation.

SUMMARY AND CONCLUSION

Africans did not share the European illusion about themselves and their culture. When subjected to colonial social reorganization, the African mind never lost a sense of its own identity. It managed to retain its own distinctive quality in an avalanche of colonial restructuring. Thus, colonialism, wherever it occurs, is doomed to failure.

This chapter leads us to two basic deductions. The first is that, regardless of the highly negative European perceptions of the African mind, the Africans had a highly evolved sense of self, even when they were being subjected to colonial violence and degradation. This positive self-image was crucial to the African struggle for survival in the colonial setting. Europeans refused to acknowledge that Africans had as much intellectual potential as they. In doing so, they fractured the bridges to human understanding, producing a perfect recipe for conflict. Methodist Bishop Ralph Dodge understood the ultimate consequences of this human folly when he wrote: "He who is dominated by another spiritually, economically, academically, or politically, will never develop his full potential until the condition of domination is removed. Because consciousness of self cannot be dominated, the dominated will realize their self actualization as a final act of freedom from domination."[40] This is what sustained the African mind during the colonial period.

The second deduction is that the Europeans' inability to recognize the cognitive abilities of the African mind led to political action that would later mean the demise of the colonial governments in Africa. In December 1945, soon after the war came to an end and the African consciousness was beginning to reemerge, E. F. Paget, bishop of the Anglican Church in colonial Zimbabwe, seemed to reflect on past colonial attitudes and the consequences to follow them when he wrote, "Stern days lie ahead of us when we must inevitably sow the seeds of either disillusionment and racial strife or of goodwill expressed in sincere justice and genuine freedom of the mind of all people."[41] If such a warning had come when the European nations were subjecting Africa to colonial adventure, perhaps it would have been possible to salvage a sane line of thinking in the interest of better relationships between the Africans and the colonial systems. In 1945 this kind of message was a lost cause; it would not appeal either to the colonial governments or to the Africans. The African mind had gained too much pride in itself to seek compromise with colonialism. How the African mind managed to retain its sense of self during the height of the colonial power is the subject of the next chapter.

NOTES

1. Indeed, in the United States of the 1990s criticism was widely expressed that some IQ or placement tests were heavily biased against students of certain ethnic groups and that admission to colleges must not be determined solely by the results of these tests.

2. In July 1983, when this author was making plans to conduct research in Zimbabwe, a high-ranking white college official who held a doctoral degree in history asked him, "Why are you going to Zimbabwe in the summer; do they run schools in the summer down there?" The official did not know that because Zimbabwe is in the Southern Hemisphere, July is part of its winter season. Knowing the official quite well, this author is certain that if it were an African who had shown this lack of knowledge of geography the official would have made an issue of it.

3. W. McIntyre, *Colonies into Commonwealth* (New York: Walker and Co., 1966), p. 106.

4. Mungazi, *Colonial Policy and Conflict in Zimbabwe: A Study of Cultures in Collision, 1890–1979*, p. 7.

5. Peter Gibbs, *Flag for the Matabele: An Entertainment in African History* (New York: Vanguard Press, 1956), p. 31.

6. Ibid., p. 34.

7. J. S. Green, *Rhodes Goes North* (London: Bell and Sons, 1936), p. 95.

8. British South Africa Company Records, No. 369/2468–60. Zimbabwe National Archives.

9. On learning of Helm's betrayal of his trust and of Rhodes's behavior, Lobengula reacted, "The white man is the father of lies" (Mungazi, *Colonial Policy and Conflict in Zimbabwe,* p. 9).

10. For the full text of the agreement, see Mungazi, *Colonial Policy and Conflict in Zimbabwe*, p. 143.

11. British South Africa Company Records, No. 369/2469–68. Zimbabwe National Archives.

12. William van Til, *Education: A Beginning* (Boston: Houghton Mifflin Co., 1974), p. 13.

13. Courtland Cox, *African Liberation* (New York: Black Education Press, 1972), p. 82.

14. Ibid., p. 15.

15. Placide Temples, "La philosophie Bantoue," in Paulin Houtandji, *African Philosophy: Myth and Reality* (Bloomington: Indiana University Press, 1983) p. 35.

16. Michael Gelfand, *Growing Up in Shona Society* (Gweru, Zimbabwe: Mambo Press, 1985), p. 26.

17. Kwanisi Wirendu, *Philosophy and the African Culture* (Cambridge: Cambridge University Press, 1980), p. 48.

18 Ibid., p. 50.

19. Mungazi, *The Struggle for Social Change in Southern Africa*, p. 53.

20. The term *chief* is a misnomer created by the colonial governments. The appropriate title was *king*. But to make a distinction between the Western and African concept of king, the colonial governments decided to refer to the highest level of African administrative system as chief.

21. V. M. Turner, *Schism and Continuity in an African Society* (Manchester: Manchester University Press, 1957), p. 18.

22. Lawrence Vambe, *An Ill-Fated People: Zimbabwe Before and After Rhodes* (Pittsburgh: University of Pittsburgh Press, 1957), p. 318.

23. Michael Gelfand, *Diet and Tradition in African Culture* (London: E. and S. Livingstone, 1971), p. 10.

24. Ibid., p. 11.

25. W. Raynor, *The Tribe and Its Successors: An Account of African Traditional Life and European Settlement in Southern Rhodesia* (New York: Frederick A. Praeger, 1962), p. 49.

26. Ibid., p. 51.

27. J. F. Holeman, *Shona Customary Law* (London: Oxford University Press, 1952), p. 3.

28. Ibid., p. 7.

29. M. Gelfand, *Diet and Tradition in African Culture*, p. 24.

30. Ibid., p. 27.

31. C. K. Omari, *The Family in Africa: Ujama Safari* (Geneva: World Council of Churches, 1974), p. 6.

32. An elderly African during an interview with the author in Mutare, Zimbabwe, May 16, 1974. The man declined to be identified because, he said "I do not wish to appear to support an institution that some people seem to believe has no longer any place in modern African society." See Dickson Mungazi, "The Change of Black Attitudes Toward Education in Rhodesia, 1900–1975," Ph.D. diss. (Lincoln: University of Nebraska, 1977).

33. Lawrence B. Goodheart, ed., *Slavery in American Society* (Lexington, Mass.: D.C. Heath and Co., 1993), p. 237.

34. For details, see Kitty Kelley, *Nancy Reagan: The Unauthorized Biography* (New York: Simon and Schuster, 1991), p. 431.

35. Michael Gelfand, *African Background* (Cape Town: Juta and Co., 1965), p. 24.

36. Gelfand, *Diet and Tradition in African Culture*, p. 45.

37. Southern Rhodesia, *The Report of the Director of Native Development* (Salisbury: Government Printer, 1930).

38. An African during an interview with the author in Mutare, Zimbabwe, May 15, 1974. For part of the interview, see Dickson Mungazi, "The Change of Black Attitudes Toward Education in Rhodesia, 1900–1975."

39. An elderly African, during an interview with the author in Harare, Zimbabwe, August 14, 1989.

40. Ralph Dodge (Methodist Bishop in Zimbabwe from 1956 to 1964), "The Church and Freedom," an essay, 1964. Old Mutare Methodist Archives.

41. E. F. Paget, "Native Welfare Society Must Act Fearlessly," an address to the African Welfare Society, Salisbury, Rhodesia, December 13, 1945. Zimbabwe National Archives.

3

The African Mind and Adaptation to Colonial Conditions: A Strategy for Survival

> Driven beyond the boiling point, the colonized are seized by anger as they break their chains and feel neither responsible nor guilty and as they utilize their adaptation to colonial conditions to end colonization.
>
> *Albert Memmi, 1965*
>
> It is a basic biological rule that creatures which fail to adapt to a new environment perish.
>
> *Godfrey Huggins, 1954*

THEORETICAL CONSIDERATIONS OF ADAPTATION

European nations resorted to extreme violence to subject the African mind to colonial rule, and they utilized extreme violence to sustain the imperial and colonial governments they instituted. Thus, the Africans were left with two choices on how to respond: (1) resist by resorting to the same form of violence as the colonial governments had inflicted on them, or (2) seek ways of adapting to new conditions they could not control. After considering these two choices, the Africans in a majority of countries made the painful decision to adopt the second choice.[1]

The Africans who decided to fight against the colonial invaders were able to see the adverse effects of subjecting themselves to colonial conditions without a struggle. From 1886 to 1900, during the time Africa was being subjected to colonial rule in accordance with the provisions of the Berlin Conference,[2] the Africans carefully weighed the merits and disadvantages of their options. This suggests a high degree of cognitive ability. The

Africans decided to exercise the better part of valor, and so, instead of risking their own genocide, they chose to adapt to a new way of life.[3]

To know why the Africans chose adaptation as a strategy for their survival under colonial conditions we need to understand some theoretical considerations relevant to it. A few examples follow. In his study, *The Colonizer and the Colonized*,[4] Albert Memmi theorizes that people subjected to colonial conditions adapt to them in order to survive. In the introduction to this study, Jean-Paul Sartre, a close associate of Memmi and philosophical collaborator at the Sorbonne, concludes that the colonizer can only exonerate himself in the systematic pursuit of the dehumanization of the colonized by resorting to violence in order to legitimatize his oppression.[5] This is the only way he can claim to have authority over the colonized. Unable to liberate himself from the oppressive conditions so arbitrarily imposed, the colonized is left with only one choice—to use his mind to seek ways of adapting to them so that he can survive.

Memmi concludes that this strategy gives the colonizer a false sense of belief that the colonized has accepted colonial imposition as a paternal act designed to salvage him from his presumed primitive culture. While this is happening, the colonized himself has an opportunity to elevate his mental powers to a new height by designing a new strategy to deal with the problems of colonial domination. Memmi also concludes that once the colonized is able to exercise the upper reaches of the rational process, he is unlikely to give up his envisaged self. In his own mental process and the application of reason to survive, the colonized creates conditions that will later prove the ultimate demise of the colonizer himself.[6]

Unknown to the colonizer is the fact that the colonized can never accept oppression. Assured that his security is best ensured only under his own power, the colonized becomes aware of the need to survive so that one day he will be able to restore his society in his own image. This awareness becomes more entrenched with each passing day of colonization. Memmi suggests that, while survival is the principal purpose of the colonized, he must retain an ability to see the value of his own culture compared to that of the colonizer. This comparative analysis is done while having to function in an alien environment. The ability to function without being socialized is how the colonized adapts to subjugation in order to guarantee his survival.

Consider this question: Is cognitive resistance sufficient for the colonized to make this critical adaptation as a strategy for survival? David Hapgood thinks so and provides a theoretical answer when he states that the colonized must endeavor to live a life of meaning between two worlds. The first world is that of the colonizer, and the second is that of his own culture.[7] Hapgood argues that the colonized's ability to utilize basic and essential components of the colonizer's culture will ensure his or her adaptation as a potent strategy for survival. It will also give the colonizer a false sense of security as he begins to base his actions on the illusion that the mind of the colonized has been controlled and he or she will function according to the dictates of the colonizer and so no longer worries about resistance or revolt. Hapgood suggests that the adaptation of the colonized is facilitated in three crucial areas of the colonizer's culture: educational, socioeconomic, and political.[8] This chapter focuses on these three areas which formed a new environment that demanded an exceptional African mind to adapt to conditions to assure its survival. Specific examples are discussed to show how this strategy of cognitive resistance posed other implications for the colonial society.

Memmi states that when constantly faced with a negative image of itself, as depicted by the colonizer, the mind of the colonized begins to use its resourcefulness to remove the psychological conditioning imposed on it by the colonizer. This in turn galvanizes his determination to retain the essential elements of its precolonized self-image.[9] Cognitive resistance is a strategy by which the mind of the colonized refuses to be what its colonizer says it is—an inferior creature that must always be under his domination. To ensure the success of this strategy, the mind of the colonized will seek educational, socioeconomic, and political adaptation, as defined by the colonizer, thereby giving him a false sense of total control. That the mind of the colonized seeks adaptation through cognitive resistance in a suppressive environment dispels the myth of the colonized's limited intellectual capacity.

This dyad also constitutes a new environment in which relationships between the colonizer and colonized are cast in their proper perspective, an oppressor—oppressed setting.[10] Memmi sums up the ultimate result of the oppressive nature of the behavior of the colonizer and the reaction of the mind of the colonized, saying that the unfairness of the laws imposed by the colonizer become testimony to the severity of the conditions they create for the colonized in order to make them feel inadequate. "But driven beyond the boiling point the colonized are seized by anger, break their chains and feel neither responsible nor guilty as they utilize adaptation to colonial conditions to end their colonization."[11]

Memmi is actually saying that, when in an environment in which it finds its options limited, the mind of the colonized strives to achieve one goal—adaptation to ensure its survival. Nothing else seems to matter. The will to survive eventually translates into a strategy for self-liberation. The entire relationship between the colonizer and the mind of the colonized is based on a pervasive contradiction between the two, with the colonizer wishing to impose his will and the mind of the colonized wishing to maintain its sense of self through cognitive resistance. The mind of the colonized has no doubt as to what it wishes to accomplish through adaptation, and there is misconception in the mind of the colonizer. This represents a classic case of conflict between the two distinct cultures of oppressor and oppressed.

Adam Curle theorizes that as a result of the colonization process, in which the colonizer attempts to control the mind of the colonized as a strategy for seeking to control his action, the mind of the colonized inadvertently perceives the necessity to make an adaptation in order to survive in a hostile and oppressive environment. In its desire to survive, the mind of the colonized makes concerted efforts to secure an education, which, though designed by the colonizer to serve his own political interests, will make it possible for the colonized to adapt to new socio-economic and political realities.[12] Curle concludes that, although the colonizer forces the mind of the colonized to seek his form of education in order to create habits of thinking that develop a dependency, he or she is unable to determine its actual impact on the mind of the colonized. This inability leads to an illusion that the mind of the colonized has accepted colonial conditions. In all its functions, the mind of the colonized is motivated by a central desire to survive, not to accept colonization. This misinterpretation makes it possible for the colonizer to confuse acceptance with adaptation.[13]

These theoretical considerations make it quite clear that the colonial governments wanted to control the African mind in order to avail themselves of Africa's vast raw materials. In doing so, they exhibited a serious misconception of its presumed inability to facilitate adaptation in order to survive independently of its colonizer's influence. This illusion was evident in the policies they designed and implemented. The formulation of the British policy of *indirect rule*, the Portuguese policy of *Estado Novo*, the French and Belgian policy of *evalue*, and the German policy of *Deutsche Kolonialbund* all had the same unanticipated effect on the African mind—its ability to adapt to colonial conditions in order to survive.

While these policies were designed to serve the interests of the colonial governments, their applications had implications for the African mind enabling it to adapt in ways that their authors never envisaged. The main problem created for the African mind in the colonization process is that colonial systems became institutionalized by the mere act of the Berlin Conference. Thus, the Africans could not try to fight against the injustice without facing a lethal reaction. The knowledge of this reality is what the African mind utilized to make its adaptation possible.

THE AFRICAN MIND AND THE PERILS OF ADAPTATION

The ability of the African mind to adjust to colonial conditions in order to survive is a tribute to the struggle of a people to retain the distinctive features of their culture. Many examples show that the Africans were able to demonstrate their ability to reject the colonial governments' efforts to subjugate them to a mental condition in which they would be effectively controlled. For example, the Portuguese *Estado Novo* policy was meant to divide the Africans into two socioeconomic and political groups, the *assimilados* and *indigenas*. The *assimilados* were expected to discard their cultural traditions, including language and lifestyles, in favor of adapting those of the Portuguese. They had rights similar to those of the Portuguese nationals. The *indigenas* were those uneducated Africans who had no rights at all; they formed the bulk of the cheap labor force. But to its surprise the Portuguese colonial government found that the leaders of the struggle for the liberation of the African mind came from Eduardo Mondlane, Samora Machel, Agosthino Neto, Jonas Savimbi, Holden Roberto and Eduardo dos Santos, all of them *assimilados* whose thinking the *Estado Novo* policy was expected to convert into alignment with the Portuguese colonial culture. The Portuguese government never thought to acknowledge the error in that policy and make adjustments.

In 1961 Antonio Salazar, the Portuguese dictator (1932–1968), was at a loss to understand why the *assimilados* rejected the policy of *Estado Novo*, saying, "A law recognizing citizenship takes minutes to draft and can be made right away. But a citizen that is a man fully and consciously integrated into civilized political society takes centuries to achieve."[14] Salazar's reaction substantiates the conclusion that the effect of adaptation is felt profoundly differently by colonizer and colonized. Salazar did not realize a critical dimension of adaptation that only the African mind could understand.

The African mind did not see the implications of *Estado Novo* in the same way as the Portuguese colonial officials had when they designed it. The perils of adaptation were felt by the colonial society itself. Indeed, Salazar's refusal to recognize the prowess of the African mind substantiates the conclusion that the colonial governments' inability to recognize the viability of the African mind, existing in its own cultural setting, proved to be their ultimate demise.

The African adjustment to colonial conditions presents yet another peril. Some Africans became vulnerable to subtle colonial tactics to control their mind, and in such an environment the dangers of adaptation became real. A case in point is Leopold Senghor's role in the struggle for the liberation of the African mind in Senegal. His birth in October 1906, his early education in Senegal, his teachers' recognition of his ability, their help in 1925 in securing more education for him in France, and his determination to acquire the basic elements of the French culture under the policy of *evalue* in order to function in the colonial setting—all combined to create a climate of the perils of adaptation that he was not able to overcome. His desire to function in a French national milieu instead of the African cultural setting eroded the elements that he needed to sustain his African identity.

Not surprisingly, as president of Senegal from 1960 to 1980 Senghor's behavior was that of an African who had learned to think in terms of French cultural imperatives.[15] His election to the prestigious l'Académie française for his literary contribution to the advancement of French culture shows that Senghor's commitment to the colonial culture threatened the purpose of adaptation. The contradiction between Senghor's thinking, his personality, his family background, his literary efforts, and his political philosophy reveals an individual who thought his place in society was determined by a combination of what he was, what was expected of him, and what he did. The danger of this contradiction is reflected in the behavior of some African leaders today and has taken a heavy toll on their sense of national identity.

Other disturbing aspects of Senghor come to light when we consider his efforts to adapt to colonial conditions. On the one hand he systematically sought to assimilate himself into the French culture in order not only to survive and function under colonial conditions, but also to assert himself in a fashion that compelled him to question the values of his own African cultural identity. After his arrival in France in 1920, Senghor decided that his future was inseparably intertwined with French culture. Any relationships that he might have with his own native Senegal were intended solely to reinforce his perception of himself as a French national whose origins happened to be African. Slowly Senghor began to drift into the dark shadows of the colonial corridors where his acceptance by the French was by no means guaranteed and his relationships with his own people were strained beyond repair. Senghor was in the proverbial "no man's land"; he was a man without a country. This is a dilemma that the peril of adaptation poses for some African leaders.

On the other hand, realizing that he had lost contact with himself and his own culture, Senghor groped for rescue where there was none. Claiming in 1948 that "Western technology and culture might set in motion change that would shake African society to its foundations,"[16] Senghor used his acquired French cultural discomfort to launch a movement he called Negritude. He did this to redirect the thought processes and to stress what he called the positive attributes of African culture, including socialist ideological precepts. He claimed to reject the capitalist and material greed of the West. But when he was seeking his own comfortable place within the French cultural setting, superimposed on him by his African sense of destiny and identity, Senghor "castigated as deserters of Negritude those Africans who espoused Marxism."[17] This contradiction alienated Senghor and badly tarnished his image as a continental leader who was seeking to assert his leadership role in a tragic vacuum created by the fall of Kwame Nkrumah.[18]

Senghor would never fully recover from this crushing dilemma. This suggests the vulnerability of the adaptation process and the confused mind of an individual whose perception of self had been lost in the inevitable cultural conflict in a limiting environment. Senghor was losing both himself and the course he had helped chart for the development of a new African mind envisaged in the demise of the colonial systems. The question that one must ask is: Was Senghor French, black, or African? He himself did not seem to know the answer, which demonstrates the critical nature of the perils of adaptation.

In 1984, four years after Senghor had retired as president of Senegal and sensing the predicament in which he found himself, the French did what they thought they had to do to restore the tarnished image of their favorite cultural agent and to give him back some of his lost sense of self: they voted him into the prestigious l'Académie française, the only African to have received this honor. That this action further alienated Senghor from the mainstream of African thought simply compounded the crisis he was facing in his seemingly endless search for a lasting personal and historical identity.

When Abdou Diouf succeeded Senghor in 1980, he was fully aware that he had to bring Senegal back into the circle of the African continental family. This was a priority needed to restore the refinements of Senegalese culture. Senghor, however, was an exception to the rule. The vast majority of the Africans living under colonial conditions fully understood the purpose of cognitive resistance: to ensure their survival and to have an opportunity to design an effective strategy for ending colonialism. Let us look at how this happened.

THE AFRICAN MIND AND ADAPTATION TO COLONIAL CONDITIONS

In spite of colonization, the Africans never abandoned their own culture. Now, faced with the reality of colonization, they recognized that the imperative of survival and adaptation was the best strategy available. This was not an easy task because they considered colonization an act of invasion and thus an imposition. Paulo Freire argues that in the kind of relationship that emerges between the oppressor and the oppressed, or the colonizer and the colonized, the contradictions become more evident when the oppressor forces the oppressed to submit to domination and to acquire his basic cultural values and practices in order to serve his own political and socioeconomic interests.[19] This notion is not embraced by the colonized, however, and so it creates a climate of conflict between the two, with the resulting need to adapt.

For colonial governments in Africa to recognize that they were, in effect, the oppressor in the process of designing a set of national socioeconomic and political policies to compel the Africans to function in the colonial environment, they would have to recognize its harmful consequences and identify themselves with their plight. Freire argues that this is impossible because the oppressor is invariably motivated by self-interest in his interactions with the oppressed. Therefore, unable to resolve the contradictions that were inherent in their policies, the colonial governments forced the Africans to submit to their will by means of educational, socioeconomic, and political interventions. In response, the Africans began to search for an identity that they hoped would make their adaptation to colonial conditions tolerable. Because the colonial governments erroneously concluded that the Africans accepted colonial rule itself, the Africans had an opportunity to design a strategy for their own survival in ways that the colonial governments did not anticipate. Two questions arise: What factors influenced the Africans to seek ways of adapting to colonial conditions in order to survive? What strategies did they design in order to retain their sense of self?

Because the colonial governments did not appreciate the important features of African culture, it was therefore up to the Africans themselves to make some hard choices in order to survive. Would they continue to resist the invasion of their society and culture and reject a Western type of educational, socioeconomic, and political adaptation to enable them to function, or would they try to acquire these skills as part of their adaptation process in an environment in which they had no choice? For them to continue to resist these three aspects of Western culture would lead to another military confrontation following colonization, and the Africans were not ready for another round of violence.

In some countries this confrontation would come later. The only option for now was to use the white man's definition of civilization, which included these three elements, even though the Africans knew that they would be trained to function under conditions in opposition to their sense of self and development. For this reason the period from the inception of the colonial systems to 1939 witnessed the Africans' effort to secure basic skills in order to function under conditions defined for them by the colonial governments.

In Zimbabwe, for example, some Africans began to pursue the British curriculum when Robert Moffat (1796–1883) opened the first formal school for them at Inyati in 1859. Nonetheless, like Africans all over the continent, most continued to oppose it until 1901, the year the Education Ordinance of 1899 made financial incentives possible. From 1890 to 1923 a number of events proved to the Africans that the white man was there to stay, in Zimbabwe as in all of Africa. In order for them to survive in a society that he controlled, they needed to make some sort of adjustment to colonial conditions as a matter of dire necessity for survival.

These events included the overthrow of King Lobengula[20] in 1893, the introduction of the infamous Hut Tax Ordinance in 1894, the Native Registration Regulations of 1897, the Education Ordinance of 1899, the Land Ordinance of 1900, the Education Ordinance of 1901, the publication of the Rolin Report in 1913 which discussed the highly negative attitudes among whites toward the mind of the Africans, describing them as "stupid animals,"[21] and the national referendum of 1923.[22] During that time the colonial legislature enacted a series of laws that were intended to convince the Africans that the British had, indeed, every intention of remaining permanently in Zimbabwe, as well as other parts of Africa, and that the sooner they recognized and accepted this new reality, the better they would adjust to the conditions that now controlled their lives.

The Africans' new effort to secure skills to enable them to function in these three areas of colonial culture after the colonization was completed suggests their ability to adapt to new conditions. The search for education seemed fundamental to the utilization of the other two components. The figures in the accompanying table show an increase in the percentages of Africans attending school in colonial Zimbabwe for the years indicated.

Africans Attending School in Colonial Zimbabwe, 1901–1930

Year	Total African Population	Total School Enrollment	Percentage of Population in School
1901	710,000	265	0.03
1913	800,000	15,466	1.9
1919	840,000	23,598	2.8
1924	915,000	77,610	8.4
1928	1,132,000	99,535	8.7
1930	1,430,000	96,000	6.7

Source: Zimbabwe, *Monthly Digest of Statistics*, 1981.

In order to appreciate more fully the efforts the Africans were making to adapt to colonial conditions, we must remember Paul Freire's theory: that is, during the initial stage of colonization (oppression), the colonized make efforts to adapt to the new situation by trying to acquire the social practices of their colonizers as a new model of humanity. Freire states that because colonization constitutes invasion, it creates a phenomenon that "derives from the fact that the oppressed adopt an attitude of adhesion to the oppressor"[23] in order to survive. Adhesion and perceiving the colonizer as a model of humanity do not in any way suggest acceptance; they merely imply the colonized's ability to adapt.

From 1900 to 1939 the Africans adapted to colonial conditions in three ways: the need to acquire basic literacy, the need to function in socioeconomic settings, and the need to perform in political settings. Let us briefly discuss how the African mind used these three features of colonial culture to make adaptation to colonial conditions tolerable and to retain its sense of self as a strategy for its survival and eventual resurrection.

THE NEED FOR BASIC LITERACY: RESETTING THE AFRICAN MIND

For the Africans of the 1900–1939 period adaptation to the colonial condition demanded specific behavior patterns that were dictated by three important factors. The first was that in order to function effectively in the colonial society, it was necessary to acquire an ability to read and write in both the vernacular and in European languages. The Africans' achievement and capacity to learn surprised even themselves.

During that time Christian missionaries, with the aid of the Africans, translated the Bible and other religious literature into local languages. They then employed Africans as teachers, whose only qualifications were an ability to read and write in either European or local languages. The self-confidence generated from acquiring an ability to read and to write was so great that it motivated them to stay in school longer than at any previous time.[24] This enabled the Africans to learn the thinking of the white man and it put them in the strategic position of being able to predict colonial behavior when the time came for the struggle for their liberation.

Slowly the African mind was being transformed into something new. What started as an act of survival in the colonial setting slowly led to an endeavor that enabled the African mind to see an entirely new world. The Africans were steadily gaining an ability to adapt to colonial conditions and to look critically at their world. This was not only because of the fundamentals of the education that they received, but also because they were forced to think critically about the reality of the conditions under which they were living. The colonial governments were never able to comprehend the ability of the African mind to see what the Africans were able to see—that the colonial conditions they were living under helped to transform their world in profound ways. A respected African leader in Zimbabwe put this critical development into the context of the events of that time:

By creating conditions which forced the Africans to acquire a restricted education to serve their own political interests, the white men inadvertently provided them an opportunity which they used to sow the seeds of the rise of self-consciousness. The combination of practical training and basic literacy was a pointer to things to come. In the ability of the Africans to read and to write lay the ultimate threat to the white man's political domination. The African mind was being reset in ways that transformed its world from the one the colonial conditions controlled to the one the Africans began to envisage for themselves. The Africans were able to adapt to colonial conditions in their own way.[25]

The Africans' need to secure basic literacy in order to adjust to colonial conditions, as restricted by the colonial governments, often caused friction within the African culture itself, especially prior to 1924. This was caused by the confusion that the process of adaptation brought with it, due to the variability it required in all situations. The chameleon nature of the perils of adaptation were very real, as shown in two examples in colonial Zimbabwe. In 1905, Josiah Chimbadzwa, a young man from Mtasa village, a short distance north of Mutare, decided that he needed to go to school in order to adapt to existing colonial conditions. Like many Africans, he knew that the future would be different from the past. But Josiah's parents, having some serious doubts about accepting the white man's education, were against this idea and urged him to remain in the village. They argued that Western education was incompatible with African instruction and cultural values.

Believing that learning to read and write would open his mind to future opportunities, young Josiah followed his intuition and went against his parents' advice, entering the Old Mutare Methodist School, which had opened nine years earlier. Charles Coffin and Eddy Greeley, missionaries in charge of the school, were happy to have him, but in enrolling him the two missionaries created yet more serious problems between the two cultures.

Josiah's parents were so displeased with what had happened that they came after him. However, the two missionaries succeeded in persuading them to allow their son to remain in school, arguing that Western education offered the Africans a new opportunity to prepare for the future, reinforcing the belief that African education was inadequate because it was cast in a primitive culture. Soon Josiah demonstrated a brilliant mind as he learned everything his teachers had to offer. He eventually went on to study theology and became an outstanding preacher and teacher. In 1968 Reverend Chimbadzwa remembered the events that had shaped his mind and influenced his life, as well as the destiny of the African people:

I cried because I wanted to stay in school to learn to read and to write. This was the only way for us to survive in the society which the British controlled. We had no choice, either we had to learn to read and to write or the white man would continue to take advantage of us. The ability to read and to write did not stop the white man from exploiting us, but it made it possible for us to become more aware of it than we had been in the past. Therefore, while the white man wanted to use our ability to read and to write to force us to become more productive laborers, we ourselves saw other benefits which accrued to us and which the white man could not see.[26]

Reverend Chimbadzwa became one of the greatest preachers the Methodist Church of Zimbabwe has ever produced. He taught his people to have personal pride and to learn to improve themselves in every way possible. While Josiah and his parents' conflict about the value of Western education manifested a critical dimension of the perils of adaptation, it later translated into a greater awareness which the Africans used to see their world from a perspective of formally educated Europeans. This enabled the African mind to elevate their perception of self to a higher level than had existed prior to and during the colonial era. In 1989 a retired African Methodist preacher, whose knowledge of historical events was as sharp in 1989 as it had been at the beginning of the twentieth century, told me:

Our minds were slowly becoming clear that our efforts to adapt to colonial conditions were not merely directed towards gaining abilities to function under prohibitive colonial conditions but to see ourselves in a different light from the dark shadows the colonial government was placing us. While we sought to adjust to these conditions, we were also able to retain critical elements of our mind in a way the colonial governments could not understand. This was important to our future. Although the perils of adaptation were a constant threat to our strategy for survival, we had to overcome them to retain our sense of self. While the colonial governments gave us an education that it wanted us to function as laborers we ourselves saw other benefits.[27]

The second example also occurred in 1905 and in the same village in which Josiah Chimbadzwa lived. Young Tenze Mtasa, a cousin of Josiah's, informed her parents that she, too, had decided to go to Old Mutare Methodist School to learn to read and write. When her father told her that she must not contemplate such a step because no young woman could make important decisions without her parents' approval, a serious conflict and a parting of the ways occurred within the family. In vain Tenze tried to convince her parents that acquiring fundamental literacy skills was the best way to prepare herself for the future and to adjust to the new social conditions. When her father made it clear that he would not allow her to bring shame and disgrace to the family and the community by her rebellion against the respected traditions of the African culture, the conflict took on critical dimensions.

Unable to resolve the dispute, Tenze disappeared during the night and went to Old Mutare, just as Josiah Chimbadzwa had done a few months earlier. She stayed there for four years, learning as much as she could, not only to read and write, but also about things such as sewing, cooking, and new social values. In 1909 Tenze was ready to return to the village she had left in shame and under conditions that made her a cultural rebel and an outcast. Because of her strength of personality and character, Tenze was able to reconcile with her parents during the years that she was in school. In this manner her mind had reached a new level of maturity and clarity—of seeing the position of African women in a way that enabled them to take positions on issues.

Tenze's return to the village became an important occasion for a community celebration. The African mind had been transformed beyond the level intended by the colonial conditions. The perils of adaptation now fell into the background as an exciting and challenging vision surged forth to give the Africans a newly charted direction to self-actualization. In 1910 a new school was opened with Tenze as its teacher. For years she devoted her life to implanting a new consciousness among the Africans. She helped them perceive colonial conditions as they were—oppressive and inhibiting. They now envisaged themselves as a people with a vision for the future. In the same year S. J. Coffin, the missionary who was Tenze's teacher for the four years she was in school at Old Mutare, described her as follows: "Whether it is the blood in her veins or for some other reason, Tenze has proved herself to be a wonderful inspiration to other African women. She is a superior girl whose happy laugh rings out every possible occasion. She is bright, pretty, and, what is better, she is good."[28] This recognition of the prowess of the African mind early in the colonial period signaled the emergence of a cultural conflict that was far more devastating than it had been in the past. The African mind would prove mightier than the gun. In her own way Tenze played a pivotal role in transforming the perils of adaptation into an African season of hope.

These two examples show that critical consciousness was becoming a new phenomenon among the Africans, a resetting of the African mind. With all their knowledge and power, the colonial governments were not able to foresee this outcome of their educational policies. The African mind's ability to retain the crucial components of itself under prohibitive conditions indicates that the assumed permanent establishment of the white man's culture in Africa forced the Africans to adjust or perish. That they elected to adjust reveals their ability to eliminate the perils of adaptation. The desire to adjust, to survive under colonial conditions, slowly began to translate itself into a new reality that neither the white man nor the colonial governments ever anticipated: the emergence of an awareness among the Africans that was different from their initial reaction to the colonization of their lands.

In Zimbabwe the threefold increase in the percentage of Africans attending school—from 2.8 percent in 1919 to 8.4 percent in 1924—set the stage for them to see the importance of acquiring skills in basic literacy all over Africa. This perception arose from the need to survive and retain a sense of self under colonial conditions.[29] This endeavor was particularly true of the period from 1925 to 1939. Albert Memmi states that the colonized's ability to utilize features of the colonizer's culture in order to retain their own sense of self, apart from the one perceived by the colonizer, will inevitably lead to conflict both within the culture of the colonized and between the two cultures.[30] This hints at the conclusion that the mind of the colonized recognizes the perils of adaptation and needs to minimize the adverse effects of colonization in order to survive. This development set new experiences in the search for a new direction in forming the mind of the colonized.

Although the colonial policy left the Africans with no easy choices, the period from 1900 to 1939 gave them an opportunity to develop and sharpen three basic instruments to carve out a new identity and character destined to shape their future. These instruments were: accepting Western religious values, acquiring new socioeconomic competency, and acquiring basic literacy skills. The decision to acquire the fundamentals in these three areas of the colonial culture was not an easy one for the Africans, but it was one that they had to make in order to survive in the colonial setting. The ability to read and write enabled them to adapt to colonial conditions.

Therefore, the Africans became keenly aware of the need for a Western type of education as a means of adaptation during the years from 1900 to 1939. For example, in colonial Zimbabwe starting with the administration of Leander Starr Jameson in 1890 and extending to that of Godfrey Huggins beginning in 1933, colonial officials argued that the only way the Africans could hope to improve themselves was by becoming "beasts of burden" in the colonial enterprises that the white man controlled, such as the mines, agriculture, industry, domestic service, and animal husbandry. Colonial officials all over Africa also argued that these areas provided an environment that promoted their best interests. But as it turned out the Africans saw other possible outcomes that the colonial governments were unable to see—that is, they equated their search for education with an instrument for sharpening their mind beyond the peripherals that the colonial regimes intended for them. Such was the nature of the African mind. Much to the advantage and delight of the Africans, the colonial systems were unable to comprehend this idea.

In their need to acquire skills in basic literacy, the sub-Saharan Africans of the period 1900–1939 encountered a new problem from a group of people whom they had once thought was trying to promote their advancement. This was opposition from the Christian missionaries, who felt that literary education combined with practical training was a wrong objective for Africans to pursue. They would have preferred a combination of religious instruction with literary education because they were trying to persuade the Africans to accept Christian values as a basis of a new life. In colonial Zimbabwe, for example, the commission of inquiry into African education of 1927 recorded this point of view among the missionaries: "Some of the missionaries are opposed to literacy instruction, not because it is not called for, but because in principle they do not agree with elements of it."[31] The Hadfield Commission also made the following recommendations regarding the education of the Africans:

1. That, recognizing the need for religious education, literary education must, at the time being, be left in the hands of missionary institutions and religious bodies at present undertaking it.

2.   That every endeavor be made to prevent Natives from proceeding beyond
      South Africa for any class of education which is within their reach within its
      boundaries.

3.   That the importance of industrial education be regarded as paramount, and
      that such education be directed towards the teaching of (a) the knowledge
      of proper methods of tillage and the rearing of stock and (b) elementary
      handicrafts.[32]

The Africans, the colonial governments, and the missionaries recognized
the importance of acquiring basic literacy as a prerequisite for other forms
in developing the African mind. But neither the colonial governments nor
the missionaries knew that the more the Africans had access to any kind of
Western education, the more they appreciated and applied its meaning to
other areas of their lives and endeavors to survive under colonial conditions.
However, the more the Africans continued their efforts to acquire literacy,
the more the colonial governments seemed willing to assist them in acquiring it because they believed that it would help them become better laborers.[33]

To make this objective possible and all the while being unaware of the
implications of their action for the African mind, the colonial governments
encouraged the hiring of better trained teachers, especially for those beyond
the elementary grades. In this context the seeds for the expansion of the
African mind were planted. In addition, the colonial governments encouraged the development of the rudiments of Western education among the
Africans by offering financial aid through legislation and philanthropy. In
colonial Zimbabwe, for example, the accompanying table shows the number of schools by class, number of pupils earning grants, enrollment, and
the amount of grant given for 1927.

Government Grants for African Schools in Zimbabwe, 1927

Class of School	No. of Schools in Each Class	No. of Pupils Receiving Grant	Enrollment	Grant for 1927
1st	60	3,609	4,100	$2,890.70
2nd	67	4,506	6,470	6,288.00
3rd	1,351	55,758	86,421	3,940.90
Evening	65	1,821	2,484	910.50
Equipment grant				3,706.00
Total	1,534	65,694	99,535	17,736.10

Source: Southern Rhodesia, *Annual Report of the Director of Native Development,* 1928.

These figures suggest that the limited outcome of the colonial educational policy made available through grants was radically exceeded by the colonized. The colonial governments' failure to foresee and control this result attests to their arrogance and neglect. Clearly, the African mind viewed the rudiments of Western education in a very different light from the way the colonial governments intended it.

This difference of perception and utilization gave the African mind an opportunity to shape its own destiny in an oppressive colonial environment. Thus, the African mind was going through a process of transformation uncontrolled by the colonial conditions. However, the real effect of this development would not be felt on the continent until the end of the war in 1945. What was important for the time being was that acquiring skills in literacy enabled the African mind to adapt to colonial conditions in a way that the colonial officials did not anticipate and could not manipulate.

THE NEED TO FUNCTION IN SOCIOECONOMIC SETTINGS: HELPING THE AFRICAN MIND TURN ADVERSITY INTO ADVANTAGE

The controversy that was emerging between the colonial governments and religious organizations, especially in sub-Saharan Africa, regarding the question of what constituted proper education for the Africans was a game that only the white man could play. The Africans themselves had no part in it. They knew that the ability to read and write would open new doors to economic opportunity. They harbored no illusions that the white man would extend this opportunity to them in the same way he had extended it to his own children. The fact that acquiring literacy was increasingly becoming an important condition for employment helped the Africans to equate literacy with self-sufficiency.

This is where the African mind was at its best in designing a strategy for survival. In designing policies that were intended to train Africans to function as laborers, the colonial governments hoped to maintain a socioeconomic stratification between the races. For instance, in colonial Zimbabwe this view was strengthened by the report of the Land Commission of 1925, which stated that, however desirable it might be that members of the two races live side by side, the conditions that placed the Africans in an inferior socioeconomic position must dictate a course of action that would require caution in allowing them to make socioeconomic changes to new conditions through formal education.[34]

The ability to function in business and commercial settings influenced the acceptance of Western education in order for the Africans to understand

and participate in colonial economics. The interdependence between socio-economic competence and acquiring the rudiments of Western education came spontaneously in the course of the Africans' endeavors to survive in the colonial environment. In this development whether socioeconomic adaptation influenced education or whether education influenced socioeconomic adaptation was really not important to the Africans. What mattered was that the more education they received, the more socioeconomic adaptation they were able to realize.

Conversely, the more socioeconomic adaptation they achieved, the more they needed Western education. Success could not be achieved in one area without success in the other. These developments show that only the development of the African mind subjugated to the colonial environment could make this possible. It is equally true that from 1900 to 1939 the need for socioeconomic adaptation influenced the development of education more than the other way around because whatever form that education took it became a critical instrument for socioeconomic adaptation. The opportunity to earn an income was all the Africans needed to make economic adjustments to colonial conditions possible. In colonial Zimbabwe the Land Commission of 1925 recognized this fact when it observed, "A feature of outstanding importance attracted the attention of this commission, the desire of all sections of the native population for education for their advancement is directly related to the desire for socioeconomic benefits occurring to all and can be gratified in a practical manner."[35]

To gratify the Africans in a practical manner was to use economic benefits to reward them for making efforts to acquire skills in literacy. This recognition by the colonial governments was not an admission of error in judging the level of intellect among the Africans; rather, it was a reality that the Africans forced on them through rational and logical thinking.

The period from 1900 to 1939 was also very important regarding the efforts the Africans made to adapt to colonial conditions by acquiring the fundamentals of Western education. Having failed to arouse in them an interest in the claimed value of practical training and manual labor, the colonial governments were once again in error in their belief that African interest in education would assure their sought-for abundant supply of cheap labor.[36]

The Africans regarded Western education as a way to broaden their horizons far beyond the objective of adapting to colonial conditions. They also saw education as a means of enriching their minds in order to live a fuller life with dignity and purpose. Therefore, with regard to acquiring Western formal education as a means of adapting to colonial conditions, the Africans and the colonial governments were set on an irreversible collision course. Jomo Kenyatta prophetically recognized the effect of colonial education in 1945. He foresaw the inevitable serious conflict between the Africans and the colonial governments.[37]

THE NEED TO FUNCTION IN POLITICAL SETTINGS: OPENING THE AFRICAN MIND TO NEW REALITIES

To appreciate the Africans' efforts to secure Western education and facilitate their adaptation to colonial conditions within the framework of colonial policies, we must understand the nature of the colonial geopolitical behavior following the Berlin Conference. In colonial Zimbabwe the Orders-in-Council of 1898, which authorized the formation of a representative form of government, did not specify the qualifications that the citizens must meet in order to claim the right to vote. However, the Orders-in-Council authorized the British high commissioner in South Africa to formulate necessary specifications and have them made known to the prospective voters.

After consulting Earl Grey, administrator from April 2, 1896 to December 4, 1898, the high commissioner announced these qualifications by issuing Proclamation Number 17 of 1898. The proclamation outlined the requirements that had to be met. It gave all white males over the age of twenty-one the right to vote, provided they also met the following additional qualifications:

1. They were British subjects who had taken the oath of allegiance to Queen Victoria.
2. They must be able to sign their names and write their address without assistance.
3. They had not been imprisoned for any criminal offense during the previous five years.
4. They owned immovable property worth seventy-five pounds sterling or had an annual income of fifty pounds sterling.[38]

These qualifications remained unchanged until 1919 when white women, whose husbands were qualified to claim the right to vote, were allowed to register as voters.[39] The Africans were barred from claiming the right to vote until 1928 because colonial officials believed that, as members of an uncivilized culture, they would not understand the electoral process.[40]

This political action would later cause irresolvable conflict between the Africans and the colonial governments. The legislative council of 1898 consisted of eleven white members, of whom five were appointed by the administrator, four were elected by white voters, one was appointed by Britain, and the administrator himself.[41] This practice remained in force in all British colonies in Africa. The belief that the African mind was able to comprehend and participate in Western political practices created concern among colonial officials.

In British colonial Africa the Royal Charter in 1889 made provisions for the colonial governments to respect African cultural traditions, but it failed to specify exactly how they could be protected against the wave of exploitation carried on by British entrepreneurs who zealously pursued their own socioeconomic and political interests. The amendment prior to the elections of 1898 made provisions that, though intended to safeguard the Africans' interests had, in effect, the opposite results.[42] As a result of the amendment, the Africans were not considered sufficiently educated to participate in the electoral process, but their cultural values would be protected, even though the colonialists did not respect them; the political power of the whites was to be strengthened to sustain Western cultural values and institutions; and no reference must be made to the war of 1886 in the treatment of the Africans.

Although these amendments had little impact on the white man's political behavior they had a profound effect on the African mind and its search for a new political identity. In reminding the Africans that they were not allowed to participate in the electoral process because they were not educated in the same way as the whites, the colonial governments were psychologically trying to condition them to submit to a new form of political oppression. Such an action is always present in relationships between the colonizer and the colonized.[43] The wars between the Africans and the colonial systems immediately following colonization had convinced the Africans that the white man's military superiority proved his political and educational superiority as well. They heard the white man make political speeches which reinforced the illusion that they were destined to serve him forever as their master. It was inconceivable that the colonial governments and the Africans could exchange ideas on issues of great national and continental importance. Instead, the Africans became a favorite topic of political debate among colonial politicians who "ridiculed and degraded us in every way possible."[44]

The political deprivation that the Africans suffered as a result of colonial political maneuvering was absolute in every way. The veteran African politician in Zimbabwe, Willie Musarurwa, concluded that the colonial politicians' action was taken to prove that the white man was invincible and to force the Africans to submit to his political power. Musarurwa adds,

"Africans were induced to believe in the invincibility of the white man and to accept his form of government as inevitable. The desire to challenge the white man's government had been obliterated and the Africans had to make the best out of a bad situation by asking the white man to rule them well."[45] This game of brainwashing played by the colonial politicians would change dramatically following the end of World War II.

Indeed, in hoping against the reality that the white man would treat them well, the Africans could only pray that their adaptation to colonial conditions would be less painful. Paulo Freire describes this behavior on the part of the colonized as coming from a "basic element in the relationship between the oppressor and the oppressed."[46] Actually, he states, it represents a reaction to the imposition of the oppressor's will on the oppressed, who have no other way of alleviating their suffering except to retain the distinctive quality of their mind.

Musarurwa might have therefore added that for the Africans to ask the colonial governments to rule them well was to recognize the futility of their opposition to the conditions imposed by colonial governments. This is why during the period from 1900 to 1939 they did not question the whites' absolute power to rule the country as they saw fit, not because a change in conditions was not called for, but because the Africans did not have the physical means of bringing it about. They knew that they were a conquered people and that they were at the mercy of the whites. That this situation would begin to change only a few years after the end of the war in 1945 indicates the magnitude of the African intellect, not the goodwill of the colonial governments.

This forced submission created a need for education among the Africans in order to receive a modicum of respect from the white man. His form of education, which the Africans of the period from colonization to 1910 had rejected, found new meaning during the period from 1911 to 1939 and beyond. From 1900 to 1939 the Africans watched from the sidelines as the white man made important political decisions affecting their future. In colonial Zimbabwe when the Royal Charter expired in 1923, the British South Africa Company had one of two choices to make: to join South Africa as its fifth province or to opt for responsible government. The second choice would allow the colonial government to exercise a semiautonomous political status. The British Imperial Government required that the issue be resolved by referendum rather than by plebiscite in order to limit the number of qualified voters to the Caucasian colonists.

Following an emotionally charged debate, the legislative council opted to use a referendum because a plebiscite would have allowed the Africans to participate. They were barred from participating in the referendum for the same reason that they were barred from the elections of 1898: that is, they did not meet the property and educational qualifications to claim the right to register as voters. When the referendum results were known on October 23, 1923, no one, not even the British government, had considered the fact that only a total of 14,773 white voters had participated out of the total Caucasian population of 35,900 and that 1.3 million Africans did not participate because they were considered to lack an understanding of the electoral process.

Indeed, the colonial government was not surprised that the Africans did not participate in the elections because it was responsible for the fact, This is, indeed, one of the self-serving sides of colonialism in Africa. In the state of their helplessness, the Africans then began to view the Western form of education as a means of giving them new political direction and purpose. The days of colonial educational and political blackmail were clearly numbered.

The elections of 1898 and the referendum of 1923 further strengthened the Victorian myth of African inferiority that the white man had been using as a justification to deny equal rights to the Africans. But the reason behind that action, that the African mind did not understand Western political processes, was a weak excuse. In 1929 that myth was still alive and well as colonial politicians attempted to justify their negative attitude by claiming, "The Native people can profit only by industrial and elementary education, that they reach a phase of mental stupidity by the time they are adolescents."[47] The African did not care much about being eliminated from the elections of 1898, but they had an entirely different reaction to the referendum of 1923. With less that 0.03 percent of the population in school in 1898, they felt that the elections were nothing more than a white man's exercise of his assumed cultural and intellectual superiority.

But with 8.2 percent of the population in school in 1923, the Africans felt that their exclusion was a deliberate denial of their political rights because the school process was to the whites themselves an acceptable way of adjusting to socioeconomic and political conditions that the colonial society had stipulated. Thus, as my uncle told me in Zimbabwe in 1983, the Africans felt that

Our elimination from the political process was an eye opener to things to come. We felt that by making an effort to secure the education which the white man had enjoyed, we demonstrated our genuine desire to adjust to the demands of the colonial government. Unfortunately, the colonial politicians did not see our efforts from this perspective. It was therefore time for us to design a new strategy to resolve the problems of our existence in the colonial setting. Seeking more education to make our adjustment to colonial rule was the only course of action opened to us. In doing so we reopened our minds to new realities.[48]

The Africans of 1923 could not meet the property and educational requirements to qualify for the right to vote. But in 1928, with 99,535 African students, or 8.7 percent of the population in school in colonial Zimbabwe,[49] the political landscape had been transformed. To demonstrate their willingness to adapt further to the political system controlled by the whites, sixty-two Africans met the educational qualifications required to claim the right to vote, which they did exercise. The following table shows the number of voters who participated in the elections of 1928 and other years, as indicated:

Number of Voters in Colonial Zimbabwe, 1928–1956

Year	African Voters	White Voters	Total
1928	62	21,938	22,000
1939	70	27,930	28,000
1952	380	44,620	45,000
1956	560	51,440	52,000

Source: F. M. Wilson, *Rhodesia: Parliamentary Elections, 1898–1962* (Harare, 1964).

These figures merit some elaboration. The sixty-two Africans who voted in the elections of 1928 did so with an absolute conviction that their participation in the political process would bring them the respect they sought from the white man as proof that they, too, were civilized (as the white man defined civilization) and that they, too, understood this process as practiced by the white man. The elections of 1898 and the referendum of 1923 had raised serious questions by 1928 about the white man's claim that colonialism was aimed at raising the Africans from their presumed primitive culture to an acceptable level of involvement in national affairs.

Having been criticized by church leaders that the 1923 referendum had made a mockery of the civilized standards that the colonialists claimed to be their exclusive prerogative, the British government demanded that the colonial officials make provisions for Africans to claim their right to vote in 1928, even though their numbers were so small that they really did not make any difference in the outcome of the elections. But it was the very idea of having them participate in elections that opened the African mind to new realities that demanded an appraisal of old practices in which it was interwoven.

Even more important to the Africans was their awareness that their participation in the elections of 1928 was synonymous with their ability to understand the political process and to adjust to colonial conditions. Therefore, the experience of casting a ballot under the same conditions as the white man showed they were capable of functioning within an environment they did not conceive. To possess the education that helped them qualify to claim the right to register as voters became a majestic symbol of adaptation and the ability of the African mind to discern political activity as a phenomenon comprised of multiple dimensions. For this reason, the pursuit of Western education acquired a new meaning. It had a practical value in their struggle to gain some ability in socioeconomic areas in order to survive under colonial conditions. In this setting, political consciousness and involvement by the Africans became new schemata in their minds and lives.

These developments represented an exciting period in the struggle of the African mind for survival under colonial rule. Thus, the hostility that manifested itself from the invasion and colonization of Africa and the bitter racial wars that followed had, by 1928, given way to the recognition of the need to adapt to new conditions. This strategy enabled the Africans to make a bona fide effort to cooperate fully with the colonial governments in order to sustain their successfully tested and corollary perspective from which to proceed. But one must not rush to the assumption that these developments constituted a resounding victory for the African mind, for the white man began to be fearful of where this new African involvement in the political process would eventually lead.

Indeed, the Africans did not know that the whites were beginning to have serious doubts about educating them beyond the level of manual labor, practical training, and basal literacy.[50] Some African leaders such as Albert Luthuli, Sekou Toure, Benjamin Burombo, Charles Mzingeli, Charlton Ngcebetsha, Julius Nyerere, and Thompson Samkange demonstrated a political ability that alarmed the whites who dreaded the prospect that the Africans would use their education to threaten white political power.

The increase in the number of African students from 23,598 in 1919 to 27,610 in 1924 must have been unsettling for the colonial governments and their white constituency. By 1927, some colonial officials such as Tawse Jollie and Hugh Williams, influential members of the legislature in colonial Zimbabwe, argued that education of the Africans must be controlled in order to prevent the development of a political consciousness that would threaten the political power of the whites. However, during the period from 1900 to 1939 the Africans strengthened their resolve to adapt to colonial conditions by promoting change from within the system that governed them. Indeed, the Africans recognized that throughout human history society has been a product of political and social change that is beyond the control of any one factor, that it is a reflection of a combination of individual and collective variables. In colonial Africa these variables included the ability of the African mind to make necessary adjustments to conditions they did not produce or could not control.

As much as the Africans recognized that colonialism, like slavery, was decidedly more destructive than constructive, more debilitating and disabling than enabling, and more negative than positive, they were compelled to make necessary adjustments to shape conditions for the future. There was little else the colonial governments could have done to limit this burgeoning awareness other than to demand that their education and socioeconomic opportunities be restricted in order to prepare them to function solely as laborers. For this reason, the character of educational, economic, and political opportunities for Africans was created almost entirely by the ability of African students and their teachers to make the most out of a set of debilitating conditions. Each student was made aware of his or her individuality. One African remembered the implications of this development: "That all Africans could contribute to the future motivated students to get the most from the colonial government that governed his or her life. The rise of this consciousness was a development that the colonial governments did not appreciate and could do little to eradicate."[51]

The underlying importance of the Africans' educational, socioeconomic, and political awareness during this period was shown in two fundamental considerations. The first was an inner feeling of self-respect and reverence of what was essential to their sense of future and self. This concept of self made it possible for them to determine the means of self-fulfillment. The second consideration was that in the process of determining the concept of self, the Africans shaped a new collective search for a political identity that was uniquely African. This enabled them to refuse to acquiesce to colonial purposes. In this context, the Africans knew that adaptation to colonial conditions was not the same thing as accepting colonial domination. The limited colonial environment provided a means of sustaining the concept of self because it gave them an opportunity to renew their sense of self in order to map out a new direction in the fulfillment of their aspirations. Without the ability to adapt to colonial conditions, the Africans might not have been able to recognize the importance of designing these strategies. The colonial governments were unable to recognize the implication of these realities and so a new environment was created in which the continental domino effect of cultural conflict began to take shape with the formation of African nationalist organizations all over Africa beginning in 1934.

The developments during the 1900–1939 period helped the Africans gain new political experience as a result of their ability to accommodate to colonial conditions. In turn, they set their hearts and minds on what "they believed they could accomplish in response to the colonial political realities. We took advantage of the refusal of the colonial governments to recognize the high level of our mind to design a set of strategies for elevating ourselves to new heights of rational thought process. If the white still wanted to pretend not to know our mind, that was his problem, not ours."[52]

More important was the fact that the Africans recognized that their efforts to secure education to enable them to function in other social settings would be futile unless they valued what was most precious at the time—adaptability. This reality enabled every student to advance as far as he or she could through the opportunity educational success afforded. On their own, the Africans were able to discover "inherent abilities and interests which they utilized to promote their own development"[53] within the context of conditions imposed by the colonial culture and society.

Above and beyond this level of intellectual achievement, the Africans of that period converted their intellectual prowess into practical use, formulating new ideals and principles that altered the character of race relationships in the mid-twentieth century when conditions were right. They were able to discern a comprehensive meaning from the educational, socioeconomic, and political processes different from what the restricted, rudimentary Western education had intended.

The Africans saw that socioeconomic efficiency and political involvement afforded them a better future, and so they began to view their world from an entirely new perspective. Perceptions generated from educational, political, and economic experience enabled them to understand the effect of colonial conditions on their lives. By forcing them to submit to colonial rule and by offering them limited educational, economic, and political opportunities, the colonial governments were, in the words of a respected African in Zimbabwe, indirectly assisting the Africans in their endeavor to

carve a new image about ourselves, our future, our minds, our survival, our political consciousness. Our concept of self was a new reality which was outside the ability of the white man to control because only people subjected to this form of oppression can perceive their situation as reality, not imagination, as one which needed radical change. What could the white man understand about our need to survive under the cruel conditions which he had created? To retain our sense of self and chart a new course, we had to have the ability to adjust to his rule in order to see our situation from its proper perspective. Without this adjustment, we would not be able to rescue ourselves from the jaws of colonialism. This is the reason why we decided that we needed to respond affirmatively to the limited education that colonial governments offered us. This could not be done without an inherent ability to convert adversity into an advantage. For a new generation of Africans this realization opened our minds to new realities. It was a revelation of the high level of our intellect.[54]

As the Africans of that period regarded their pursuit of Western education as an act of survival, they began to see the other benefits afforded by that strategy. One of these benefits was gaining experience in planning for the future. The awakening of a new interest, collective and individual, in their future, even though they recognized the limitations of the colonial conditions and rule, was the best survival kit they carried with them on their long road to self-fulfillment. They now knew who they were in relation to the colonial conditions.

It was not the intention of the colonial governments to have them experience this ability. The principal of an African school, who completed his primary education in Zimbabwe in 1940, recalled the Africans' ability to set new objectives with regard to a Western-type education during that time in order to accommodate colonial conditions:

The main objective of my parents in sending me to Old Mutare in 1937 was to be able to function, to adjust, to survive in an African country which was under the political control of the white man. Ability to read, to write, to speak some English, all symbolized our efforts to gain maximum adjustment to the culture of the white man so that we would design a strategy of easing our oppression. Without an ability to adjust to this condition we would be unable to end it. The basis of the success of our efforts was the misconception the white man had about the abilities of our minds.[55]

A practicing attorney, who began his primary education in 1938, also in Zimbabwe, added:

Because we were a conquered people, we were forced to endure the adverse conditions of colonialism in painful ways. We were made to believe that everything which the white man did represented perfection in human endeavor and achievement. Therefore the white man's culture, with all its imperfections, served as a guide, a model of our efforts and adjustment. But the white man himself was not aware that in forcing us to endure this colonial oppression we made an adjustment which gave us the time to design a strategy of ending it. Fortunately for us, the white man misunderstood that adjustment as our acceptance of colonial rule.[56]

These examples suggest that adapting to colonial conditions by accepting the rudiments of Western education was a slow, painful journey to a new path of self-discovery among the Africans. The colonial governments demanded from them nothing less than complete severance from their culture if they hoped to be treated better. The Africans' unwillingness to do this helped them retain their sense of self and cultural identity, which enabled them to perceive colonial conditions from a comparative analysis of both cultures.

They concluded that, however much they desired to adjust to the culture of the white man, it would be detrimental to their own development to make a clean break with their own. They therefore used the educational, economic, and political opportunities available to them to concurrently maintain their cultural identity and adapt. The contradiction between accommodation and cognitive resistance culminated in the discernment of the harshness of colonial rule itself. There is no doubt that the African mind was now coming of age in the colonial setting.

SUMMARY AND CONCLUSION

The period from 1900 to 1939 was a time of critical growth for the African mind and its ability to survive under colonial conditions. In providing limited educational, economic, and political opportunities to train them to function in accordance with their prescribed purposes, the colonial governments misjudged the ability of the African mind to remember who and what it was. This was a time when Africans needed to design strategies to envisage a future different from the past. Inhibiting economic and political conditions were controlled by the colonial institutions, but they did not control the African mind in the way they were intended. This highlights the ability of any human mind to survive under adverse conditions.[57] The Africans were no exception.

Adaptation was not an easy task, but the Africans had few options if they were to retain their sense of self. Events that began to unfold with the colonization of Africa, in accordance with the specifications of the Berlin Conference, to the beginning of the Second World War in 1939, forced the Africans to recognize that the Europeans intended to stay permanently. In order for them to survive and retain the crucial elements of self-consciousness as a people, they had to acknowledge the reality of the white man's political power.

For the Africans to continue to resist the colonial systems would have given the whites an opportunity to destroy the very fabric of the African culture, and it may well have led to genocide. The whites tolerated the Africans' early twentieth-century culture because they believed that the Africans had submitted to the colonial political will and now embraced colonial institutions. After all, the white man was superior and he lived the way others wanted to. He was the envy of the human race, the supreme creation of God.

Whereas the Africans submitted to colonial conditions, they did not accept colonial rule itself. This level of self-consciousness among the oppressed is manifested in similar situations in contemporary society. It is the part of human intuition that enables passengers in a hijacked plane to want to identify with their captors and cooperate with them in their actions. This does not mean that the passengers accept the hijacker's behavior: they are only adapting to a situation they cannot control in order to live. The Africans of the 1900–1939 period saw their predicament in a similar manner: they were hostages of a situation they could not control, but they had to survive. Some Africans, however, encountered the perils of adaptation, and they were not able to overcome its socializing power.

Three basic areas influenced the African mind to make necessary adjustments to colonial conditions in order to survive: literacy, socioeconomic involvement, and political development. Because there was an important difference between the Africans and colonial governments' cultural values, it was not realistic for the whites to expect the Africans to discard their cultural traditions in order to make the kind of adaptation demanded by the colonial governments.

If the Africans had so adapted, they would have been reduced to the status of a people with no sense of direction or self. This is why the Africans sought to adjust to colonial conditions in their own way. But in sustaining their uniqueness, the Africans sent wrong signals to the whites, who began to see them as inherently unable to progress. What was important to the Africans was to understand that accepting features of Western culture, including the rudiments of education, was "essentially an act of practicing the white man's culture."[58] They could hope that some day they would live in a social environment that negated cultural exploitation and instead promoted cultural diversity as an enrichment of human institutions. For the time being, however, they opted to play the game of socioeconomic and political survival according to the rules the white man had set.

In the Africans' efforts to acquire the rudiments of Western education, neither the Africans nor the colonial governments could predict the effect such efforts could have on future race relationships. One African observed in July 1983:

The ability of the Africans to question the assumed superiority of the white man began with their introduction to the education which the colonial governments wanted us to have in order to serve their own socioeconomic and political interests. It did not occur to colonial governments that while they colonized our personhood, they did not colonize our minds as well. By denying us the kind of education we needed to play a dynamic role in society, the colonial government opened the possibility of the rise of consciousness among us beyond its ability to control.[59]

The adaptation that the Africans were trying to make during the 1900 to 1939 period had another important dimension that the colonial governments did not understand. If the Africans had been unable to accept features of Western culture, they would have denied themselves an opportunity to prepare for the social change that was to come and would never have been able to learn about all the behavior patterns of the whites. To observe and study is to predict. The more the Africans accommodated Western socio-economic and political systems, the more they valued education, the more they assimilated the rudiments of Western education, and the better they came to understand themselves in relation to the conditions they found themselves in. For the Africans education was for living, not for preparing for life, as it is universally understood. They needed to sustain themselves economically, socially, and politically before they could make a living in the context of the colonial conditions. This was the ultimate strategy of their survival.

The Africans' efforts to adapt to colonial conditions were recognized by some leading members of the colonial government. For example, T. R. Stanning observed in 1967: "The Africans had to adjust to a new outlook and be very careful to work with the system which was already there. The adjustment which they made in order to function in a colonial setting shows the educational benefits that accrued to them."[60] Stanning fully recognized the Africans' ability to adjust to colonial conditions in order to survive in a situation that would have destroyed their sense of self. But he also saw what other colonial officials refused to see: the adaptation the Africans made was not merely a process of survival, but a means of reasserting themselves and the rightness of their demands for equal treatment in society in order to prevent future racial conflict.[61]

The adaptation the Africans made in acquiring Western cognition from 1900 to 1939 had a far-reaching effect on their lifestyle. Again, this was not a choice they made freely, but one that circumstances forced them to make. Out of this experience the Africans learned valuable things about the colonial culture, while the colonial governments refused to learn to appreciate the worth of the African culture. This state of affairs placed the colonial governments and white man in general at a great disadvantage. The Africans' recognition that their lives would no longer be the same reflected their ability to see things as they were.

The problems that the colonial governments created for themselves by designing a limited set of national policies inadvertently helped the Africans sharpen their perception of their future because these policies were conceived in egocentric ignorance. As a result, the white man's culture was no longer a model of manhood at the end of the war in 1945, which it had been made to be from the period of colonization to 1939. The outbreak of the war in 1939 created an entirely new situation. This compounded the problems of racial relations that the colonial governments had neglected prior to 1945.

To appreciate the Africans' ability to adjust to colonial conditions, we must understand Paulo Freire's notion that when survival becomes crucial among the oppressed, adaptation becomes a necessary strategy for survival.[62] But in making this adaptation, the oppressed send a message to their oppressor that it is not the same thing as acceptance of oppression. In this kind of setting, the oppressor is forced to resolve the contradiction that characterizes the relationships between him and the oppressed in his own way. When the Africans slowly began to make demands for immediate self-government following the end of the war, they were trying to resolve that contradiction in their own way. This is how conflict between the two cultures became inevitable. The colonial governments were at a loss to understand the basis of the influence that was motivating the African. They did not know that the adjustment process of the years preceding the war was experiential education for the emergence of a powerful nationalism that could no longer be subdued.

The African mind's ultimate success in adapting to colonial conditions to ensure its survival was its ability to recognize the dangers of wholeheartedly accepting the culture of the colonizer without first critically appraising all its dimensions and the perils of adapting to it ignorantly. This was the dilemma that only the Africans could resolve in their own way by utilizing cognitive processes. Godfrey Huggins, the prime minister of colonial Zimbabwe from 1933 to 1952, acknowledged this reality when he said in 1954: It is a basic biological rule that creatures which fail to adapt to a new environment perish."[63]

Huggins was clearly advising the Africans to adapt to colonial conditions in a very different way from how they themselves had wanted to do. Huggins' intolerance of the Africans' ability to adapt in their own way strengthened the determination of the African mind to retain its own sense of self. This situation created tragic relationships between the Africans and the colonial governments. It was a situation that required the rise of the African mind to correct.

NOTES

1. In some countries, such as Angola, Mozambique, and Zimbabwe, the Africans decided to resist the colonization of their land. As a result, fierce fighting broke out between the colonial forces and the Africans. Because bows and arrows were no match for the gun, the Africans had no chance of winning.

2. Apart from what has been discussed in Chapter 1, this author does not think it is necessary to discuss details of the colonization itself because they are well known.

3. Philip Curtin, *Africa South of the Sahara* (Morristown, N.J.: Silver Burdett Co., 1970), p. 63.

4. Albert Memmi, *The Colonizer and the Colonized* (Boston: Beacon Press, 1965).

5. Ibid., p. xxvii.

6. Ibid., p. 58.

7. David Hapgood, *Africa in Today's World in Focus* (Boston: Ginn and Co., 1971), p. 53.

8. Ibid., p. 56.

9. Memmi, *The Colonizer and the Colonized*, p. 87.

10. Ibid., p. 90.

11. Ibid., p. 94.

12. Adam Curle, *Education for Liberation* (New York: Wiley and Sons, 1973), p. 59.

13. Ibid., p. 61.

14. *New York Times*, March 31, 1961.

15. Janet Vaillant, *Black, French, and African: A Life of Leopold Sadar Senghor* (Cambridge, Mass.: Harvard University Press, 1990), p. 230.

16. Ibid., p. 128.

17. Ibid., p. 269.

18. See Chapters 4 and 7 of this study for a detailed discussion of Nkrumah's role in the struggle for the liberation of the African mind and the reasons for his fall.

19. Paulo Freire, *Pedagogy of the Oppressed* (New York: Continuum, 1983), p. 49.

20. The exact nature of Lobengula's death has remained controversial: the author believes that he was actually killed by the colonial forces when they invaded his village in 1893.

21. Henri Rolin, *Les Lois et l'Administration de la Rhodesie* (Bruxelles: l'Etablissment Emil Bruylant, 1913).

22. The referendum was held on October 23, 1923: 8,774 white voters favored responsible government status, and 5,999 favored joining South Africa as its fifth province. The Africans did not participate because they were considered *uncivilized* and so were presumed to be unable to understand the political process and the issues to be decided.

23. Freire, *Pedagogy of the Oppressed*, p. 30.

24. C. S. Davies, "African Education in Rhodesia," *NADA* 10 (1969).

25. A respected African during an interview with the author in Watsomba, Zimbabwe, July 17, 1983.

26. Rev. Josiah Chimbadzwa, "The Seed is Planted," an audiotape recording made by Rev. E. L. Sells, 1968, Old Mutare Methodist Archives.

27. An African during an interview with the author in Harare, Zimbabwe, August 11, 1989.

28. Methodist Episcopal Church, *The Official Journal* (Rhodesia: Mission Press, 1910), p. 49.

29. Southern Rhodesia, Commission of Inquiry into Native Education (F. L. Hadfield, chairman), 1927, p. 16.

30. Memmi, *The Colonizer and the Colonized*, p. 95.

31. Ibid., p. 99.

32. Ibid., p. 101.

33. Ibid., p. 105.

34. Southern Rhodesia, Report of the Land Commission (Morris Carter, chairman), 1925, para. 63. Zimbabwe National Archives.

35. Ibid., para. 80.

36. Southern Rhodesia, Annual Report of the Director of Native Development, 1928, para. 16.

37. Curtin, *Africa South of the Sahara*, p. 92.

38. British South Africa Company Records, Proclamation Number 17 of 1898. Zimbabwe National Archives.

39. British South Africa Company Records, *The Constitution of 1898*, Article 50/51. Zimbabwe National Archives.

40. Ibid.

41. Ibid.

42. Southern Rhodesia, The Land Commission, 1925.

43. Memmi, *The Colonizer and the Colonized*, p. 86.

44. Matthew Mwandiringa, during an interview with the author in Watsomba, Zimbabwe, July 29, 1983.

45. Willie Musarurwa, "African Nationalism in Rhodesia," in Robert Cory and Dianna Mitchell (eds.), *African Nationalist Leaders* in *Rhodesia's Who's Who* (Bulawayo: Books of Rhodesia, 1977), p. 7.

46. Freire, *Pedagogy of the Oppressed*, p. 31.

47. "Native Education in Africa," *Nature* (no. 124/3135), November 30, 1929.

48. P. H. Mungazi during an interview with the author in Mutare, August 6, 1983.

49. Southern Rhodesia, Report of the Director of Native Development, 1928, p. 6.

50. "Native Education in Africa."

51. Interview with an African in Mutare, July 1, 1983.

52. Interview with an African in Harare, July 10, 1983.

53. Southern Rhodesia, Report of the Education Committee, 1943, p. 60.

54. An African during an interview with the author in Harare, July 27, 1983.

55. An African principal during an interview with the author in Mutare, July 17, 1983.

56. An African attorney during an interview with the author in Harare, July 29, 1983.

57. Memmi, *The Colonizer and the Colonized*, p. 106.

58. Davies, "African Education in Rhodesia."

59. An African, during an interview with the author in Mutare, July 7, 1983.

60. T. R. Stanning, "African Farming Development in the Chiweshe Tribal Trust Land," *Rhodesia Journal of Economics* 1, no. 1 (1967).

61. Ibid.

62. Freire, *Pedagogy of the Oppressed*, p. 105.

63. Godfrey Huggins, "Taking Stock of African Education," an address to the Southern Rhodesia Missionary Conference held at Goromonzi, August 25, 1964, Zimbabwe National Archives.

4

The Rise of the African Mind and Its Effect on the Colonial Society

> The rise of the mind of the colonized derives from the very nature of the colonial situations.
>
> *Albert Memmi, 1965*

> The Africans must be in the front of the battle against imperialism. Their weapon is their invincible mind, devoted to new heights and sure in the rightness of its cause.
>
> *Kwame Nkrumah, 1945*

COLONIALISM AND THE RISE OF THE MIND OF THE COLONIZED

Colonial governments consistently fail to recognize that their systems are not destined to last forever and that the systems' demise is often the result of the colonized's actions. From the days of the Roman Empire through the Thirteen Colonies in North America to the vast European colonial empires in Africa, colonial systems were based on a single principle—they could last as long as the mind of the colonized was controlled. It is also recognized that the most effective means of exercising control over the mind of the colonized is to play a psychological game that makes the controlled party what psychiatrists call a dependency personality. This makes it possible for the colonized to believe that without the colonizer their life is fragmented and incomplete, that their very survival is threatened. It is the function of the colonizer to perpetuate this lack of confidence so that the colonized will be unable to achieve self-actualization.

But much sooner than later, the mind of the colonized awakes to the reality that it is functioning under conditions fully controlled by the colonizer. This awakening is the beginning of the rise of colonized mind and poses serious implications for both parties. The colonized now refuse to operate on colonial reality from the same perspective that the colonizer does. They refuse to have their mind controlled in the same way it has been controlled in the past. They begin to assert their own mind in their own way in a manner that the colonizer does not understand. In order for this to happen, the mind of the colonized must rise above the level to which it has been prescribed by the colonizer. This means that the rise of the mind of the colonized must occur outside the conditions stipulated by the colonizer. This elevation has a profound impact on the colonial society. The relationships between colonizer and colonized are profoundly and irrevocably altered. The colonizer sees the colonized as a rebel against properly constituted authority, and the colonized sees the colonizer as a trespasser and oppressor. The lack of compromise between these two extreme positions helps to explain the changing character of the colonial society. Once this form of interaction comes into being, it cannot be reversed. By degrees, this situation constitutes the beginning of the end for the colonizer and the end of the beginning for the soon to be uncolonized. The future for both hangs precariously on the cliff of uncertainty and conflict.

THE RISE OF THE AFRICAN MIND: SOME THEORETICAL CONSIDERATIONS

The rise of the African mind took on powerful dimensions that the colonial governments were not quite able to comprehend. Two thinkers from the Third World who understand colonial conditions, mentioned in earlier chapters, are Albert Memmi of Tunisia and Paulo Freire of Brazil. They have outlined theoretical considerations that explain the effect of the rise of the mind of the colonized on the character of the colonial society.

Albert Memmi explains why the rise of the African mind was an inevitable outcome of colonial conditions that were designed to control it. "In all of the colonized there is a fundamental need for change. For the colonizer to be unconscious of this need means that either his lack of an ability to understand that the effect of the colonial system on the colonized is immense or that his blind selfishness is more than he can readily believe."[1] Memmi argues that, while failure or refusal to understand the oppressive conditions that control the mind of the colonized is a universal phenomenon, it cannot serve as an excuse to perpetuate them. Accordingly, he concludes that the rise of the mind of the colonized is generated by knowledge of the colonial conditions themselves. This knowledge helps the colonized to understand his position in a society that these conditions create. This is what makes him impatient, and demands change as he can no longer tolerate colonization itself.[2] In acknowledging this reality, the colonized uses the techniques and thought processes of the colonizer to develop his mind truly so that he can deal with it from the perspective of a complete knowledge of the consequences of his action. Because the colonizer always operates from an illusion of the inferiority of the mind of the colonized, he is never quite able to understand the rising mind of the colonized. In this context, the colonized has an added advantage.

Paulo Freire shares this line of thinking and argues further that the colonizer refuses to understand the harshness of the conditions that control the life of the colonized because he assumes that those colonial conditions have so reduced the mind of the colonized that he cannot engage in rational thought.[3] Thus, the colonizer refuses to engage in dialogue with the colonized. Without dialogue the chasm between them gets wider. This kind of social environment generates conflict. In his assumption that the colonized is inferior, the colonizer loses an opportunity to understand the adverse effects of the conditions that oppress the colonized. These conditions, and the refusal of the colonizer to understand their effect on the colonized, combine to create a new situation in which confrontation becomes inevitable. Freire explains in precise terms why only the mind of the colonized can grasp the essentials of what it must do to regain itself:

The oppressed, having internalized the image of the oppressor and adopted his guidelines, are fearful of freedom. But sooner or later he will understand that freedom of his mind would require him to reject this image and replace it with autonomy. Freedom is acquired by conquest, not by gift of the oppressor. He understands that freedom is an indispensable condition for the quest for human completion.[4]

Two conclusions can be reached about the application of these theoretical considerations to the rise of the African mind and its effect on the character of the colonial society. The first is that it doesn't take long for the mind of the colonized to begin to reassert itself in ways that the colonizer does not understand. Once it takes this course of action, it cannot be reversed, and the only type of relationship that now exists between the colonizer and the colonized is conflict. The second conclusion is that the colonizer either refuses to understand that the conditions he has imposed on the colonized will have an adverse effect on relationships or he believes that the colonized is unable to envisage and attain his destiny without his assistance or guidance. This chapter substantiates these two conclusions. Essential to the rise of the African mind is Freire's conclusion that its freedom is acquired by conquest, not as a gift from the oppressor. In other words, Freire maintains that the colonized must assume responsibility for the rise of his or her own mind because the colonizer will not support or encourage it. Let us now discuss how this happened in Africa following the conclusion of the Second World War.

NKRUMAH'S ROLE IN THE RISE OF THE AFRICAN MIND

The return of Kwame Nkrumah (1901–1972) to the Gold Coast (Ghana since 1957) in December 1947, following his twelve-year educational *safari* in Britain and the United States, was cause for African celebration. During the years he was in school, Nkrumah developed a political philosophy consistent with the general consciousness among the Africans following their participation in the Second World War. In 1947 he wrestled with the difficult decision of whether or not to accept the invitation from a group of lawyers and businessmen who had established a new political party to be its full-time secretary. Painfully aware that some Africans, such as Leopold Senghor,[5] were losing their cultural identity as a result of their close associations with colonial establishments, Nkrumah faced a dilemma of choice. If he declined the invitation, he would not have the exposure that he needed to launch his political career. If he accepted it, he faced the real possibility that the new political party would so control him that he would become ineffective.

But in 1947 the African mind had attained a level that would resist any attempt to control or manipulate it in any way. Nkrumah was highly sensitive to the reality that he needed to be his own man to function under less than adequate conditions. If he succeeded in this effort, then he would not only convert the existing political status quo into a channel through which he would launch his own political career, but he would also give legitimacy to the rise of the African mind by having it accepted by the establishment. He operated under the assumption that, although this was a new political party, it was part of the establishment because it operated under the stipulations made by the British colonial government.

Having satisfied himself that he must be his own person, Nkrumah accepted the invitation with an added importance to his mission. From the moment he assumed his position as secretary of the new political party, the United Gold Coast Convention (UGCC), on December 28, 1947, Nkrumah decided that the destiny of the African mind fell squarely on his shoulders.

He was to be its standard-bearer. From this moment the political landscape of Africa was mapped out, and the actions of the Berlin Conference of 1885 were about to be undone. The von Soemmering-White school of thought was about to experience an encounter different from the ideas expressed by Thomas Winterbottom, and the new African mind was rising.

UGCC was formed in August 1947, as a result of the increasing disillusionment among some middle-class Africans and liberal white politicians over the claimed benefits of colonialism. The UGCC's action in naming Nkrumah as its secretary also bears out Memmi's conclusion that the oppressed ultimately demand nothing less than equality and freedom.[6] Nkrumah's uneasiness with his association with white liberals suggests his perceived vulnerability to the perils of adaptation. Indeed, white liberal politicians commonly exploited the Africans' lack of political experience to sustain the colonial status quo. Nkrumah never believed that any white liberal could fully understand the African mind and the need to eliminate colonialism entirely. Because no white liberals advocated the advent of an African government, Nkrumah felt that they were part of a system that oppressed the Africans. This is why he put distance between them and himself. By 1947 the Africans were aware of this peril of adaptation.

In assuming his position as secretary of the UGCC at a monthly salary of 100 pounds sterling, Nkrumah wanted to demonstrate to his fellow Africans that it was quite possible to work within existing political establishments run by white liberals without falling victim to the perils of adaptation and without losing the sense of self. Although the Africans had serious doubts about the wisdom of accepting this strategy, they were willing to give Nkrumah an opportunity to show that it could work. Accordingly, he distanced himself from the great socialist liberal, the charismatic George Padmore (1900–1959), a native of Jamaica who later became a successful restaurateur in Britain. The rise of the African mind had an agenda and a character all its own, and Nkrumah symbolized this new approach to colonial politics. Mellowed by experience and seasoned by hardship, Padmore had earlier become an influential mentor to Nkrumah in a partnership of wills stronger than the bonds that existed between Cecil John Rhodes and Wynwood Read. Padmore was constantly at the disposal of his protégé, giving his total commitment to the African cause; in turn Nkrumah had an immeasurable admiration for his mentor.[7]

By 1949, Nkrumah had become something of a folk hero and had become well known throughout the Gold Coast and beyond. He felt that it was now time to launch a political career that would transform the political map of his country. This was the first phase of his plan to effect the total political transformation of Africa. Throughout his political career, Nkrumah never lost sight of this objective. Whether or not he would succeed in accomplishing it would depend on other factors. He believed that the destiny of the African mind demanded that he initiate a crusade that was destined to alter permanently the course of events in all of Africa.

Therefore, Nkrumah's decision to use his position as secretary of UGCC to seek higher political office that year reflected an understanding of the rise of the African mind different from what it had been in the past. Martin Meredith concludes that as he began to campaign for the office of prime minister in 1950, "Nkrumah brought to bear formidable talents as a political activist with a sharp mind. Possessing a restless energy and great ability as an organizer, he pursued political power with obsessive determination. His fiery speeches, his flamboyant manner, his winning smile made him the most famous politician in the country, the showboy who could generate a sense of excitement, of hope, of expectation. Unerringly he used a popular touch"[8] to accomplish what he knew had to be accomplished.

In the rising star that Nkrumah represented, the ascension of the new African mind had now carved an identity all its own, powerful and assertive, determined and aggressive, clear in its perception of itself and its destiny, unwavering in its will and commitment to a cause. Nkrumah was the man of the hour. The eyes of all of Africa and the colonial world were on him. His victory in the elections, his assumption of the office of prime minister in 1950, as well as his successful campaign for the independence of Ghana in 1957, spelled the demise of the British colonial empire in Africa.

By this time, Nkrumah had withdrawn from the UGCC to form the Convention Peoples party (CPP) which, under his leadership, won two successive elections between 1950 and 1956. The party and Nkrumah became two powerful political forces unmatched by any other party or leader. David Hapgood writes of Nkrumah's rising star: "With Ghana's independence, Nkrumah became a popular hero at home and in other parts of Africa. He was called *osagyfo* (redeemer) and a huge statue of him was built in Accra to signify the hopes of the oppressed African masses all over the continent and to symbolize the greatness of his mind."[9]

Since Ghana was the first colony to gain independence in the British empire in Africa, Nkrumah played a critical role in shaping the course of events on the continent. With his enormous popularity, charismatic personality, magnetic persuasion as a powerful speaker, and brilliant mind, Nkrumah was poised to begin a new continental campaign that would elevate the African mind to new heights in human endeavor and political action. He saw political independence in Africa as a prerequisite of all other forms of development. As soon as he was secure in his political position, he directed his efforts toward independence for the rest of Africa. Using a philosophical strategy based on his paraphrasing of biblical scripture, Nkrumah urged his fellow Africans to place political independence at the top of their agenda, saying, "Seek ye first the political kingdom and all other things shall be added unto you."[10]

Nkrumah immediately took issue with the traditionally negative attitude of the colonial officials toward the Africans, underscoring his belief in the potential of the African mind. For the colonial governments all over Africa, the days of S. T. von Soemmering and Charles White were over, and the era of new thinking was under way. Some colonial officials refused to adopt a positive attitude toward the Africans. In 1953, for example, Nkrumah felt greatly insulted by the views expressed by Sir Philip Mitchell, the governor of Kenya and a colonial official whose opinions the British Colonial Office in London greatly respected.

With regard to conditions in Kenya at the height of the Mau Mau movement, Mitchell argued that the entire population of this region of Africa was still in a state of ignorance and backwardness, controlled by superstitious beliefs that made it economically weak to the point of near helplessness and totally unable to develop a civilization that could command the respect of other peoples and cultures.[11] In Mitchell's opinion of the Africans, we see a clear reincarnation of von Soemmering and White. Mitchell was totally unaware that in seven short years the mind of a people he called uncivilized would rise to such a level that they would assume responsibility for a successful independent government.

In addition, in failing to recognize the pace of change in Africa, Mitchell represented what was now becoming the new white man's burden, denial. Nkrumah and other African leaders were incensed by Mitchell's remarks, which came at a time when colonial officials were being called upon to exercise caution in their articulated views of the Africans. Mitchell helped to galvanize their sense of destiny and only increased their beliefs in the rightness of their cause.

On the first anniversary of Ghana's independence in 1958, Nkrumah outlined grandiose goals and objectives for the continent, including total equality in all aspects of national life, economic development, cultural enrichment, and the deliverance of justice in all legal cases. Nkrumah argued that these elements strengthened African national institutions and were the product of the prowess of the African mind.[12] As Nkrumah saw things, the development of Africa was virtually impossible unless its leaders mobilized the priceless potential manifested in the cognitive abilities of its people.

THE SECOND WORLD WAR AND THE RISE OF
THE AFRICAN MIND

When the Second World War came to an end in 1945, the African mind had been transformed in ways that the white man had failed to predict and comprehend. The Africans who took part in the conflict came to learn things about the white man and his culture that they could scarcely have learned in any other way. What they learned to value most was the rise of a mind that would lead to self-awareness. This consciousness enabled them to perceive themselves as people who, though under colonial rule, were capable of shaping their own future. The suppressive nature of the problems they encountered in their relationships with whites was their primary concern, and they considered them "the key to all other problems."[13]

In order to assess their position in colonial Africa, as a result of their participation in the war, the Africans convened a high-level conference in London on October 15, 1945. As a symbol of their aspiration, the organizers of the conference went to amazing lengths to adorn the conference hall with flags of Liberia, Ethiopia, and Haiti. These were the only black independent countries of the world, and the action was intended to emphasize the hope that the colonized countries of Africa would soon achieve political independence as well.

Nearly one hundred delegates arrived from the West Indies and Africa. Ras Makonnen used his position as a highly successful black entrepreneur in the West Indies to underscore the importance of the conference, saying that Africa's destiny was in their hands. Makonnen made available his Cosmopolitan, one of his chain of restaurants that served food of African origin and taste, and so became a leading personality at the conference. Jomo Kenyatta, who managed the Cosmopolitan, also played a leading role at the conference. George Padmore also played a crucial role, helping to give the conference its proper focus and credibility among outside observers and reporters.

The excitement at the end of the war was coupled with the prospects of realizing the promises the colonial governments had made for improved living conditions as a reward for the Africans' participation in the war. The Fifth Pan African Congress commenced under the glare of unprecedented publicity. This conference was quite different from the Congress's four previous conferences. It held up the vision of the emergence of a progressive way of African thinking, different from the past in that it made it possible for Africans to challenge colonial institutions and to demand fundamental change to accommodate their aspirations.[14]

A new phenomenon emerged at this conference. Prior to 1945, beginning in 1925, the Pan African Congress had been led and directed by black American intellectuals such as W.E.B. Du Bois (1868–1963). In contrast, at this conference African nationals shaped its agenda and deliberations. Although Du Bois was invited to the conference, (as Meredith concluded, essentially to carry the mantle that would give respectability to the proceedings),15 he had no more powerful a role than he had had in the past. Thus, the African mind began to realize that it must shape its own destiny.

This action silenced the critics who argued that the Africans depended on the leadership of black Americans to direct the Pan African Congress because they lacked the intellectual potential and political experience to be creative and set priorities on their own. Black Americans had not seen the African mind from the negative perspective of the white critics. They were quite pleased with the new assertiveness of the African mind, for now they and the Africans could join hands in the struggle to reach their common goals. Both groups were seriously oppressed: the Africans by the colonial conditions, and the black Americans by the denial of their civil rights. Adopting the Padmore political philosophy, the central figures of the conference now assumed radical political positions to form a generation of thinkers molded by colonial hardship, and they took an unequivocal stance against the colonial status quo. It was the best of times for the Africans and the worst of times, indeed, a political nightmare, for the colonial establishments.

The conference's agenda included a discussion of the problems that black communities in Britain were facing, such as police mistreatment, the plight of the deprived masses who were enduring enormous difficulties caused by the war, and the question of caring for illegitimate children left behind by black American soldiers stationed in Britain during the war. While these issues were undoubtedly important, the main agenda of the conference immediately became a forthright attack on colonial rule itself. Each speaker made an outright demand for political rights as a prerequisite for independence.16 When Kenyatta said, "One thing we must do, and that is to get political independence. If we achieve that goal we shall be free to achieve other things we want,"17 he was laying the groundwork for a new strategy that Nkrumah would later utilize to attain continental prominence.

Sensitive to the promises that the colonial governments had made for improved standards of living, the Africans did not think that the demand for freedom and independence was unreasonable. It was no longer possible for them to make petitions of the type they once had by acting in a nonthreatening moderate fashion. For the Africans of 1945 moderation, as Barry Goldwater put it in 1964, in the pursuit of political rights was no longer a virtue, and extremism in their demand for equality in society was no longer a vice. This is why they designed a strategy that placed them at a distance from the white liberal politicians that included the head of the British government, Clement Attlee, because they were part of the colonial establishments they were now trying to abolish. They concluded that massive political action against the colonial establishments was the only strategy that would invoke a response by the colonial governments and would lead to African autonomy.

When Nkrumah was asked to draft one of the key resolutions of the conference, he was given an opportunity to demonstrate the level of the assertiveness of the African mind beyond any doubt and to set the tone for its elevation to new heights. He stated that the colonial government must give way to the demands for independence. He concluded, saying "The Fifth Pan African Congress therefore calls on the workers and farmers in the colonies to organize effectively. The Africans must be in the front of the battle against imperialism."[18]

The colonial governments tried to control this new phenomenon but were unable to suppress it. For the Africans, this phenomenon was a highway to a political heaven, whereas for the colonial governments it represented a rough road to "the other way." The decision of Britain's Labour party to allocate 120 million pounds sterling to improve conditions for the Africans in the colonies fell far short of meeting expectations and aspirations. It only served to accentuate the Africans' demands for freedom and independence. A parting of the ways had been reached between the colonial governments and the African mind. Everything pointed to a brutal and fierce struggle of the wills.

To their amazement and disbelief, the Africans who participated in the war discovered that European nations had both the positive attributes and negative features that characterize human life all over the world. The Europeans' illusion of superiority was found to be just that, and it no longer made any difference in the efforts the Africans were making to end the misery that was the lot of the African masses. The Great Depression had left political and socioeconomic scars that would not disappear. For the Africans to discover that poverty and squalor were the lot of a great number of people in Europe was a demonstration of the fallibility of the human mind and the inability of the Europeans to create socioeconomic and political utopia in Europe.

The Africans wondered what was happening to the resources that European nations had been exploiting in Africa since the nineteenth century. They learned that for many Europeans the purported centers of civilization were also the ramshackle dwelling places of the deprived and unfortunate masses. For the Africans to discover that, indeed, some white people in

Europe were poor was "to recognize the inability of European governments to solve human problems."[19] But what was most shattering to the Africans was the idea that the European nations that had colonies in Africa (including Britain, France, Belgium, Portugal, and Spain) had implemented educational policies that effectively eliminated the African populace from the political, social, and economic affairs of their countries.

THE RISE OF THE NEW AFRICAN MIND: A DILEMMA
FOR THE COLONIAL GOVERNMENTS

As noted earlier, the Africans joined the ranks of the Allied armies to fight against the Axis powers only because, in return, the colonial governments promised to improve conditions in their countries. The Africans clearly heard Winston Churchill and Franklin Roosevelt proclaim in the Atlantic Charter of August 11, 1941, that they would be given an opportunity for self-fulfillment after the war was over: "After the final destruction of the Nazi tyranny we hope to see established a peace which will afford all the lands and all men to live out their lives in freedom from fear and want."[20] With these words, the two leaders led the Africans to believe that they were, in effect, warning against continuing colonial conditions to the detriment of the development of the people they governed. When European nations were either unable or unwilling to follow up on this promise, the Africans were strengthened in their resolve to demand far-reaching changes in colonial society.[21] The search for opportunities to advance this pledge was its ultimate manifestation. They perceived educational, socioeconomic, and political participation as basic human rights that they were entitled to as well.

While in Europe, the Africans saw what nations were doing to promote the development of their people through participation in these three areas. They observed the contradictions that were central to the way in which people lived. Some lived a life of luxury, while others lived in poverty and deprivation. Some enjoyed an opportunity to play a participatory role in society, while others had no such opportunity. The so-called Great Industrial Revolution was a mixed bag for Europeans. It had benefited some, but it had left others in the mire of deprivation and want. Opportunity was an exclusive right of a few.

Since the mass migration of Europeans to the New World beginning in 1837, the European leaders did not appear to have learned anything that would assist them in solving national problems. They were preoccupied with preserving their own political positions. This is the context in which, upon their return home, African military veterans shared their experiences

in Europe with those who had stayed behind.[22] From this informal education, the Africans began to question the legitimacy of the colonial leadership
and the assumption that only whites were capable of running good governments. Their bustling mind compelled them to refuse to accept the status
quo.

The Africans now looked to the Pan African Congress meeting in London
in 1945 as a prelude to the drama of the struggle for self. It was a pivotal
component in the strategy to resolve in their own way the problems the
colonial conditions had created for them. The lack of participation in the
affairs of their countries added fuel to the fire of their expanding consciousness as they began to articulate political views that were diametrically
opposite to those of the colonial governments. Their ability to articulate
social and political views and to formulate national goals and objectives
helped set the two racial groups on a collision course that had its catalyst
in Nkrumah's campaign for political office in 1950. The colonial governments' failure to recognize that the war had helped create a new consciousness among the Africans only accelerated their demand for meaningful
equal opportunity. They felt that they had earned it by their participation in
the war. Clearly, unless the colonial governments responded affirmatively,
an intense struggle to bring about meaningful and comprehensive change
was inevitable.

One unfortunate development of the postwar period was that the colonial
governments did not think that the lack of equal opportunity for Africans
would likely cause immediate serious problems, although some officials
seemed to recognize the potential danger. For example, in April 1945 the
duke of Devonshire, the British parliamentary undersecretary for the colonies, paid tribute to "the courage, endurance of the African soldiers and the
quality of their mind."[23] He warned members of the British House of Lords
that "the Africans are anxious to practice in civil life the various new skills
which they have learned during the war. Their grasping minds demand
nothing less."[24]

By the very nature of their existence, however, the European colonial
governments entailed a potential for their own demise "by holding on to
past traditionally negative attitudes towards the Africans."[25] The rise of the
African mind enabled the Africans to realize that social institutions needed
a fundamental change if conflict between them and the colonial governments were to be avoided in the future. At the beginning of the war, the
colonial governments had made the Africans understand that they were
asked to fight for human freedom by defeating the Axis powers, but they
returned home to experience new forms of oppression. They were made to
believe that they were fighting to ensure the liberation of the universal

human being and self-fulfillment, but they returned home to find new repression. They were made to believe that they were fighting to ensure equal rights for all, and yet they returned home to endure new forms of racial discrimination, inequality, and prejudice.

Therefore, tragic as the war was, it gave the Africans an opportunity to elevate their mind and to see themselves in relation to how colonial governments were running their countries. It soon became evident that the Machiavellian principles that were central to the policies of the colonial governments were indeed vulnerable to a united opposition and affront. But, unlike Machiavelli, the colonial governments did not think that the subjugated Africans had a mind that would enable them to "take up arms"[26] and flex the muscle of their cognitive prowess to fight sooner than they had anticipated. By colonizing Africa in the first place, the European governments created a desire for freedom among the Africans.

By exploiting the resources of the continent, they had inadvertently created an environment of racial and cultural conflict. By introducing the Africans to new social and political systems in the context of Western paradigms, they had indirectly implanted the need for the freedom of self-expression in its universal meaning. By demonstrating their political intolerance of the expansion of their mind, the colonial governments had given rise to a new thinking that all people must be treated equally in society if major conflict is to be avoided. By providing limited opportunities for the Africans to serve their own socioeconomic and political interests, the colonial governments had indirectly taught them the skills necessary to engage in new self-directed learning activities.[27]

The continuation of forced labor practices,[28] even during the war years, created an environment that strengthened the Africans' quest for self-fulfillment.[29] Having instituted forced labor in the first place beginning in 1894, the colonial governments had indirectly implanted in the Africans an irrepressible desire for freedom. When the whites forced the Africans to work on public projects such as road construction, they strengthened the Africans' will, not just to survive, but to demonstrate that they would no longer serve as beasts of burden.

The Africans, aware that whites were subjecting them to dehumanizing conditions, demonstrated that they could convert adverse situations into a strategy for their liberation. For example, the creation of the Rhodesia African Rifles during the war was an occasion that Godfrey Huggins (prime minister of colonial Zimbabwe from September 12, 1933, to September 6, 1953, and of the ill-fated Federation of Rhodesia and Nyasaland, 1953–1956) recognized as having the beginnings of a potential conflict. Huggins, however, felt that he had to create conflict in order to augment the white colonial army.[30] In doing so, he failed to measure the influence of this action on the rise of the African mind and political consciousness.

The war also helped develop the Africans' understanding of their uninhibited personality. The war had touched this personality in a way that the colonial governments could not comprehend. In the relentless pursuit of their objectives, the colonial governments failed to recognize that this generation of Africans was not afraid to take risks in assessing new possibilities for their endeavors. The emergence of this new expression of the African personality facilitated the acquisition of a pragmatic understanding of the events that were increasingly influencing their lives.

In order to fight forced labor laws, the self-serving practices of the colonial governments and their claimed right to rule, to question the legitimacy of these colonial governments, and to value the freedom of human cognitive expression, the Africans needed to demonstrate that they could utilize their emerging risk-taking trait to challenge the whites' assumed superiority. They rejected outright the Victorian myth that they had an inferior mind, and they looked forward to the emergence of a new society that would promote total equality in every sphere of national life.[31] Nothing short of this objective would satisfy the Africans.

The Africans of the postwar period considered fulfilling this objective as an absolute imperative. When the colonial governments did not see things from this perspective, the phenomenon of the rise of African mind and political consciousness only grew. The colonial governments never imagined this outcome, and in their sudden impotence they could only watch it unfold.

Yet another aspect relative to the rise of the African mind and consciousness was a result of the war. In their limited contact with whites, especially through the tragedy of the war, the Africans learned that personality was the source of self-worth. To ensure future development at the highest level, they came to understand that it was dependent on the collective and individual personalities of the African people.

To structure their quest for the future, which the expansion of their awareness helped them perceive, the Africans knew that they had to base it on values that gave new meaning to their lives, encouraging them to make sacrifices and to take risks. This level of consciousness contextualized itself from the possibility of an instant death that the war produced. To value life they had to remind themselves of the possibility of an instant and violent death. This realization translated into concrete strategies for dealing with oppressive colonial conditions. To value freedom, they had to recognize that colonial oppression was real and absolute, and that to die in overthrowing it was a necessary sacrifice for the good of the whole.

In this regard, the Africans came to realize that only a blind person can yearn for sight; only a sick person can appreciate good health; only a prisoner can cherish freedom; and only a slave can dream of liberty. Therefore, only the Africans fighting in the white man's war could aspire to the reverence of a life of dignity, self-fulfillment, and respect. Out of this realization they endeavored to develop a personality that helped them refuse to be treated as mere objects or instruments to fulfill colonial purposes. In this way, the development of a risk-taking African personality was helping to elevate the African mind and consciousness. This development caused common concern among colonial officials, but they were helpless to prevent it.

In developing this kind of personality, the Africans knew that the successful attainment of their objectives lay in discovering the power that manifested itself in their will to achieve what the colonial government considered impossible—political freedom through educational achievement. It was their will to achieve identified goals that helped them concentrate on doing their best with minimum educational opportunity. For this reason, the Africans regarded their participation in the war not only as an opportunity to fight the potential Axis oppression, but also as a staging point for the struggle against the real oppression they were enduring under colonial conditions at home. They knew that the development of a new personality and the rise of their consciousness were inseparably linked to their search for a more meaningful chance for development envisioned in the principle of freedom and independence.

This is the situation that the colonial governments failed to understand and appreciate more than any other aspect of the personality of the Africans during the postwar period. Their restless minds, their desire for development, and their sense of purpose emanated from values that only their cultural heritage could make possible. Now, in their Victorian attitudes toward African cultural values, the colonists were watching the chickens come home to roost. The African mind was now able to design ways of seeking an end to colonial conditions that had engulfed them since the Berlin Conference in 1884.

This development gave the Africans a capability to formulate goals for the future "consistent with universal human aspirations. This move became the basis of their critical examination of the white man's standards of conduct and behavior."[32] Blind obedience and loyalty to the colonial governments were no longer possible. Instead, a new form of personality became an uncharted channel through which the Africans searched for new principles that had universal application to human life outside the control of oppressive regimes.

Therefore it was becoming increasingly clear to both the colonial governments and the Africans that the Africans would no longer allow the colonials to use them as a means of sustaining their Victorian myth about them. The Europeans could no longer continue to use them to attain the objectives that they envisaged for a utopian society in both Europe and Africa. The days of Edward Long had passed into oblivion, and the colonists would try to relive them at their own peril. By creating the elements of a totalitarian environment in their relationships with Africans, the colonial governments exposed their weaknesses in ways the Africans understood as their Achilles heel, which they could exploit in the pursuit of their goals and objectives. In this way, the Africans demonstrated their capacity to confront the problems that the colonial conditions had created.

It was not easy for Africans to overcome the handicaps that the colonial governments had imposed on them, but their collective personality helped them not to allow the colonial establishments to pit Africans against one another as was happening in Senegal or to believe that the colonists had a superior personality simply because of their ability to exploit Africans politically. Instead, they recognized that the colonial governments were "guilty of warping their full development and training misfits for society"[33] at the expense of their own vision for their development. To appreciate the development of a new risk-taking personality among post–World War Two Africans is to understand the expansion of the African mind and the factors that brought it about.

Throughout human history, those who have had no viable cultural values on which to base self-motivation in self-directed endeavors have been less prone than those who do to attain the basic developmental objectives that are often a measure of human aspirations and fulfillment. To initiate goals in accordance with this realization, the Africans of the postwar period developed dependable qualities consistent with their new personality as proof of group pride. These qualities also served as a collective norm for identifying goals that would help them seek to fulfill their dreams and aspirations.

The development of a new personality and the rise of consciousness among the Africans of that period were manifested profoundly in their quest for political independence as a prerequisite for seeking other forms of development. All over Africa the formation of such organizations as the African Artisans Guild, the Council of African Chiefs,[34] and the National African War Funds did more than any other organization or institution to help postwar Africans establish new social institutions. The national African war funds created all over the continent, for example, offered the Africans an opportunity to contribute money to national funds for purposes of assisting men returning from the war to make a new beginning in life, or offer financial assistance to the widows and families of fallen soldiers.

This African GI program elevated the evolving African personality to new heights of self-consciousness. In Zimbabwe, between September 1940 and April 1945, the Africans contributed more than $52,000 to the fund.[35] What alarmed the colonial governments was not the amount of money the Africans raised, but the expanded consciousness that brought with it meaning and commitment to self-directed projects and efforts based on concrete objectives solely aimed at self-sufficiency.

While the colonial governments welcomed the Africans' contribution to the war effort, they did not appreciate its effect on the emergence of a new personality and consciousness. They welcomed their participation in the war, but not the Africans' new abilities to promote their own development independent of colonial control. This was the real meaning of self-consciousness that led to the demand for freedom and independence. In 1983 a retired white mechanic who emigrated to Zimbabwe in 1944 told me:

The colonial government faced a dilemma in asking Africans to fight in the war. It wanted them to help end the threat of Nazi domination without addressing the question of its own real domination at home. It wanted them to learn about the importance of liberation from possible Nazi oppression without letting them learn about the reality of its own oppression. How could the Africans recognize possible Nazi domination without questioning real colonial domination? How could they resist possible Axis oppression without raising fundamental questions about real colonial oppression? The emergence of a new personality and consciousness among the Africans as a result of their war experience compounded this colonial dilemma. How could this dilemma be resolved? The rise of the new African mind had reached a level the colonial governments could no longer control. We knew that sooner than later we were heading for trouble.[36]

As the Africans pondered the contradiction of colonial conditions, they felt obligated to do something to eliminate its causes. For the first time since the conflict that appeared as a result of colonization, they were increasingly questioning the claimed benefits of colonialism. By exposing the weakness of the colonial system, the Africans were quick to take advantage of it as they sought to eliminate it as the ultimate contradiction that characterized colonial behavior. The same retired white mechanic put this contradiction in the context of that reality when he observed:

The colonial governments wanted the Africans to accept their own oppression, but have them fight against that of the Axis powers. They tried to portray them as oppressors, but wished them to accept their own leaders as interested in their development. To suggest that leaders who espoused Victorian political philosophy of the Africans had suddenly changed constituted an attempt to camouflage the real colonial character. That kind of logic simply did not make sense to the Africans. I guess one could say that it was one of those cultural differences. By campaigning against possible Axis domination the colonial governments exposed themselves more about the reality of their own oppression. The Africans could no longer accept that line of thinking.[37]

By 1945 the Africans had translated their fear of a remote Axis oppression into intensified opposition to the immediate colonial oppression. The new personality that the colonial government could never have foreseen was slowly, but steadily, combining with the rise of African consciousness and the expressed need for more meaningful involvement in creating new social conditions and new national institutions. The colonial governments' unwillingness to allow the development of this new line of thinking created a pervasive climate of conflict.

COLONIAL ATTITUDES TOWARD THE RISE OF THE AFRICAN MIND: SOWING THE SEEDS OF DISILLUSIONMENT WITH COLONIAL CONDITIONS

The rise of the African mind made it possible for the Africans to convert the tragedy of the war into an impetus for a new consciousness. But the colonists attempted to use the end of the war and the defeat of the Axis powers to strengthen the Victorian illusion about African inferiority. Speaking on March 21, 1945, D. L. Smit, secretary of African Affairs in South Africa, recognized that the colonists needed to see that their belief of African inferiority was detrimental to their own future and that they must pursue policies designed to promote mutual respect in Africa. Smit added, "Our efforts to improve race relations should be guided not by extremes, but by a sane approach along the pathway of moderation. Before the community of mankind could be formed, the old attitudes, the old forms of social organizations must be replaced by a future-oriented attitude to bring all people into a single family of the universal man."[38]

Smit was, in effect, recognizing that during the war the Africans had acquired a new level of awareness that no colonial government could control. The expansion of African cognition had reached a stage where a partnership of equals was the only way to avoid future conflict between the races. Accordingly, Smit urged the white community to accept this consciousness as a development that would safeguard the long-term interests of the whites by regarding it in a positive light. Unfortunately, this was not the perspective from which many colonists viewed the rise of African self-awareness. Many saw it as a development that carried political implications that they considered detrimental to their own political interests. They could not understand that in reaching a new level of consciousness, the Africans could, as Paulo Freire put it, "no longer remain as they were."[39] This consciousness was not merely an initial stage in the process of self-liberation by only the Africans, but a necessary condition for the liberation of all people.[40]

Not surprisingly few colonial officials shared Smit's perspective. For example, Sir Alfred Beit, an influential member of the British Royal African Society which had enormous influence on colonial policy, stated that the postwar colonial government policy must not emphasize the promotion of equal political rights for the Africans. Beit argued that it would be a mistake to design policies "to set more importance for economic and political rights to a man who could not avail himself of them."[41]

Beit was assuredly thinking in terms of Victorian attitudes and had not comprehended the effect of the rise of the African mind on colonial society. For Beit, therefore, to make this claim was to be blind to the hard realities that the whites either pretended did not exist or attempted to ignore. This political indiscretion would later prove costly to the colonial governments in Africa.

Knowledge that the colonial governments were not genuinely enthusiastic about accepting the rise of African consciousness as a positive national development prompted Bishop E. F. Paget of the Anglican Church in colonial Zimbabwe to deliver a thought-provoking speech to the African Welfare Society in January 1946. Paget warned:

There is a growing suspicion as to our sincerity in seeking to fulfill our national objectives with specific reference to the development of the Africans. Stern days lie ahead of us when we must inevitably sow the seeds of either disillusionment with colonial conditions as they are today and will lead further to racial strife, or of good neighborliness expressed in sincere efforts to bring about justice and freedom for all people. The governments must resolve this dilemma by seeking to gratify the new consciousness, which has become a permanent part of the experiences of the African people as a result of the war, or seek to repress it and create conditions of further racial conflict. The African mind has come of age.[42]

For Paget to urge the colonial government to formulate good racial and educational policies with a sense of urgency suggests that he was painfully aware that the war had transformed the African mind in profound ways. This prophetic warning would not go unheeded without a price to pay.

Unable to remain silent in the wake of a growing continental controversy, various church organizations held meetings to discuss appropriate courses of action as a response. Many believed that the colonial governments' neglect of the Africans would ultimately lead to a cultural and political conflict. They felt that the colonial governments were pursuing an imprudent policy. Paget therefore broke with a popular myth and urged the reconstruction of a postwar society that would promote human understanding and better communications beyond racial boundaries. An alternative course of action, argued Paget, would be a serious racial conflict from which the colonial governments might come out second best.[43]

It was not possible to expect the colonial governments to break out of the confines of Victorian attitudes and to drop their mistaken idea about the inferiority of the African mind and instead design policies to promote the genuine advancement of all Africans, white and black. The colonial governments simply felt that such policies were not possible. Some church organizations felt compelled to help the colonial governments recognize the error of their policies. In colonial Zimbabwe, for example, meeting at Waddilove near Marondera in February 1946, the Methodist Church passed a number of resolutions urging the government to conduct a major review of its policy:

We believe that a satisfactory educational policy awaits a clearer enunciation of principles than has been the case in the past regarding the Africans' place in society, economic and political life of the country, and that the formation of definite lines of development of the Africans be initiated so that they reach the full and unrestricted citizenship which we believe is unquestionably their right.[44]

This positive response to the rise of the African mind and consciousness was not limited to the church and its leaders. It became a rallying point among many colonists who saw the development of the Africans as the only realistic way of safeguarding their own long-term interests. Some colonial officials with moderate views shared their opinion on what must be done to resolve the problems created by the inadequacy of colonial policy. One such influential individual was General J. C. Smuts (1870–1950), who had commanded South African troops in both wars. Speaking in Maputo, Mozambique, at a banquet held in his honor in July 1945, Smuts warned:

In the long run the security of the white man in Africa will depend on a *modus vivendi* based on justice and granting the Natives opportunity for development. By their labor the Natives have provided the great progress which in the space of a generation, has helped transform the face of Africa. There is room for white and black to work side by side in the spirit of mutual respect and understanding. Each makes indispensable contribution to the welfare of the country as a whole. Discrimination based upon any thinking or notion of the inferiority of the African mind creates an environment of racial conflict which would not serve the best interests of any country.[45]

Smuts and other moderate white individuals were, in effect, suggesting that the war had created a new environment that compelled the white colonists to reevaluate their attitudes about the Africans. Some were beginning to realize that there was only one hope for the survival of European influence in Africa and that was to extend equitable political and socioeconomic rights to Africans. A. M. Tredgold, a leading farmer in the Bulawayo area of Zimbabwe, a descendant of the famous Tredgold family and related to the equally famous Moffat family that settled in Zimbabwe during the nineteenth century, recognized this reality. Tredgold urged his fellow whites to move aggressively in extending equal rights and opportunities to Africans so that they could play an effective role in society. He saw this as a needed prerequisite for racial cooperation, which he believed Africa required to assure continued development.

The powerful force which the Africans exert must be felt in the educational, socioeconomic and political fields. If we deny them that right we're going to create in their minds a feeling of oppression. The sacrifices which they made to defeat the Axis forces must be regarded in tangible ways. If we fail to do this we might not suffer as a result, but our children and their children will suffer. The rise of the African mind has become a powerful factor that countries of Africa must utilize to ensure mutual racial respect.[46]

It was surprising that this apparent liberal thinking was taking place at all. However, these liberal views were expressed exclusively by those whites whose position in society demanded they demonstrate their capability to see social issues from a higher philanthropic consciousness. For them to think otherwise would have reduced them to the level of ordinary men, and they were not ordinary men. General Smuts, Bishop Paget, and A. M. Tredgold[47] belonged to this exclusive group. Its members took it upon themselves to remind their fellow white colonists that they either had to adopt new and positive attitudes toward the Africans or face the increasing certainty of racial conflict in the future.

When Tredgold tried to convince the white population that "The world opinion of 1947 is against all forms of repression"[48] of Africans or when Sir Stewart Gore-Browne suggested that "I think it is time a good thing was said about the Africans,"[49] here was clear recognition that the momentum was against them. Although the Africans put a distance between these white liberals and themselves owing to their fears of the perils of adaptation, their views had a profound effect on colonial society as a whole.

Only six years following the end of the war, members of the white community recognized that the Africans could no longer accept the idea that their refusal to adopt the white man's culture was responsible for their lack of development. D. L. Yamba spoke for many Africans when he wrote: "Africans are as capable as Europeans[50] and can easily equal all that the white man does if only they had the opportunity to learn to do those things. There is no doubt that the Africans have a mind capable of grasping critical social issues."[51]

COLONIAL RESPONSE: POLICY FOR THE AFRICAN WITH ONE FOOT IN HIS PRIMITIVE CULTURE

The disturbing truth about colonial policy that the Africans learned by 1951 was that the colonial governments' persistently negative attitudes had not changed for the better in spite of the progressive views of a few white individuals. In colonial Zimbabwe the Kerr Commission of 1951 recorded various negative attitudes and opposition to the advancement of the Africans as expressed by the white colonists who came before it. For example, the manager of an industrial concern said, "Once a Native can read and write, his one ambition in life seems to be to proceed to the nearest town to get a job in which he need not use his hands or indulge in manual labor of any kind."[52]

This development occurred only two years after Philip Mitchell's remarks about the backwardness of the Africans in Kenya had received wide publicity and negative response. It indicates the rapid rise of the African mind and its effect on colonial society. For the Africans to recognize that some whites were still thinking of them as they did in Victorian times was quite disturbing and demanded they do something to end it. However, another white witness disagreed when he told the commissioners, "The intelligent African who is denied equal opportunity will soon become sour and embittered and be anything but a good citizen."[53] This shows the nature of the controversy that was growing among whites concerning economic opportunity for the Africans.

By 1954 this controversy was beginning to worry the leaders of African colonial governments and they considered ways of ending it. The debate and position taken by white liberals furnishes yet another piece of evidence of their profound effect on colonial society, including Huggins himself. But the colonial governments felt that the whole question of African development, as perceived by white liberals, was detrimental to their own political interests. In colonial Zimbabwe on August 26, 1954, Godfrey Huggins used the annual meeting of the Rhodesia Missionary Conference, held at Goromonzi Secondary School for Africans, as an appropriate forum to attempt to correct what he believed was an erroneous notion that the African mind was equal to that of the European and to argue that the Africans were incapable of guiding their own advancement.

We have the sad spectacle of many of our so-called educated Africans wasting their energies on some completely unattainable objectives such as self-government. The African with one foot in his primitive culture presents two problems for the government. The first is how to deal with the immediate situation caused by the mis-guided and so-called African intellectuals. The second is how to develop the African so that the educated ones do not waste their time on sterile and futile nationalistic agitation. The best that we can do is to formulate a policy to assist the African with one foot in his primitive culture to emulate the white man. Our task as a government is to reverse the claimed consciousness which is believed to have come about as a result of the war and guide the African mind toward a proper end.[54]

Huggins regarded the development of the Africans as charity that only the colonial governments could extend to them. It is also quite clear that Huggins shared the Victorian perception that no matter how hard they tried, the Africans could never attach an exaggerated importance to the rise of their mind for their advancement. He saw the permeation of African consciousness and nationalism as inconsequential to colonial policies and felt that because most Africans were not properly educated, they were unable to appreciate that the magnanimous white man was doing everything possible to give the Africans opportunity for socioeconomic progress. Huggins thought the relationship between the level of educational attainment and the emergence of African consciousness must be controlled at all times to ensure the survival and continuation of the colonial system.

Consequently, Huggins argued that structured education was not incompatible with African aspirations because they were incapable of upsetting the existing social system.[55] Three years later, in 1956, Huggins's political career came to a crashing end as he discovered that he had made serious errors in judging the impact of the rise of the African mind leading to political consciousness as a result of the war.

It is a sad irony that despite all his political charisma and his popularity among the white colonists, Huggins, like his mentor Cecil John Rhodes and his protégé, Ian Smith, was unable to understand the serious cultural conflict that existed between the Africans and the whites. He perceived the Africans only from the British cultural perspective, and this arrogance dictated both his attitudes and the policy of his government, which translated into various forms of racism that shattered bridges of communication between the two races. Because he failed to respect their way of life, Huggins was unwilling and unable to initiate any meaningful dialogue with the Africans. Without dialogue based on mutual respect of the intellect of all participants, it was virtually impossible to ease the escalating racial tension between the two groups. This situation was making it hard for the two racial groups to live together in peace and to cooperate in building a dynamic society.

Misunderstanding became a crucial factor in the cultural collision that occurred in 1966. The policy of Huggins's administration, combined with the view that the Africans must not share power with the colonial governments, created a devastating climate that led to armed conflict. In pursuing this policy, the colonial governments failed to initiate effective means of communication between themselves and the Africans. Freire concludes that this situation is often an outcome of the action of politicians who speak but "are not understood because their language is not attuned to the concrete situation of the men they address."[56]

Therefore, Huggins was engaging in political action that Freire says is void of any critical awareness of the deteriorating relationships that emerge between the oppressor and the oppressed. This led to Huggins running "the risk of preaching in the desert"[57] about his own ignorance of the rise of the African mind. He also ignored the shifting paradigm that African consciousness was bringing about, which was central to the Africans' perception of their place in their own land.

Huggins's refusal was the main reason why the Council of Non-European Trade Unions issued a statement in February 1947, in which it concluded:

It is the firm belief of this Council that the present policy of preserving skilled trades exclusively for white workers is not in the interest of the country as a whole, but one that is bound to lead to racial conflict. The council urges the government to reconsider this policy in light of the adverse effects that may ensue from implementing it.[58]

The council felt that the trade unions run by white colonists were actually standing in the way of national progress by supporting Huggins's policy of denying equal opportunity to Africans for self-improvement. The council called on "all progressive trade unions of whatever race and color to deplore in the strongest terms possible the attitude and reactionary action of the white trade unions and the educational policy of the government."[59] It also recognized that these "reactionary moves are responsible for dragging the Africans down the road of underdevelopment."[60] It urged all people to work toward compelling the colonial governments to formulate national policies that would help promote equal opportunity for all people and to prepare them to engage in any trade or profession without suffering from any restrictions imposed by the deliberate action of the governments.[61]

Huggins was as much a victim of Victorian myth about African culture as the Africans themselves were. But he felt sorry for them for what he believed to be their failure to realize that total equality with the white man was impossible because they had an inferior mind. This is quite disturbing in light of the period of time when he expressed his negative views. It is not surprising that by 1966 the Africans felt that because they had exhausted every means possible to bring about mutual respect, they had no choice but to go to war to restore their rights. Huggins, angry to hear the liberals urge him to abandon his Victorian attitude, accused them of falsely raising hopes that the Africans would eventually attain their aspirations and political rights.

Huggins and other colonial government officials chose to forget that in the course of human events, no force can reverse the rise of consciousness that any group has claimed for itself. For Huggins to attempt to retard that progress was tantamount to reneging on the promise and commitment that he and the British government had made at the outbreak of the war: that is, equal opportunity for Africans after the Axis powers were defeated. Huggins made no apology for his negative views of the African mind. Indeed, he vehemently reiterated his Victorian illusions in 1954:

We must unhesitatingly accept the doctrine that our superiority rests on our technical skills, education, cultural values, civilization and heredity. We must appreciate the fact that we have a paramount monopoly of these qualities and the Natives of Africa have been denied them by their primitive culture. The best that we can do for them is to educate only a few in the hope that they will pull the rest out of the mire of that primitive culture.[62]

Huggins found it difficult to hide his Victorian views of the Africans because he had come out of the Victorian era and immigrated to Africa in 1911. But in his forthright negative opinion of the Africans, he thought that he had put an end to a growing controversy that he feared was paralyzing his government's policies. He also believed that he had a duty to remind the Africans of their proper place in colonial Zimbabwe. Although he envisaged a snail's pace development for the Africans in the future, he concluded that total equality for the time being was out of the question because the African mind was not equal to that of the white man. Within a year Huggins would regret his professed culture of ignorance. This was the eleventh hour for him as the culture of ignorance he based his political career on was coming to an unanticipated end. But it had left a legacy that his successors could not escape.

Three conclusions are possible at this point. The first is that the colonial governments and the white community in Africa would not consciously support the advancement of the Africans, even though the rise of African consciousness was a shifting reality with which they had to deal. In Britain, this condition was an issue in the general elections of 1945 in which the two main political parties, the Conservative party led by Winston Churchill and the Labour party led by Clement Attlee, took opposing views on the future of the Africans under colonial rule.

The Conservative party generally supported the policies of the colonial governments, whereas the Labour party sympathized with the aspirations of the Africans, creating an issue of international importance and debate. Churchill seemed to forget that he had helped to arouse these very aspirations only four years earlier by his role in the Atlantic Charter in 1941. Perhaps political expediency dictated a departure from that proclamation. Or perhaps the end of the war in 1945 had altered the excitement of the freedom promise that was central to the charter as a way of arousing the passion of the Africans against the Axis powers. But they would never forget its message, and Attlee wanted to remind both Churchill and the voters of that pledge.

On July 26, 1945, after winning the elections and having King George VI invite him to form the next British government, Attlee reacted: "This is a very remarkable and gratifying result. It shows that the electorate will respond to a clear and definite policy based on principles and application to the needs of the present day."[63] Attlee was referring to the fact that during the campaign the Labour party relentlessly urged the British government to honor its solemn war promise to the Africans, one that Huggins and other leaders of the colonial governments would not consider. Attlee and the Labour party also opposed the colonial status, which reflected the new reality that the rise of African consciousness had produced.

British politicians knew that they had to take this reality into account in designing a new colonial policy. The Labour party also argued that this situation could no longer be delayed. It submitted that if the whites in Africa were to do something soon to ensure their long-term interests, then it had to be the recognition of the Africans as equal partners by guaranteeing equal opportunity for all.[64] The Conservative party appeared reluctant to take this definitive stand, instilling doubts in the mind of the voters as to the sincerity of its policies and programs. Churchill, the war hero who was enjoying an unprecedented wave of popularity among the British people and throughout the Western world, found himself suddenly out of power. Such is the reality of the impact of colonial conditions and the rise of the African mind and consciousness. National leaders in Europe were no longer immune to their effects.

The second conclusion is that as products of the Victorian delusion of African intellectual inferiority, the colonial politicians could not agree to engage in dialogue with the Africans on equal terms. Huggins received clear signals from individuals such as J. C. Smuts, A. M. Tredgold, Stewart Gore-Browne, and Bishop Paget that it was imperative for their survival that equal educational opportunity be extended to Africans. Because they were denied participation in the affairs of the country, the Africans were rendered hopeless. Freire suggests that "Hopelessness is a form of silence, of denying the world and fleeing from it. It is a form of dehumanization resulting from a might order."[65]

This was a recipe for a cultural conflict that the colonial governments refused to perceive. Even though Huggins, owing to his advanced age, might not experience it, as A. M. Tredgold suggested in 1947, the next generation was certainly bound to face it sooner than later. Once it became a reality, the rise of the African mind and consciousness was a political factor that the white politicians had to learn to take into immediate account. There was no other course.

The third conclusion is that the colonial government and the Africans saw the impact of the war from diametrically opposite perspectives. The Africans saw it in the way Aldon Mwamuka (1911–1972), president of the African Teachers Conference in colonial Zimbabwe, saw it. Speaking on July 26, 1945, at the conference held in Mutare, Mwamuka observed: "During the war we have been called upon to assist in every way possible to fight against the forces of darkness, tyranny and racism. Our men in the Rhodesia African Rifles are shedding blood in order that men everywhere may be free from racial domination."[66] Clearly, Mwamuka was expressing the views that the delegates to the Pan African Congress conference held in London were also to emphasize in October of that year. Conscious of the impact of what he was saying, Mwamuka chose his words carefully as: "With the end of the European war, all liberty-loving people of the world, in which the evils of social injustice have been recognized as the major cause of the war, will demand that they be eliminated."[67] Mwamuka was, in effect, criticizing the colonial governments for adopting negative policies toward the development of the Africans.

Huggins could not tolerate such criticism, and the Africans could no longer acquiesce to the totality of that policy. Inevitably, then, the two cultural groups were heading toward an unprecedented political showdown. The colonial perspective, as expressed by Alfred Beit and Godfrey Huggins, hastened that showdown. In stating his belief that the rise of African consciousness was "the greatest curse of all of Africa,"[68] Beit was in effect saying that the advancement of the Africans was detrimental to the interests of whites. Nothing was therefore more damaging to future cultural and racial relationships than a colonial preoccupation with the myth that the Africans were not equal to the white colonists. The rise of the African mind and consciousness forever altered the complexion of that political landscape.

SUMMARY AND CONCLUSION

In failing to recognize the reality of the rise of the African mind and consciousness, the colonial government and the white community placed the two races on a cultural collision course. The only way to avoid that impact was for the whites to accept this situation as a positive feature of national development. But by its very character, colonialism is unable to see things this way. The Africans were willing to give the white community time to make adjustments, just as they themselves had done from 1900 to 1939 in order for the two races to live together in peace.

Indeed, the delegates to the Pan African Congress were willing to allow the colonial governments time to accommodate the rise of the African mind. The colonial governments' unwillingness to consider that possibility indicates that conflict could not be avoided. And, too, as long as they felt that they enjoyed the support of the white community, the colonial governments acted as if there was nothing that the Africans could do to change things. They also were quick to blame the ascent of the African mind for the deteriorating race relationships.

In turn, the Africans blamed the colonial governments for failing to bridge the differences that ultimately led to the struggle for political independence. Indeed, colonial officials in all of Africa recognized that the war had produced in the Africans a new determination quite different from their opposition to the occupation of their countries in the nineteenth century and the subsequent wars that followed colonization in some countries. In 1970 J. R. Taylor, a high-ranking official in colonial Zimbabwe, fully recognized this fact when he observed, "The change of attitude which has produced in the Africans an increasingly insistent demand for education and other forms of opportunity since the post-war years stems from their broadened outlook from the war service."[69]

Kwame Nkrumah's role in all this was crucial. For the colonial governments to argue otherwise was to pretend that the war had no impact on the rise of the African mind and the way the Africans reflected on their situation. This rise ultimately had a profound effect on colonial society. It also signaled the beginning of a new phase in the relationship between the colonial governments and the Africans. Was it possible for the colonial governments to recognize, as Albert Memmi observes, that the rise of the African mind originated in the conditions established by the colonial governments themselves? Where else could that rise lead other than to the struggle for self? This is the subject of the next chapter.

NOTES

1. Memmi, *The Colonizer and the Colonized*, p. 119.

2. Ibid., p. 120.

3. Freire, *Pedagogy of the Oppressed*, p. 89.

4. Ibid., p. 31.

5. See Chapter 3 of this study for details.

6. Memmi, *The Colonizer and the Colonized*, p. 62.

7. Nkrumah so admired Padmore that he dedicated his book, *Africa Must Unite*, to the memory of George Padmore in 1963, four years after Padmore's death.

8. Martin Meredith, *The First Dance of Freedom: Black Africa in the Post-war Era* (New York: Harper and Row, 1984), p. 48.

9. Hapgood, *Africa in Today's World Focus*, p. 82.

10. Kwame Nkrumah, *Africa Must Unite* (London: Panof Press, 1985), p. 50. (See also Matthew 6:35 and Luke 12:30.)

11. Meredith, *The First Dance of Freedom: Black Africa in the Postwar Era*, p. 53.

12. Kwame Nkrumah, *Africa Must Unite*, p. 120.

13. Southern Rhodesia, Report of the Education Committee, 1943, p. 55.

14. Meredith, *The First Dance of Freedom: Black Africa in the Postwar Era*, p. 7.

15. Ibid., p. 8.

16. Ibid., p. 9.

17. Ibid., p. 8.

18. Ibid., p. 9.

19. Ndabaningi Sithole during an interview with the author in Harare, July 22, 1983.

20. Prime Minister Winston Churchill and President Franklin Roosevelt, *The Atlantic Charter*, August 11, 1941, British Embassy, Harare, Zimbabwe.

21. N. Sithole interview, July 22, 1983.

22. Indeed, the author remembers that while he was a student at Old Mutare in Zimbabwe, E. D. Chasinda, who had been a sergeant during the war, came to speak of his experiences in Europe and drew large crowds with accounts of life in Europe.

23. *The African Weekly*, April 18, 1945.

24. Ibid.

25. A white man during an interview with the author in Mutare, Zimbabwe, August 12, 1989.

26. Christian Gauss, *Machiavelli: The Prince*, Trans. Luigi Ricci (New York: Signet Classics, 1952), p. 127.

27. Robert July, *A History of the African People* (New York: Scribner and Sons, 1974), p. 28.

28. Indeed, forced labor remained a major component of colonial policy in Zimbabwe until 1943. For details, see Dickson A. Mungazi, "The Change of Black Attitudes Towards Education in Rhodesia, 1900–1975." Ph.D. diss. (Lincoln: University of Nebraska, 1977), p. 52.

29. Ibid.

30. Charles C. Davies, "African Education in Rhodesia," in *NADA* (1969): 25.

31. Rhodesia, *The Report of the Education Committee*, 1943, para. 2, p. 55.

32. Ibid.

33. Ibid., para. 45, p. 50.

34. Examples of countries in which the councils of African chiefs played a critical role in the rise of the African mind include Ghana, Nigeria, Zimbabwe, and Kenya.

35. *The African Weekly*, April 18, 1945.

36. A retired white mechanic during an interview with the author in Mutare, August 6, 1983. The man declined to be identified because he said, "I do not wish to appear to be a liberal man who seems to reject his own British heritage."

37. Ibid.

38. D. L. Smit, Secretary of African Affairs in South Africa, "Black and White in Southern Africa," *The African Weekly*, Vol. 1 (No. 28), April 18, 1945.

39. Paulo Freire, *Pedagogy of the Oppressed* (New York: Continuum, 1993), p. 47.

40. Ibid., p. 40.

41. Sir Alfred Beit, "Government Policy and African Development," in *The African Weekly*, Vol. 1 (no. 28), December 13, 1945.

42. Bishop E. F. Paget, "Native Welfare Societies Must Act Fearlessly," address to the African Welfare Society, January 11, 1946. Old Mutare Methodist Archives.

43. Ibid.

44. Methodist Church, *The Waddilove Manifesto: The Educational Policy of the Methodist Church*, February 9, 1946. Old Mutare Methodist Archives.

45. J. C. Smuts, "Fair Play for the Africans," address given at a banquet in his honor in Maputo, Mozambique, as reported in *The African Weekly*, Vol. 2 (no. 9), August 1, 1945.

46. A. M. Tredgold, "Recognition of Africans' Rights to Citizenship Is the Only Hope of European Survival in Africa," address to the Farmers Union, Bulawayo, November 11, 1947. Old Mutare Methodist Archives.

47. Two other members of the Tredgold family were quite active in colonial Zimbabwe during that time in promoting the development of the Africans. Robert Tredgold (1899–1979), who served as chief justice of the Federation of Rhodesia and Nyasaland from 1955 to 1960, often espoused liberal views and so came into conflict with the colonial officials. His sister, Barbara Tredgold, was also very active in promoting the development of African women. Her service as advisor to Helen Mangwende was resented by the colonial government.

48. A. M. Tredgold, "Recognition of African Rights to Citizenship," November 11, 1947.

49. *The African Weekly*, Vol. 4 (No. 12), November 12, 1947.

50. As it was used in colonial Africa, the term *European* meant anyone who was white.

51. D. L. Yamba, "Lost Opportunities for Africans: The White Man's Problem," letter to the editor of *The Bantu Mirror*, No. 23, February 19, 1947.

52. Southern Rhodesia, Commission of Inquiry into Native Education (Alexander Kerr, Chairman) Para. 41, 1951.

53. Ibid.

54. Godfrey Huggins, "Taking Stock of African Education," an address to the Rhodesia Missionary Conference, Goromonzi, August 26, 1954. Old Mutare Methodist Archives.

55. Ibid.

56. Freire, *Pedagogy of the Oppressed*, p. 85.

57. Ibid., p. 86.

58. Rhodesia, The Council of Non-European Unions, Statement of Goals and Objectives, February 18, 1947. Old Mutare Methodist Archives.

59. Ibid.

60. Ibid.

61. Ibid.

62. Godfrey Huggins, speech delivered during an election campaign, May 1954. Zimbabwe National Archives.

63. British General Election Results, July 26, 1945. *The African Weekly*, July 26, 1945.

64. Ibid.

65. Freire, *Pedagogy of the Oppressed*, p. 80.

66. Aldon Mwamuka, president of the African Teachers Conference. Old Mutare Methodist Archives.

67. Ibid.

68. *The African Weekly*, Vol. 1 (No. 28), December 13, 1944.

69. R. J. Taylor, *African Education in Rhodesia* (Salisbury: Government Printer, 1970), p. 6.

5

The Mind of Black Africa and the Struggle for Self

> Between freedom and colonial slavery there can be no compromise.
>
> *Patrice Lumumba, 1961*
>
> In many ways Jomo Kenyatta was the African Bobby Kennedy of 1946.
> He saw some Africans viewing the colonial conditions as they were
> and asking why. He dreamed of conditions that never were and asked
> why not.
>
> *An African graduate student, 1991*

THEORETICAL CONSIDERATIONS

In his study, *The Colonizer and the Colonized*, Albert Memmi argues that relationships between colonizer and the colonized come to a head when the colonized can no longer submit to the will of the colonizer.[1] Even more important is the notion that once the colonized decide they want to assert their legitimate independence, they put themselves in a frame of mind in which they will no longer compromise their principles. The strength of their mind and the conviction that motivates them will lead to an outright struggle for these principles. Memmi also maintains that although the colonized have no idea about how long that struggle will last, the outcome is always predictable in their favor.[2] The essence of the action taken by the colonized to assert their freedom is an outcome of the rise of their mind. This expansion of awareness makes it possible to see things in a very different light from what they used to. This is a phenomenon that neither the colonizer nor the colonized can predict.

For Memmi the main reason why the colonized often win the struggle of the minds is that the colonizer underestimates their willful determination to regain their lost pride. The colonizer also assumes that since he has imposed domination on the colonized for many years they are unable to exercise any independent thinking, critical or otherwise, because dependency has reduced their mind to the level where it can be controlled. With the mind of the colonized under effective control, the colonizer no longer worries about resistance. Reliance on the belief that because the mind of the colonized is domesticated, they are unable to initiate independent thought and action, often leads to the demise of the colonizer. Memmi also concludes that the colonized is often faced with two choices stemming from the rise of their mind in an action to set itself free.

The first is to accept assimilation into the culture of the colonizer so as to feel secure in the belief that his colonizer will always protect him as long as he serves his interests. The second choice is to assert individuality and independence of mind. Memmi states that while, in the initial stages of colonization, the colonized might be left with no choice but to merge themselves in the environment established by their colonizer, there comes a time when they will realize that to liberate themselves they must decide to seek an end to oppression because it is not possible to avoid confrontation.[3] The impetus for this decision is born in the raising of consciousness in the mind of the colonized.

Memmi's theory may be substantiated by the study done by James H. Oldham, an official of the International Missionary Society based in London, in 1930. In *White and Black in Africa*, Oldham deduced that the Africans were not developing as rapidly as they should because the colonial governments exercised so much control over their mind that they were not allowed to initiate self-fulfilling activity independent of that control.[4]

Oldham predicted that in time the Africans would have to make one of two choices: (1) To accept their condition of colonization and try to function as best they could under stipulations made by the colonial governments, with serious consequences arising from the control over their thinking; or (2) to risk confrontation with the colonial governments in order to restore their sense of self. Exercising the second choice would demand that the Africans reclaim their right to exercise the freedom of human thought.[5] This would be the choice the Africans were likely to make in the future.

Oldham concludes that given the character of any colonial system it was just a matter of time before the Africans began to recognize the detrimental effect of colonization on their mind. This recognition would constitute the first essential step they would take to achieve their freedom of thought as a prerequisite to political independence.[6] In initiating this action, the Africans would take advantage of the vulnerability of the colonial governments' overconfidence which was based on the illusion that the African mind was inferior and that Africans were incapable of initiating anything on their own.

Because the colonial governments were interested primarily in training the Africans to function efficiently as laborers, they were not likely to do anything that would awaken the Africans to new realities. This is why in their limited contact with the colonists, the Africans would try to assert their own mind to ensure not only their survival, but also their individual and collective development.[7] The need to ensure this development would create a social environment in which confrontation with the colonial governments would become inevitable.

In his study conducted nineteen years earlier in 1911, *The Future of Africa*, Donald Fraser, who, like Oldham, was an influential member of the International Missionary Society, concluded that colonial systems in Africa would last only as long as they were able to control the mind of the Africans.[8] Fraser argued that sooner or later the Africans would begin to realize that the colonial systems entailed more negative features than any claim of benefits. Once the Africans reached this level of mental perception of their position and the means to articulate it, the colonial governments would no longer be able to impose the total control they once did.

This development would constitute an entirely new stage in the relationships between the colonial governments and the Africans in that the Africans would begin to assert the viability of their mind and cognition. These two elements would combine to enable the Africans to consider taking action to improve their conditions. The knowledge that colonial systems were not destined to last forever would be the reality that the Africans would consider to recognize the inhibiting side of their existence and eventually to demand their end.[9] They would opt to speed up the inevitable.

Fraser warned the colonial governments that unless they gained the Africans' confidence by designing a set of policies intended to assure equal opportunity in society, the Africans would develop a frame of mind from which they would believe that they were being exploited. This conclusion would lead them to design a strategy to free themselves from colonial domination. Once they became conscious of the need to free themselves, the colonial governments could do little to reverse the trend, apart from utilizing military force to stop them.

This development would generate a new social and political climate from which a major armed conflict would ensue, leading to a struggle for independence because the Africans would no longer allow the colonial governments to control their mind.[10] In applying these theoretical considerations, this chapter examines specific examples of how the Africans struggled for independence in the British, Belgian, and Portuguese colonial empires. Because these theoretical considerations came early in the colonial period, the colonial governments did not seriously think about them until after the Second World War, when it was too late.

INDEPENDENCE FOR GHANA AND THE THRESHOLD OF THE AFRICAN MIND

This study has proposed that by the outbreak of the war in 1914 Africa had been subjected to colonization, in accordance with the provisions of the Berlin Conference, to the extent that there were only three noncolonized countries on the continent. These were the old and unstable feudal empires of Ethiopia, Liberia, and South Africa, which achieved independence from Britain in 1910 and was then under an oligarchy controlled by extremist Boers.

By 1945 the number of independent countries in Africa had increased to four; in addition to these three, Egypt had taken control of itself in 1922. By the end of the Second World War, then, the political map of Africa was very much the same as it had been at the conclusion of colonization in 1900. Although the rise of the African mind was instrumental in bringing independence to Libya in 1951, and to Morocco and Tunisia in 1956, the devastating and protracted struggle in Algeria slowed the movement toward independence throughout the French colonial empire.

The brutality that characterized the struggle for the African mind in the French colonial empire in Africa was misunderstood by some Africans. For example, Leopold Senghor who decided to identify himself with the French, rather than remain and operate within his African cultural heritage, claimed in 1953 that Africans in the French colonial system were not taking up arms to seek their political independence because they considered themselves better off than the Africans in the British colonies such as the Gold Coast, Liberia, or British Gambia.[11]

Clearly, in his desire to adapt to the French colonial setting in order to survive, Senghor lost his African identity. For him to claim that the Africans were happier under the control of the French than those under conditions controlled by other colonial systems was to misrepresent the actual facts because no colonial system makes its subjects happy. In fact, while Senghor was making his ludicrous claim, the Africans under French colonial control were waging a struggle for independence, placing the government of Charles de Gaulle in a severe political bind.

Certain developments in the French colonial system might have given Senghor an illusion of happiness among Africans. In 1956 the French government accepted Senghor's advice to increase the number of deputies from Africa in the French Assembly to thirty-three and the number of voters to 6 million. Having done this, the French government included four African ministers and secretaries of state. Their function was mainly to coordinate the payment of subsidies on export crops. This practice increased the dependence of French colonies on French revenue and so submitted them to French political control.

By 1958, over "seventy per cent of the total public investment and more than thirty per cent of the annual running costs were financed by France."[12] While the French government was able to buy time by temporarily setting back the African mind, it was not possible to retard it permanently, regardless of Senghor's claim. Because Senghor was not aware of the perils of adaptation, these developments gave him the illusion of happiness among the Africans.

While this was happening, Nkrumah was doing his best to help the African mind come of age. His assumption of the office of prime minister of Ghana in 1950 positioned the African mind at a level of observation and influence that had not been reached before. Although Ethiopia and Liberia were under black leadership, their leaders, Emperor Haile Selassie and William Tubman,[13] respectively, had assumed office at a time when the African mind was not fully cognizant of the realities that compelled later leaders, like Nkrumah, to set specific goals and a corresponding agenda for achieving them.

Therefore, it can be said that Nkrumah was the first African leader to develop an intellectual perspective that gave postwar Africans a sharpened sense of who they really were in colonial settings as well as what they had to do to rediscover themselves as a people with vision for the future. There is no question that in assuming the office of prime minister Nkrumah lifted high the mantle of the African destiny cast in an array of new aspirations.

The process of shaping a new destiny for the Gold Coast as a prerequisite for shaping the destiny of Africa was by no means an easy task, but Nkrumah was equal to it. In 1954, while he was planning to move aggressively to achieve independence for his country within a few years, Nkrumah encountered a new problem that seemed to threaten his agenda, the formation of an opposition political party, the National Liberation Movement (NLM). Because the NLM consisted mainly of the powerful Ashanti, it demanded a federal-type constitution for the country. Keep in mind that Nkrumah did not belong to the Ashanti clan. Their demand was made before Britain was asked to consider the question of independence.

This kind of constitution would mean that the central government would be limited in the application of its constitutional power and that the provinces would possess the lion's share of power. It is quite clear that NLM was fearful, based on the aggressive manner in which Nkrumah was pushing his agenda, that he would easily assume a dictatorial measure of political power. Without a constitutional provision to stop him from doing so, he would do it sooner than later. Only time would tell. However, NLM managed to convince the northern territories and Togoland to see the rapidly moving events from their proper perspective. In this setting, NLM and Nkrumah's Convention People's Party (CPP) engaged in a political struggle that appeared to question the absoluteness of Nkrumah's savvy as a political genius in the new African era.

When the NLM–CPP struggle led to violence, the British government was caught in the middle, not knowing what course of action to take. This seemingly difficult political problem put Britain in a dilemma. If it refused to set the date for independence, it would increase the prospects of national violence on a scale that would require a massive military presence. Such a step would have serious political implications for the British government. If it hastily granted independence without making adequate constitutional preparation, solving all the pertinent constitutional issues, the Gold Coast would degenerate into a state of anarchy. This would set a terrible precedent for the rest of British colonial Africa. In this dilemma, the African mind was having a profound effect on the thinking of the colonial government officials, making the white man's burden almost unbearable. For the British government there was no easy answer.

After pondering the dilemma for nearly two years, the British government decided to allow the people of the Gold Coast to resolve the issue through the electoral process. It therefore decided to call new general elections, scheduled for July 1956, to determine which of the two major political parties represented the actual wishes of the people, the NLM or the CPP. When the results of the elections showed that CPP had won 72 seats in a legislature of 104, although only 58 percent of the voters had participated, Britain was satisfied with the results and set March 6, 1957, as the date for independence. NLM faded into political oblivion as Nkrumah's star was illuminated to a new level of brightness.

Nkrumah immediately began to chart a new course for his country and the rest of black Africa. His success in the elections and the independence of the Gold Coast as the new state of Ghana placed the African mind at a new threshold. From this vantage point, the Africans looked to the future with great expectations and to the past as only a phase in their history. The process of dismantling colonial empires in Africa had begun, and the African mind had come into its own, asserting its rightful place among the respected minds of the world. In this context, Nkrumah's leadership in

Ghana's struggle for independence for Africa became an influential model for oppressed people all over the world.[14]

Events began to move rapidly. In Accra at midnight on March 6, 1957, the Union Jack flying over the parliament building was lowered and was replaced by the new red, green, and gold flag of Ghana. The huge crowds surged and roared into a frenzy and danced all night. Nkrumah was over-whelmed by it all. Mingling through their midst, as he was carried from the parliament building on the shoulders of his political associates, Kwame Nkrumah was humbled by the avalanche of admirers whose political destiny, and that of the rest of Africa, he was now responsible for. To symbolize the fact that the African mind was once imprisoned by colonial conditions, Nkrumah came in "wearing a convict's white skull cap embroidered on the front with the letters PG—the prison graduate badge for those nationals who, like himself, had once been jailed by the British."[15]

To Nkrumah physical imprisonment was far less painful than imprisonment of the African mind. He wanted his fellow Africans, not only in Ghana but also throughout British colonial Africa, to know that Ghana's independence represented a new phase in their struggle for freedom. The threshold to which Ghana's independence had placed the African mind was now converted into the portals to launch a great human endeavor. With tears running down his sturdy face and mindful of the painful days of the past, Nkrumah used this brief moment of triumph to challenge his enthusiastic audience to accept the task of liberating the African continent from the psychological shackles of colonialism. In a voice variegated and quivering with emotion, but strong and sure, Nkrumah made an impassioned appeal, saying, "At long last our country is free forever. From now on there is a new day in Africa to show that the black man has a mind quite capable of running his own affairs. But our independence is meaningless unless it is dedicated to the total liberation of the African continent."[16]

To show that he was future-oriented, Nkrumah announced that he intended to convene a conference in Accra which would be attended by African nationalist leaders in order to map out a new strategy for entirely liberating the African mind from colonization. As crowds roared their approval, Nkrumah's image as a true son of Africa was seen across the continent; he was brilliantly poignant in stature and serenely articulate in composure. Nkrumah was at the apex of African aspirations. He saw the independence of Ghana as invariably intertwined with the destiny of Africa, and so he projected himself as a continental leader, a statesman whose vision of his continent remained unmarred by colonial conditions.

In December 1958, Nkrumah ushered in the first stage of his strategy for the liberation of Africa, with the assistance of his mentor, George Padmore.

Nkrumah convened the first All African People's Conference, structured along the lines developed by the Fifth Pan African Congress and brought to Accra an impressive list of African nationalists whose thinking he inspired to seek their own liberation. The British colonial entrepreneurs could only watch the unfolding of this rare human drama.

Among the conference attendees were Hastings Banda of Nyasaland, Kenneth Kaunda of Northern Rhodesia, Joshua Nkomo of Southern Rhodesia, Patrice Lumumba of the Belgian Congo, Holden Roberto of Angola, Amilcar Cabral of Guinea Bissou, and others. Tom Mboya of Kenya, a brilliant young politician, was elected presiding officer of the conference. With this unusual African mind converging on Accra, colonial society in Africa was altered permanently. In his own charismatic and powerful way, Mboya warned the colonial governments in Africa to undo the scramble for Africa because the time was rapidly coming when Africa must achieve independence.[17] Before the conference adjourned, the delegates committed themselves to this goal: the liberation of all of Africa.

There was no other course of action to take. The struggle for survival between the colonial mind and the African mind was now about to begin in earnest on a continental scale. Nkrumah had been the catalyst for its beginning.

THE AFRICAN MIND, THE WIND OF CHANGE, AND THE FALL OF BRITISH COLONIAL AFRICA

The British government knew that its decision to grant independence to Ghana would lead to the same demand from other colonies. Harold Macmillan, the leader of the Conservative party and government from 1957 to 1963, was aware that the British government had no alternative but to adopt a flexible policy toward the people in its African colonies, especially their desire to attain political independence. Thus, three years following Ghana's independence, Nigeria, the most valued British colonial possession, gained liberation through the same kind of resistance that had earlier sent Nkrumah and his associates to prison.

By this time, Britain had come to a better understanding of the African mind. The cooperation, enthusiasm, and ability to articulate positions on critical issues all combined to give the Africans in Nigeria an added advantage over Ghana. Indeed, top officials of the British government had come to accept the real meaning of what Nkrumah had expressed on March 6, 1957, that the Africans had a mind quite capable of governing itself.

Nigerian history set the stage for the short delay in gaining its independence. British annexation of Lagos Island in 1861 was the impetus for the colonization of Nigeria. In 1888, three years following the conclusion of the Berlin Conference, Britain learned that France was attempting to acquire western Nigeria as its own. Believing that its acquisition of Lagos Island entitled it to claim the mainland, Britain made treaties with the local Yoruba chiefs in order to protect its colonial interests. This allowed the British government to extend control of Nigeria from 1888 to 1897. During this time, Britain also mobilized its military forces to enforce its antislave law that had been in effect since 1807. This created the perception that the British were benefactors because slavery was rampant in non-British colonies. This action influenced the character of Nigerian culture and social structure.

In 1900 Britain set up a chartered company known as the Royal Niger Company to administer its possession. The Yoruba chiefs, however, insisted on a provision that recognized the British presence for what it was intended—to ensure the position of Nigeria as a protectorate, not as an outright colony. This hints at the speculation that Britain came face to face with the prowess of the African mind from the beginning of their colonial ventures. In 1903 the Yoruba refused to allow what was happening in the rest of Africa to occur in Nigeria. Thus, in 1906 all of the Nigerian homeland became a British protectorate, not its colony.[18] Yoruba's foresight in protecting the interests of their land and people surprised the British. In 1914 the northern and southern parts of Nigeria were joined to form one common protectorate.

In 1946 Nigeria decided to establish councils for purposes of coordinating their developmental programs. This gave the Africans an opportunity to learn the functions of a western form of government. Although these councils exercised advisory powers and nominated members to the central legislative council, they came to understand the real aspirations of their people. Slowly but steadily, they began to articulate the objective of attaining independence in clearer terms than they had voiced in the past. In 1951 the councils asked Britain to increase the responsibility of the local governments, and the central legislative council was named the House of Representatives in accordance with the wishes of the people. Could the British government continue to doubt that these developments represented the astuteness of the African mind at its very best?

It was also clear to all parties concerned that these historical developments were a prelude to the major events that placed Nigeria on the road to independence. In 1954 Nigeria became a federation, giving each of the four major regions considerable power to run their own affairs without any interference from the central government. In 1959 the federal legislature was divided into the House of Representatives and the Senate, a system modeled after the United States. The Senate included representatives from the four regions. With this remarkable development, Nigeria was now ready to follow Ghana in achieving freedom.

Following the general elections held in 1959 in which the Northern People's Congress (NPC) led by Abubaker Tafawa Balewa obtained a majority of seats, Britain set October 1, 1960, as the date for independence. In 1963 Nigeria, through its own volition, became a federal republic within the British Commonwealth of Nations. The independence of Nigeria furnishes yet another example of the African mind's coming of age and of bringing the British colonial empire in Africa to an end.

Nigeria's demand for independence must be seen from the perspective of events that began to unfold with the conclusion of the war in 1945. As everywhere else in colonial Africa, those returning from the war were appalled by the poor economic conditions of Africans. Low wages, unemployment, and a general decline in the standard of living had plunged the Africans into an abyss of despair, while conditions affecting the whites steadily improved. The educated Africans bitterly complained of racial and job discrimination.

The British government came under constant attack in the press, Nnamdi Azikiwe and Abubaker Tafawa Balewa provided the national leadership that helped to mobilize the rise of the African mind. In 1943 the British government described Azikiwe as "the biggest dangerous threat of the lot"[19] to its colonial interests because he operated at a level of intellect that had a profound influence on the thinking of Africans. The colonial governments' recognition that the Africans had a mind of their own finally compelled them to recognize the legitimacy of their claim to political independence. The independence of Ghana and Nigeria validated this conclusion. Britain was on its way to losing its vast colonial empire in Africa, and with it its global empire. The sun was setting on the British Empire.

KENYA: CONFLICT BETWEEN THE AFRICAN AND COLONIAL MINDS

Jomo Kenyatta returned to Kenya in 1946, following his years of study in Britain. Like Nkrumah, Azikiwe, and Balewa, Kenyatta became an instant folk hero and legend upon his return. After spending years studying in Europe, all three had acquired a comprehensive analysis and understanding of the thinking patterns of the whites.

This development, coupled with their ability to express the aspirations of their people, made the Africans especially difficult to manipulate. Their ability to understand the novels of Charles Dickens, their interpretation of historical themes discussed by Edward Gibbons, their comprehension of the social implications of the plays of William Shakespeare, and the political philosophy of John Stuart Mill, Thomas Hobbes, and Benjamin Disraeli—all placed the Africans in a unique position of understanding the West far more than the Westerners could understand the African thought process. These African nationalists had learned about the strategies that the impoverished European masses had designed during the turbulent Industrial Revolution to improve their lot. They had read with enthusiasm the works of Karl Marx, Rudyard Kipling, Victor Hugo, and Jean-Paul Sartre. How could the colonial governments pretend that the Africans did not have a mind capable of restoring itself?

Kenyatta was a brilliant student and savvy politician. Back in Kenya, his people had learned about his role in the Fifth Pan African Congress, and they had known about his years of struggle to gain a meaningful education in political science. They learned his political philosophy through his book *On Facing Mount Kenya*, which critics heralded as brilliantly written. They had heard of his restless and imaginative mind that dreamed of creating conditions that never were. They knew of his simple and unassuming personality, anchored in a sharpness of mind and an unshakable strength of character. They knew of his ability to articulate issues about a composite fragile colonial environment in which his mind was cast. An African graduate student from Kenya in 1991 described Kenyatta as follows:

In many ways Jomo Kenyatta was the African Bobby Kennedy of 1946. He saw some Africans viewing the colonial conditions as they were and asking why. He dreamed of conditions that never were and asked why not.[20] Indeed, Kenyatta's mind was a bustling creature of enthusiasm. It was revolutionary to the core. It enabled him to grasp the adverse character of the colonial system and the need to end it without further delay. The African people listened to his message and supported him in giving it a new meaning. His dedication to the restoration of the African personality manifested the quality of the African mind at its very best.[21]

Martin Meredith agrees with this assessment of Kenyatta. Meredith states that Kenyatta's life overseas and the knowledge and experience he acquired about British politics had earned him great prestige. He used this prestige with remarkable success on his return to Kenya to arouse a sense of great expectation among the Africans. The nationalist campaign he had launched in Britain was now beginning to yield tangible results in Kenya.[22]

When Kenyatta arrived back in Kenya, huge crowds of Africans came to greet him. In Mombasa, the harbor was packed with Africans and porters who crowded around to see him. The harbor security had a difficult time trying to control the crowds. During his train journey to Nairobi, huge crowds waited to catch a glimpse of the man who symbolized everything they had dreamed of. As soon as he arrived in Nairobi, crowds carried him shoulder high as the people cheered and roared their acceptance of their hero and inspirational leader. For Kenya this was a new day, the coming of age of the African mind. The British colonial government, led by the arrogant and flamboyant Philip Mitchell, could not fully understand this phenomenon. The African world and the colonial world that had engulfed African existence since 1888 were about to collide with such force that a new world would emerge. Cognitive parity for Africa had arrived.

Wishing to determine his appropriate role in shaping political developments and mapping out the course to independence, Kenyatta wasted no time in seeking a meeting with the governor, Philip Mitchell. Because Mitchell was highly regarded at the Colonial Office at Whitehall, fundamental questions arose in the minds of the Africans about the character of the colonial mind. For more than thirty years, Mitchell's policy and approach to colonial administration had endeared him to his superiors more than any other official. With a sense of his popularity, authority, and claimed knowledge of the Africans, Mitchell decided to hold the meeting with Kenyatta under the glare of enormous publicity in both Kenya and Britain.

Mitchell's main purpose was to reduce Kenyatta's ego and to remind him of his assigned place within colonial society. Arrogant and sure of himself, Mitchell had little respect for Kenyatta. Mitchell figured that if he could minimize Kenyatta's mind to the level of that of other Africans, then Mitchell would stand as a giant in the history of British colonial Africa as the man who demonstrated to the Africans that they were indeed inferior to whites. The battle lines were now being drawn for one of the most serious conflicts ever between the African and colonial mind.

Kenyatta, conscious of his rare opportunity to demonstrate African cognition, was equally determined to dispel both the myth and the colonial arrogance that Mitchell represented. The behavior pattern exhibited by Mitchell was typical of colonial officials all over Africa, and Kenyatta wanted to expose them for what they really were—delusions of colonial grandeur. Mitchell had assumed office as governor of Kenya in 1944, two years before Kenyatta, but this gave him no advantage in understanding how the expansion of African awareness was influencing the character of colonial society.

Mitchell was surprised to discover that Kenyatta not only exhibited adeptness of mind, but also clearly articulated positions on pertinent issues such as African representation in the legislature, a specific agenda to ensure the political advancement of the Africans, the question of land distribution, especially relocating some Africans in the fertile central highlands from which they were evicted following colonization in 1888, and a timetable for independence. For Mitchell to listen to an African he considered inferior espouse a political philosophy similar to that of Edmund Burke was a nightmare for him. He was infuriated not by Kenyatta's understanding of the issues, but by the brilliance of his mind.

The conflict between the African and colonial mind took a perilous turn in the events that followed. In failing to recognize African nationalism as a powerful movement arising from the Africans' increased rational thought process,[23] Mitchell showed his inability to acknowledge the mind of the Africans as a new reality for the colonial government. Mitchell's attitude and response demonstrated the colonial culture of ignorance. It was an insult to the African intellect and widened the chasm between the two sides.

Mitchell's Victorian perspective on the African mind did not play well in the forthcoming struggle. Given the nature of this irreconcilable difference, the meeting between Mitchell and Kenyatta achieved nothing except to entrench their respective positions. Kenyatta argued that the African mind was capable of assuming national responsibility outside the control of the colonial system, whereas Mitchell held on to the belief that the Africans were incapable of assuming such a responsibility because they did not have a recognized civilization.

Back in London, the British government of Clement Attlee expressed great concern over Mitchell's inability to keep up with events. In Kenya itself the Africans began to emphasize that they were quite capable of functioning independently of the colonial establishment. Within a few years events could compel Mitchell to regret his low regard for the African mind. He was so preoccupied with his desire to sustain the colonial status quo that he was unaware of, or refused to acknowledge, the implications of the rise of the African mind.

Mitchell's uncompromising view that the white man must retain all forms of political control over the Africans was a product of another tragic aspect of the colonial systems. British colonial Africa, according to Mitchell, had been transformed from primitive cultural societies into modern industrial states solely by the whites' intellectual power and entrepreneurial knowledge. He neglected to acknowledge the core truth that the Africans had been forced to endure socioeconomic and political exploitation to make that possible and that all they were now demanding was to share in the fruits of their labor and toil. Deprivation was no longer acceptable.

These circumstances provoked resentment and indignation among the Africans, especially those of the Kikuyu tribe, to which Kenyatta belonged.

They had been forcibly removed from the fertile central highlands to make room for white farmers. Although a sense of guilt among some of these white farmers compelled them to treat their African servants with a paternalistic attitude, to the Africans this atonement represented scorn and contempt for their mind and an insult to their ability to comprehend issues of human interaction.

Since the vast majority of Africans who were removed from the central highlands were members of the Kikuyu tribe, within a few years they would play a decisive role in the drama of the conflict of the minds. Africans all over Kenya received Mitchell's view that the Africans must not be allowed to reclaim the central highlands with derision. They also were contemptuous of any suggestion that whites should retain possession of the best land in the country.

Jomo Kenyatta was thrust into a political setting where compromise on fundamental principles was virtually impossible. For him, maintaining the political status quo was a painful reminder of the past. As a boy, he had watched the white man usurp the land of his ancestors and force him and his family to relocate to desolate places. The colonial entrepreneurs had also forced the Africans to work for them to ensure their own socioeconomic and political security. He had watched the colonists make fun of his culture and castigate Africans in such a manner that the vast majority of them began to doubt their own worth. Kenyatta was determined to turn things around and to revitalize the African mind which had been shattered by colonial conditions. It was time to restore the African to the position of greatness it had had before 1888. Like Nkrumah, Kenyatta felt that these principles could not be compromised. The colonial mind had to give way to the coming of age of the African mind.

In 1949 a group of white colonial politicians, sensing what was likely to happen in the near future, published the *Kenya Plan*, which affirmed the presumed inferiority of the African mind. The group went on to add a clause that shattered any hope of racial cooperation:

Any attempt to hand over political power to an immature race must be resisted. To the Africans we offer sympathetic tutelage and guidance because they have a mind still to be developed. In time they will participate in government and in the affairs of the country. The white race is here to stay and other races must accept this premise with all that it implies.[24]

Through this Victorian attitude, increasingly political restrictions and socioeconomic hardships were imposed on the Africans. Agricultural production was controlled to allow white farmers to sell their produce without any competition. Africans were required to carry identification cards they considered a symbol of colonial oppression. It is one of the ironies of colonialism that the culture of ignorance becomes a major influential factor of the colonizer.

Since the end of World War II, the whites had seen activity surrounding the political thinking among the Africans as coming from a group of primitive people. Colonists totally refused to acknowledge that the African mind had reached a level of development unequaled by that of any other period in its history. This culture of ignorance became a major cause of conflict between the colonial governments and the Africans; events in Kenya would substantiate this conclusion.

In this increasing climate of conflict and the colonial government's refusal to acknowledge the African mind's coming of age lay the elements that led to Kenyatta's call for political action. He reactivated the faltering Kenya African Union (KAU) originally formed in 1944; without proper leadership when nearly eight thousand Africans were participating in the war, the KAU had lacked an effective political agenda to convince the colonial government that it must be taken seriously. This is what Mitchell had in mind when he suggested in 1953 that the Africans were incapable of implementing an agenda based on rational planning independent of the whites' assistance. A parting of the ways had been reached, and everything pointed to a protracted struggle of determined wills.

As thousands of Africans returned home after the war in 1945, they faced enormous socioeconomic and political problems. Nairobi was crowded with thousands of unemployed Africans, including war veterans, as they watched their former white comrades assume positions of power. In July 1947 an African member of the legislative council, Eliud Mathu, sent an urgent memo to Mitchell warning of an impending major national confrontation between the Africans and the government unless he took quick action to resolve the causes of discontent among the Africans. In characteristic fashion, Mitchell dismissed the warning, arguing that the Africans had neither the will nor the capability to wage a confrontation along the lines Mathu suggested in his memo. In January 1948, a white member of the same legislative council presented a motion expressing deep concern over government failure to see a major national crisis brewing, caused by its refusal to acknowledge the aspirations of the Africans. Again, Mitchell ignored this concern.

Before the end of that year, the district commissioner of Nakuru in the Rift Valley made the first official acknowledgment of a major national conflict and urged Mitchell to defuse the situation before it exploded. But the warning came too late, for the Mau Mau uprising was already under way. The colonial government had outlawed the Mau Mau in 1950, but the African mind had reached a point from which there was no return. In the words of a graduate student from Kenya:

The savagery and brutality with which the colonial military forces attempted to suppress it can only be compared to the atrocities committed by the Nazi in an effort to exterminate the Jews. In a publicity campaign to portray the leaders of the Mau Mau movement as monsters, the colonial government inflicted a devastating damage to not only the Kikuyu, but also to the Africans in Kenya as a whole. But the Africans had put themselves in a frame of mind in which they were determined to bring to an end their oppression. Their mind could no longer be recolonized. This was a moment of truth for both the Africans and the British colonial government, a time of reckoning for the colonial society. This was the last time for a conflict of this magnitude between the African mind and the colonial mind, and Mitchell might as well start packing. The imprisonment of Jomo Kenyatta and the hanging of Dedan Kimathi simply reinforced the determination of the Africans to fight to the bitter end to liberate themselves. There was no going back for the African mind.[25]

In this tragic drama, it is sad that the colonial government did not realize the effect of its own action until 1956. During the struggle it had employed eleven infantry battalions, 21,000 police, and thousands of air force aux- iliaries, and had drafted 43,000 Africans. It was like the Second World War all over again. In the process, 80,000 Africans were detained, and 11,500 were killed compared to only 95 whites. Kenyatta was arrested, tried, convicted, and sentenced to life imprisonment because he was believed to have masterminded the uprising.

Kimathi was executed. If the British colonial government had hoped that this carnage would silence the African mind and that it would resubmit to its will, it needed to understand the conclusion that Albert Memmi reaches: that is, once the colonized reach a point at which they decide to get rid of the colonizer, nothing can be done to reverse that decision.[26]

In spite of the great loss of life, the African mind remained focused. Instead of diminishing the Africans' resolve to attain political inde- pendence, this conflict only intensified it. The release of Kenyatta from prison on August 14, 1961, set the stage for Kenya to achieve liberation following his victory as the leader of the Kenya African National Union (KANU) in the elections held in May 1963. Six months later, Kenya achieved independence. Three years earlier, the British government had recognized the inevitable collapse of its colonial empire as a consequence of its decision to grant independence to Ghana in 1957 and to Nigeria in 1960.

Speaking on February 3, 1960, to the Joint Session of the South African Parliament in Cape Town, the legislative capital city of the notorious policy of apartheid, Harold Macmillan warned of the consequences of refusing to acknowledge the rise of the African mind: "The wind of change is blowing through the continent of Africa. Whether we like it or not, the growth of nationalistic consciousness is a political factor and we must accept it as a fact. Our national policy must take account of it."[27]

With this admission, the British government had finally discerned the coming of age of the African mind and was on its way to dismantling its colonial empire in Africa. Mitchell's controversial and turbulent political career came to an abrupt end, while that of Jomo Kenyatta was just beginning. With his reputation at Whitehall badly tarnished, his reputed savvy questioned, and his political philosophy in disarray, Mitchell had no choice but to retreat into political oblivion. It was an unceremonious anticlimax to a series of events he did not seem to understand and an ironic turn of events he did not have control over. Only after it was all over did the British government recognize its gross error of judgment in placing its total confidence in a colonial zealot.

THE STRUGGLE FOR RHODESIA AND NYASALAND: CLOSING THE COLONIAL MIND

With the independence of Kenya fully established, the struggle between the British colonial establishment and the African mind shifted elsewhere. The conflict between the colonial and African minds now centered on the struggle for what was called the Federation of Rhodesia and Nyasaland, consisting of the British colonies of Northern Rhodesia, Southern Rhodesia, and Nyasaland. The exploration undertaken by David Livingstone beginning in 1842 had taken him, by 1859, to the shores of Lake Nyasa. There the beautiful landscape had been ravaged by the brutality of the slave trade. With the assistance of the London Missionary Society, of which he was a member, Livingstone managed to reduce the effect of slavery on African attitudes by seeking to convince the Africans that Western missionaries were their friends.

But what the Africans did not know was that missionary activity was laying the foundation for the British colonial empire in accordance with the provisions outlined by the Berlin Conference. This does not imply that the Africans were incapable of recognizing the subtle intent of the missionaries.[28] The missionaries, themselves, might not have seen this consequence as a critical component of their government-sanctioned mission in Africa. By 1864 events would show that Livingstone and other missionaries had other purposes besides bringing Christianity to Africa. As I quoted in Chapter 1, Livingstone made a speech at Oxford University in that year to show why it was necessary to promote other objectives in Africa besides Christianity. He stated that efforts to introduce Western civilization to Africa must include more than attempts to convert the Africans to Christianity. Rather, they must entail an aggressive program of commercial enterprise because that aspect of Western civilization was more likely than anything else to convince the Africans of the need to accept Western culture.[29]

In 1891, when conditions were seen as right, Britain declared Nyasaland as its colony. This area's main economic activity was agriculture, and tea its primary crop. The administration of the colony was vested in the British Colonial Office. In 1904 the establishment of tea plantations experienced a dramatic development, made possible by investments from wealthy British businessmen who were profiting from the Industrial Revolution. By 1928 emigration to Nyasaland had increased the British colonial population there and along with it their political confidence. In 1929 the British government sent a commission to study the possibility of establishing Nyasaland, Northern Rhodesia (which became a British colony in the same year as Nyasaland, 1891), and Southern Rhodesia, which had been colonized a year earlier, into a federation.

The British Colonial Office argued that through the agricultural potential of Nyasaland and Northern Rhodesia, and the mineral wealth of Southern Rhodesia, the federation would generate higher economic development and productivity than they could as separate colonies. But by this time the African mind vigorously asserted itself in opposing the proposed federation. The Africans argued that the whites would use the status of "responsible government," which had been attained in Southern Rhodesia in 1923, to impose even more oppressive conditions. Therefore, the proposed federation fell on its face, a victim of the alertness of the African mind. But the British Colonial Office would not take defeat so easily. It tried again in 1938, this time waging a vigorous campaign among the Africans to convince them of the claimed economic benefits of the federation. Again, the African mind rose to the occasion to alert the Africans to the colonial self-serving nature of the proposed federation. Unable to accomplish their objective, the colonial establishments in the three colonies let the matter rest until 1950.

Soon after the British proclaimed these three territories as its colonies, the drama of conflict began to unfold in Southern Rhodesia. The deception of the Rudd Concession of 1888, the secrecy of the Royal Charter of 1889, and colonization itself in 1890 were among the events that combined to bring the colonial and African minds into disagreement. The introduction of the infamous Orders-in-Council and the assassination of King Lobengula, both in 1894, accelerated this clash of minds. Because Charles Rudd (1844–1916), the leader of the Rudd group representing Cecil Rhodes, was not honest in dealing with King Lobengula, the king refused to honor the terms of the agreement as stated in the Rudd Concession.[30]

Slowly but steadily, King Lobengula and his people became painfully aware that the whites were not being honest in any aspect of their relationship. From that point until the advent of an African government in Zimbabwe in 1980, the Africans would not trust anything that the colonists did. Nothing was more damaging to future relationships between the two races than for the African to know that they could not believe the white man.

King Lobengula's refusal to submit to the control tactics of the colonial mind and Rhodes's determination to pursue his objectives created a climate that led to the war of 1896. In that conflict, 451 colonists and many more Africans lost their lives.[31] Rhodes set out to prove that divine providence had placed into his hands the destiny of the British entrepreneurs in Africa. This explains why he undertook a daring financial and political gamble to show that he was the quintessential colonist and a loyal son of Britain, that he was to be entrusted to place his country on the pedestal of African power, enshrined in the belief of Caucasian superiority. But in doing so Rhodes invoked in the African mind an awareness of the colonial entrepreneurs' insidious intent.

The referendum of 1923 called for the establishment of an all-white government. It was to decide whether Southern Rhodesia should join South Africa as its fifth province or assume a semiautonomous political status. The Africans could not participate in the voting, and the event demonstrated to the Africans the true character of the colonists. This was the situation that led to the expansion of African awareness beginning with the end of the war in 1945. The Pandora's box had been opened, and the British could not close it. For Southern Rhodesia the die was cast for the inevitable struggle between the two racial groups. The constitution of 1961 lit a fuse that could not be extinguished.

In Northern Rhodesia as well, conflict had also become inevitable. To follow the road this conflict took, we must understand the structure of precolonial African societies and how the colonial system violated them.[32] The Africans' ability to organize an effective society based on trade, agriculture, and social systems, all rooted in accepted values, had elevated the Africans to a point of development that was far too complex for the colonial entrepreneurs to discern. Their way of life had evolved over centuries by interacting with their natural environment. When the colonists appeared on the scene, cloaked in European culture, the Africans appeared to be disintegrated in a culture considered primitive. Money, as it was known in Western concept, did not exist in Africa.

Wire and copper, however, were widely used as a form of currency because they were in great demand as standard items of trade exchange for arts and crafts.[33] That the stability and progress of the African society were disrupted by the white man is not in doubt. The Industrial Revolution astronomically increased the need for raw materials and labor for production. At the Berlin Conference, Britain claimed the territory that later became known as Zambia. This colony was placed under the guidance of Cecil Rhodes in the same way that he had implemented colonization in Southern Rhodesia in 1890.

Believing that Nyasaland, Northern Rhodesia, and Southern Rhodesia were under its control, the British government now tried to strengthen its hold on these three resource-rich colonies by trying to form a federation, first in 1929 and then in 1938. The Africans in Nyasaland and Northern Rhodesia refused to cooperate in a scheme that would violate their way of life. They also showed that, in spite of the military power the colonial governments used to subject them to political domination, their mind was articulate and uncompromising in its clarity of purpose. This position remained unchanged until 1953. The conviction of the African mind was so strong that when matched against the obsessive determination of the British colonial entrepreneurs to have their own way it would prevail. In that year the British government took part in the colonists' plan to create the federation that the Africans passionately hated.

Having excluded the Africans from the earlier debate and referendum of 1923, the colonial governments of the three territories coordinated their efforts so as not to allow the Africans to undermine the plan. Thus, against opposition from the Africans, the federation of the two Rhodesias and Nyasaland came into being in 1953. An historical twist of fate came into play in this conflict of ways of life. The Africans of Southern Rhodesia, feeling that the federation would treat them more humanely than the so-called responsible government, did not oppose it as much as those in Northern Rhodesia and Nyasaland, who felt that the federation would stand in the way of their development because it would be controlled by the white colonial bureaucrats. Neither the British government nor the leaders of the federation knew that it was doomed from the beginning.

The events that finally rent the veil of British colonial empire in Africa began with those in Nyasaland. During the years that Hastings Banda (1902–) practiced medicine in the Gold Coast, he showed no apparent interest in the political events that were taking place in his homeland of Nyasaland. Even when Kwame Nkrumah invited him to the independence celebrations for Ghana in March 1957, Banda declined to attend. The demand for independence expressed by Godfrey Huggins and Roy Welensky, the leaders of the federation, created a situation the Africans considered detrimental to their interests and a challenge to their mind. In March 1957, Banda received a letter written by Henry Chipembere, a brilliant and articulate young college graduate and member of the legislative council. In his letter Chipembere expressed the need for an effective leadership of the African National Congress, which was experiencing leadership problems because of constant harassment from the colonial government. The colonial government threatened to outlaw it and arrest its leaders if their political activity proved to be in conflict with its own principles.

Chipembere emphasized to Banda that he was urgently needed back home to invigorate the African mind and so help the Africans to refuse to submit to the will of the colonial government. Banda, nearly sixty years of age, did not at first see the urgency of the situation in the way that his people did. Continuing efforts by Chipembere and other African leaders in Nyasaland finally persuaded Banda in 1958 to return home to lead the struggle for independence.[34] But soon after achieving independence in October 1964, Chipembere and other African leaders would regret their decision to urge Banda's return because Banda immediately assumed the position of dictator. He turned against many of the people who supported him and sent them into exile. Like many other African leaders, Banda betrayed the people he needed to build a dynamic and vibrant society.[35]

Responding to mounting pressure from his home people, Banda began to feel a sense of responsibility to help shape the emerging African mind. Now convinced that he had an obligation to his people in Nyasaland, Banda gave up his medical practice in Ghana and began to make preparations that would lead to the demise of the federation, something the British government never anticipated. On June 13, 1958, Banda led a delegation of Africans from Nyasaland to hold discussions with the British colonial secretary, Alan Lennox-Boyd. The talks centered on the future of the country, with a specific stated objective of seeking independence outside the federation. To their disappointment, members of the delegation discovered that Lennox-Boyd sympathized with and enthusiastically supported Roy Welensky, who had succeeded Huggins in 1956 as prime minister of the federation. Welensky, a former boxer, was known throughout the federation more for his periodic emotional outbursts than for rational thought. His unpopularity among the Africans and some whites raised fundamental questions not only about his mental stability, but also about the mediocrity of the leadership of both the federation and the colonial hierarchy.

Faced with growing opposition from the Africans and with doubts from the members of the Dominion party, as well as from the Labour party in Britain, Welensky became totally engulfed by events he could neither understand nor control. These events reduced him to reactionary thinking, which was the ultimate manifestation of the decline of the colonial mind. Placed in a difficult situation in which he could not exercise rationality, Welensky was forced to resort to emotional outbursts that did not go over well with the British government. Lennox-Boyd's support of Welensky also raised questions in the mind of the Africans about just how far Britain was prepared to go to respond to the Africans' political aspirations. Britain did not appear to have any specific plans for it until the delegation raised the question of independence.

The meeting between the delegation from Nyasaland and Lennox-Boyd indicated that as the colonial secretary, Lennox-Boyd secretly advised Welensky to stop Banda from returning to his homeland because he was planning to accomplish two objectives. The first was to break the imposed federation because it was detrimental to the Africans' political interests. The second objective was to achieve political independence for Nyasaland.[36] Although Lennox-Boyd warned Banda that he would be arrested if he tried to do that, Banda was not intimidated. To this threat Banda responded that the road to political independence passed through colonial political prisons. Kwame Nkrumah, Jomo Kenyatta, and, later, many other African leaders endured the pain of this colonial institutional system. All it did was accomplish the opposite: it elevated the African mind to the point where it had to ensure its own freedom. On July 6, 1958, Banda returned to Nyasaland and immediately became the major focus of political activity in the federation and beyond. Not surprisingly, as soon as he arrived Banda's first political message was *Kwacha* (freedom). He immediately became the Kwame Nkrumah and the Jomo Kenyatta of the Federation of Rhodesia and Nyasaland. The Africans' determination to restore their way of life had been given a tremendous boost by Banda's return. Rifles were being loaded on both sides.

On his return from the All-African Peoples Conference held in Accra in December 1958, Banda was more determined than ever to help his countrymen to restore their sense of worth. For him and the people he led, there was no turning back. Arriving at Salisbury Airport in Southern Rhodesia, Banda was questioned for an hour and his baggage searched at Welensky's orders. The colonial government in Nyasaland, under the governorship of Robert Armitage, Welensky's colonial brother, canceled Banda's flight to Blantyre. Indignant and defiant, Banda used his extra time to campaign for the breakup of the federation. Speaking in Highfield, outside Salisbury,

Banda challenged the Africans in all three federation colonies to reinforce their commitment in the forthcoming struggle:

I came prepared for anything, even death. I am not afraid of anything. I will fight the federation from prison, even from the grave. Throughout history of the world there is no incident where so-called moderation has helped achieve anything. We mean to be masters of our own destiny. Our minds are set, our objectives are clear. We will not go back. The high road to independence and self-determination has been mapped out, now we must construct it. In doing so we will close the colonial mind forever.[37]

Armitage, Lennox-Boyd, and Welensky were determined to sustain the colonial status quo in a new age of rising African consciousness. In January 1959, the year a general state of emergency was declared in Southern Rhodesia, Banda was arrested and secretly sent to a political prison in Gweru in central Zimbabwe. Instead of derailing the course of a movement that was gaining momentum, the arrest had the opposite effect. Throughout Nyasaland, the Africans were united in their thinking, and they brought government operations to a halt. Alarmed by what was happening, the British government, in accordance with tradition, appointed Sir Patrick Devlin, a high court judge in Britain, chairman of a commission to investigate the situation. Behind this move was the fear that any delay in taking action might lead to a situation in Nyasaland similar to that which had caused the Mau Mau movement in Kenya. When the Devlin Commission submitted its report in 1960, its conclusions sent shock waves through both Armitage and Welensky.

The Devlin Commission warned Armitage that because he had instituted a police state it was reasonable to expect future trouble unless his administration's efforts to restrain African political activity were eased. It also declared that Banda was released and was allowed to take his rightful place of leadership. For Welensky, the Devlin Commission was even more blunt in its warning that the opposition to the federation among the Africans was so great that it would require massive military force to sustain it.

The Devlin Report sealed the fate of the two colonial zealots, Armitage and Welensky, both of whom had refused to see the ramifications of the rise of the African mind. The end of their political careers was near, with neither man able to measure up to the challenge issued by the expanding African awareness. Like Nkrumah in Ghana and Kenyatta in Kenya, Banda was the man of the hour. His star, too, was rising to a point that neither Armitage nor Welensky could tarnish or control it during the historical events of the next ten months. On April 1, 1960, Banda was released from prison. He had earned his diploma as a prison graduate in a colonial institution.

In order to play a safe political game in an explosive situation, the Devlin Commission decided against discussing the central question of its mandate, the fate of the federation itself. However, Harold Macmillan knew what was coming when he indicated during his grand tour of Africa in 1960 that he was going to appoint a new commission under the chairmanship of Sir Walter Monckton, a distinguished British jurist, to study the future of the federation. When the Monckton Commission submitted its report in 1961, it concluded that, although the federation was worth preserving, the weight of African opinion in Nyasaland and Northern Rhodesia was such that it could be sustained only with massive military force. It recommended that any territory must be allowed to secede. The fate of the federation was sealed when Britain decided to dissolve it on December 31, 1963, paving the way for independence for Nyasaland as Malawi and Northern Rhodesia as Zambia in October, 1964. The colonial mind had lost the first round in the struggle to dissolve the federation.

The granting of independence to Malawi and Zambia forced a perilous twist in the events that were to unfold in Southern Rhodesia, the last remaining vestige of the federation. There, the whites had enjoyed rights and privileges protected by the constitution of the so-called responsible government that came into being as a result of the referendum of 1923. There was no change in that status until a new constitution was introduced in 1961, which for the first time allowed fifteen African members in a legislature of sixty. The struggle of the minds was evident in the arguments that both the Africans and the colonial politicians expressed. The Africans argued that, having been denied equal political representation for so long, fifteen seats in a legislature of sixty was an insult. The colonial politicians countered that allowing the Africans to sit in the legislature was the first step toward an African government. The two sides did not share the British government's view that this constitution represented a compromise. Unmoved, Britain required that new elections be held under the existing constitution as the first phase in increasing the number of African seats by the time of the next elections.

The elections of 1962 were among the dirtiest in the history of politics in colonial Zimbabwe. The right-wing Dominion party, having lost the struggle to preserve the federation, decided to disband and form the Rhodesia Front (RF). The men who led the RF were of such an extreme racial philosophy that the country was politically paralyzed due to their efforts. The last elections had been held in 1958 when Edgar Whitehead's white, moderate United Federal party (UFP) won the majority of seats in the legislature by appealing to both whites and Africans to come together to build a country in which race would not be used to determine a person's place in society. The Dominion party saw this as a threat to the colonists' position and so decided to contest the elections of 1962 as members of the Rhodesia Front. The trouble with the Rhodesia Front is that it was led by fanatical racists, and as a result the struggle between colonial and African minds took on an added dimension. Winston Field, Ian Smith, David Smith, Lance Smith, Arthur Smith,[38] Peter van der Byl, William Harper, Lord Graham, and the other members of the RF readily identified the rise of African consciousness as the most serious threat to the colonists' position since 1890.

Using fear tactics, the RF portrayed Whitehead (1905–1971) and his UFP as the colonial Neville Chamberlain seeking to appease the Africans for short-term political gain and added that if the RF was voted into power it would put a stop to African nationalism once and for all. The RF warned the white voters that if the UFP won, they might as well start packing because the African government that would be installed would deprive them of all their rights, privileges, and possessions. Because only 5 percent of the total registered voters in the country were African, the RF concentrated on the white vote. The victory that the RF scored in the elections held on December 18, 1962, was an ominous event that was destined to lead the country to a bitter thirteen-year civil war between colonists and Africans that lasted from April 1966 to December 1979. To add insult to injury in April 1964, Ian Smith led a political coup that removed the first RF prime minister, Winston Field (1904–1969), because Field showed a willingness to follow the British demand to accelerate the political inclusion of the Africans.

As soon as Smith assumed office, events took a turn for the worse. Smith was appalled that his government had to deal with the African governments in Malawi and Zambia which were led by people he considered inferior. He and his RF followers decided that an African government would never become a reality in their lifetime. Smith, committed to the political philosophy of the inferior African mind, argued on November 11, 1965, during a unilateral declaration of independence intended to stop the advent of an African government: "The mantle of the pioneers has fallen on our shoulders to sustain civilization in a primitive country."[39] Smith was clearly trying to relive the days of von Soemmering, White, Rhodes, and Huggins in a time when the African mind was asserting itself to gain parity. How could anyone, even Ian Smith, succeed?

The Africans, recognizing the seriousness of the situation under the RF, rose up and challenged the legitimacy of this offensive neo-Nazi regime. Herbert Chitepo (1923–1975),[40] a brilliant lawyer, politician, and president of the Zimbabwe African National Union (ZANU), exhorted his fellow Africans to rise up and confront the RF in the struggle for their minds: "In the existence of the colonial policy we are faced with a situation of violence. It is now time to change tactics in order to confront our oppressor. We can no longer cooperate with our oppressor in his efforts to reduce us to the level of bare existence. The RF represents colonial violence at its worst, it must be stopped in order to restore our mind to its proper position."[41] On April 30, 1966, the final phase in the struggle between the African and colonial minds in Rhodesia began with a fierce battle that signaled the start of a brutal civil war that cost thousands of lives by the time it ended in December 1979.

Washington Malianga, a spokesman for the African nationalist guerrillas, put their case before the court of world opinion when he said:

This is the beginning of our struggle to liberate ourselves. We are going to intensify the struggle until the enemy is utterly destroyed. We shall wage the struggle without backing down. The hour has come to fight to end the oppression, the subjection, and the humiliation which we have suffered for many years under colonial conditions. The colonial denial of our political and educational rights can only be ended by eliminating the cruel colonial conditions which have been imposed on us since 1890. It is no longer possible for us to acquiesce to colonial purposes.[42]

In December 1979 Smith was forced to sue for peace and agreed to attend a conference held in London to arrange the transfer of power to the Africans, a people he once described as primitive. Robert Mugabe, the African he described as uncivilized, became the new president of the independent state of Zimbabwe on April 18, 1980.

These events show that the British colonial empire had at last been checkmated in its African colonial chess game. The colonial mind was vanquished. Under Harold Wilson and Edward Heath, the British government, having satisfied itself that it had done all it could to advance its interests in Africa and having been disappointed with its efforts to bring Western civilization to a people it considered less civilized, now decided to turn its attention to its relationships with the rest of Western Europe by seeking membership in the European Economic Community. The days of its vast colonial empire in Africa were over. The sun had finally set, and the so-called brooding spirit that John Stuart Mill, Rudyard Kipling, Wynwood Read, Cecil Rhodes, Philip Mitchell, and Godfrey Huggins had symbolized for decades had at long last come to an end.

THE RISE OF THE AFRICAN MIND AND THE
COLLAPSE OF THE BELGIAN COLONIAL EMPIRE

To understand the effect of the rise of the African mind on the Belgian colonial empire in Africa, we need to go back to the Berlin Conference of 1885. The activity of European nations following the conclusion of the conference attracted the imagination of an ambitious and adventurous leader, King Leopold II (1835–1909) of Belgium. Wishing to engage in the rush for lands, Leopold sought to establish himself as the dominant figure in the colonization of Africa. His decisions were not impulsive, for he carefully calculated his moves and deliberately formulated his plan of action and policy to ensure their success. In doing so, Leopold envisioned all of Southern Africa under his personal control. In this regard, Leopold and Cecil Rhodes had one thing in common: their grandiose ambition and obsession to build a vast colonial empire in Africa in order to control the African mind. In this way, the vast resources of the continent could be utilized to benefit Europe.[43]

Leopold saw the founding of a Belgian colonial empire in Africa as a means of providing a life of luxury for his countrymen in both Africa and Europe. His goals and methodical approach for attaining them attracted intelligent and knowledgeable men to serve in his administration, among whom was Henry Morton Stanley (1842–1902). Stanley was born in Denbigh, Wales, as John Rowlands. When his father died, John was only two years old. His world shattered, he was forced to spend his youth in a workhouse where he endured great hardships. At the age of eighteen, he was a drifter without any goals or direction. A few months after his eighteenth birthday, Rowlands sailed to New Orleans, Louisiana, where he met a prosperous merchant, Henry Morton Stanley. This man grew to care for John, and he eventually adopted him. He gave him his own name by which he is historically known to the world.

With a new identity and a new country, Stanley served in the Confederate Army during the American Civil War. He was captured by Union forces, but he was soon released and joined the Union Navy where he served faithfully. At the end of the war, Stanley became a newspaper reporter, which set the stage for his part in African history. In 1869 the *New York Herald* selected him to undertake a mission of great importance—to find David Livingstone, from whom nothing had been heard for several years. After a brief period of hesitation, Stanley accepted his assignment as a divine mission that he felt only he could accomplish. Recognizing the circumstances of his own early life and the hardships he had endured in both Britain and the United States, Stanley set out for Africa, not only to find

Livingstone, but also to embark on a religious pilgrimage in search of himself. After months of searching, Stanley found Livingstone on October 28, 1871, at Ujiji in present-day Tanzania. Stanley greeted the revered Livingstone with the famous words, "Dr. Livingstone, I presume." Livingstone is reported to have answered simply, "Yes."

Stanley felt that his mission in life had been accomplished by locating Livingstone. Stanley's achievement in Africa made him an instant celebrity, and colonial entrepreneurs believed he was someone whose knowledge of Africa could be utilized to carry out their objectives. In 1876 Leopold established an organization that could be used to promote his goals in Africa. He named himself president and chief stockholder of the International African Association (IAA), a commercial enterprise designed to make profit for Europeans. He envisaged the development of a huge commercial enterprise that would employ large numbers of Africans in extracting raw materials, especially rubber, to feed industries that were being built all over Europe. But before he could undertake this task, Leopold commissioned Stanley in 1877 to explore the equatorial region of Africa. Stanley's mission was to come up with methods for implementing Leopold's plan to bring the region under his control.

In his report Stanley hints at how the African mind was likely to respond to the European presence. He advised Leopold not to involve the Belgian government in his intended enterprise because the Africans bitterly resented any schemes that were initiated by European governments. Accepting Stanley's advice, Leopold established the Congo Free State (CFS) in 1878 as his personal property and directed its business in accordance with his own objectives. In 1885 the Berlin Conference recognized Leopold as the sole and sovereign ruler of CFS. Leopold was ecstatic. He immediately began to formulate a new and more ambitious administrative structure to fulfill his desire for economic gain. Among the first steps he took to solidify his claim to the huge territory under his control was to appoint a board of advisors. For the day-to-day administration of CFS, Leopold appointed a governor who reported directly to him. He also divided CFS into fifteen administrative provinces and appointed an administrative assistant over each.

Then, Leopold took a step that was certain to lead to conflict: he eliminated the authority of the local African chiefs and appointed a Belgian colonial zealot, Leon Roget, captain of an army he had created to defend CFS interests. Roget also assumed the position of commander of a special military unit known as Force Publique, which soon became notorious for recruiting "local militia frequently from Africans with a reputation of cannibalism."[44] Two things are evident in this strategy. The first is that using

Africans as an instrument of controlling the African mind was a strategy commonly relied on in colonial Africa, and Leopold knew how to utilize it for his own benefit. The second is that using the Africans to control them enabled them to see the negative attributes of colonialism much faster than they would have done otherwise.

In order to make profits, Leopold instituted a policy that deprived the Africans of any control over their lives. He prohibited them from collecting ivory and rubber unless they were sold directly to CFS at a price he stipulated. He required all Africans over the age of sixteen, both men and women, to register in order to make sure that he had a sufficient labor pool. He ordered a strict daily production quota for each laborer and provided severe penalties for failing to meet it. For example, "During the colonial period a common punishment for a village's failure to meet Belgian rubber quotas was the random cutting off of hands."[45]

Failure to register or to report for work when ordered to do so carried serious consequences for both one's family and self. Leopold's obsession with quick profits proved to be the demise of his CFS. Humanitarian organizations in Europe were alarmed by reports showing that Leopold had introduced conditions that actually turned the Africans into slaves. In 1893 the Aborigines Protection Society asked the British government to investigate the charges. For the society to ask Britain to undertake this task would be equivalent to the American Medical Association or state bar being asked to investigate a doctor or lawyer, respectively. Although Britain treated the Africans in its own colonies no better, it was forced to respond by instructing Roger Casement, its consul in Leopoldville (named after Leopold himself), to investigate the charges and submit his report. When Casement submitted his report in 1903, he confirmed the CFS's gross mistreatment of the Africans.

Naturally, Leopold was angered by the criticism and argued that, by its very nature, colonialism was oppressive. But the Casement report had an impact on the African mind that Leopold could not have foreseen, a feeling of consciousness for when the time was right. But what is interesting in Leopold's reaction to the Casement report is that he observed that criticism of his poor treatment of the Africans came from European nations, such as Britain, which had vast colonial empires in Africa and were treating the Africans no better than he was doing. It was a case of fingerpointing at one another for ill treatment of the Africans. For the British to admonish Leopold for his mistreatment calls to mind the adage that people in glass houses shouldn't throw stones. Indeed, in 1913 the Belgian government commissioned law professor Henri Rolin to study the application of British colonial policy in Africa. Southern Rhodesia was chosen for the study. When Rolin reported gross mistreatment of the Africans by the British colonial governments, the Africans saw all colonial systems as instituted to enslave them. This general continental consciousness was bound to have serious implications for colonial systems all over Africa.

Bad publicity together with the desire to exploit the Africans had a devastating effect on the CFS's activities. In 1907 Leopold, advancing in age, lost so much money that he felt compelled to give up the operations of CFSA and asked the Belgian Colonial Office to assume responsibility for running it. On October 18, 1908, the Belgian Parliament passed legislation authorizing the government to accept the administration of CFS as a Belgian colony of the Belgian Congo. Leopold would never recover from his failure. He withdrew from public life, even though he was king of Belgium, and died in 1909, a bitterly disappointed man. Like Rhodes, Leopold left a legacy of racial bitterness that was destined to influence race relations for years to come.

As soon as it assumed its new responsibility of administering the Belgian Congo, the Belgian Colonial Office decided to operate under the view that the new colony should generate sufficient economic activity to yield profits. It therefore initiated a new policy that encouraged European migration to provide the technical skills needed to generate a higher rate of production. A number of private companies substituted IAA with its system of monopoly. Such companies included Compagnie de Chemin de Fer du Congo, which later became the Congo National Railways, and Comte Special du Katanga. Each was given special privileges to make profits. The formation of these companies gave them political power that they had not had in the past. It was the same political environment that gave the Africans an opportunity to reconstruct their own political identity. They were aware that, although colonial systems imposed on them conditions that oppressed them physically, they refused to have their minds enslaved as well. They knew that in the change of administration from Leopold to the Belgian Colonial Office, they had merely exchanged one face of oppression for another.[46]

The outbreak of the First World War witnessed a dramatic change in the thinking and pride of the Africans as they demonstrated their unquestionable skills to fight and survive in a hostile environment. In 1920 they felt so exploited by the colonial government that they turned the experiences they had gained during the war to initiate self-improvement projects. Among these was the emergence of a new religious experience different from that of the Europeans. In 1921 Simon Kimbangu convinced his fellow Africans that they must reject the religious organizations of Western missionaries because they were in full cooperation with the colonial government in oppressing them. He organized mass meetings and demonstrations against the exploitation to which the colonial government subjected the Africans. This climate began to give the African mind a new vision of itself.

Within a very short period of time, this religious fervor elevated Kimbangu to a position of power and influence. What alarmed the Belgian colonial government about this new religious movement was the fact that it was rapidly turning into political activity that hovered on extreme action with clear anticolonial sentiments. Unwilling to allow the course that this movement was taking to continue, the colonial government quickly moved in to arrest Kimbangu and charged him with treason and rebellion. Before he could be tried, Kimbangu escaped from prison, but he returned on his own to face charges. A massive manhunt had failed to locate him, increasing the Africans' belief in his divine power. The sudden rise of Kimbangu and the influence that he had on the expansion of African awareness presented the Belgian colonial government with an explosive situation and the very difficult problem of how to deal with him. If it tried and executed him, he would immediately become a martyr. If it confined him to prison, his charisma and power would increase rapidly. Kimbangu was eventually tried, convicted, and sentenced to death, but the sentence was commuted to life imprisonment.

This kind of behavior on the part of the colonial systems in Africa helped to elevate the African mind. The arrest and trial of Kimbangu produced exactly the result the colonial government feared. Between 1921 and 1950 Kimbanguism mushroomed in a way that frightened the colonists and the colonial government. It helped to generate a new level of political consciousness that was not known before. By 1951 the religious consciousness that had brought Simon Kimbangu to a position of influence and power now translated itself into a new political phenomenon. As part of the general consciousness that swept through Africa following the end of the Second World War, African leaders came forward to help shape new directions. The formation of Association des Classes Moyennes Africaines (the Association of the African Middle Class) led by Patrice Lumumba, Joseph Kasavubu, Arthur Pinzi, Gaston Siomi, and Joseph Ngalulu rapidly moved from seeking to promote a new political consciousness to demanding independence.

Lumumba turned out to be a shrewd political strategist, a visionary with high energy. After traveling throughout Africa and Europe, he sought the advice of Kwame Nkrumah on how to achieve, without further delay, independence for the Congo. Early in 1959 Lumumba delivered a moving speech at a political rally that called for immediate independence. He exhorted the Africans to unite and demand an end to colonization. Although the colonial government was impressed with his ability to articulate issues, it was alarmed by the implications of his speeches. Throughout the country, the colonists regarded Lumumba as too radical and began to raise questions about the colonial policy of excluding the Africans from the political process. If this was an admission of failure of the colonial system, it was too late for the colonial government to correct these errors.

A series of rapidly moving events took place during the next six months that caught the colonial government completely by surprise. The culture of ignorance was now having a traumatic and far-reaching effect on the character of Belgian colonial society. Demonstrations, rallies, strikes, and outbursts of violence brought government operations to a halt. Nothing else mattered as the Africans demanded independence without any further delay. Caught between the rising tide of the African demand and continued chaos resulting from widespread strikes, the Belgian government agreed to grant the Congo independence on June 30, 1960. This would follow the outcome of elections from which Lumumba emerged as prime minister and Joseph Kasavubu served as president. In these developments, the Belgian colonial empire came to an end as the mind in equatorial Africa came of age. In 1961 Lumumba put the rise of the African mind in proper context when he said, "Between freedom and colonial slavery there can be no compromise. We chose to pay the price of freedom."[47] Only the rise of a mind in new settings can perceive itself within a new sense of pride and worth.

THE RISE OF THE AFRICAN MIND AND THE FALL OF THE PORTUGUESE COLONIAL EMPIRE

The road to conflict between Portuguese colonists and the rise of the African mind took a perilous twist when Antonio Salazar assumed the position of autocrat in Portugal in 1932. Salazar immediately reactivated the colonial policy of *Estado Novo*, an old policy that had been reformulated in 1926 to strengthen control of the African colonies of Guinea-Bissau, Angola, and Mozambique. As noted earlier, a central feature of this policy was its division of the Africans in these colonies into two socioeconomic classes, *assimilados* and *indigenas*.

Based on provisions of the Colonial Act of 1930, Salazar began to implement a policy that regarded its African colonies as overseas provinces in order to camouflage its real oppressive intent. By 1952 the Africans' position had deteriorated so badly that five hundred Africans in Angola signed a petition requesting the United Nations (UN) do something to alleviate the hardships imposed on them.[48] In 1953, when the UN failed to take any action, the Africans formed a political party of their own, the

Struggle of Africans in Angola (PLUA), permanently altering the character of Portuguese colonialism.

To their dismay and disbelief, the Portuguese colonial officials soon discovered that instead of dividing the Africans, as intended, the policy of *Estado Novo* united them. Both the *assimilados* and *indigenas* joined forces to launch a struggle against colonial oppression. As throughout all of Africa, the awareness of the native peoples in this region could no longer be suppressed by the culture of ignorance as had been done in the past. The *assimilados*, the educated and upper class Africans that the policy was designed to isolate from the *indigenas*, provided the leadership the Africans required to understand the character of the colonial society from its proper perspective.

In so doing, they could then design a prerequisite strategy for freeing themselves. Alarmed by the accelerating events it could not impede, the colonial government tried various methods, including arrests, torture, and harassment to foil the surging African mind. This was all done in vain. In December 1956 PLUA met in Luanda with representatives of the Popular Movement for the Liberation of Angola (MPLA), which had just been formed, and agreed to merge under the leadership of Agostinho Neto, an *assimilado*. MPLA adapted PLUA's main principles and objectives, among them the liberation of Angola. This event was the catalyst for the demise of the Portuguese colonial empire in Africa.

In 1959 MPLA leaders were arrested, but refusing to give up the goals that the rise of their mind dictated, the Africans moved their organization to Conacry in New Guinea to avoid further interference. At the same time, other African political organizations were being formed in Angola. Among these were the Union of the Populations of Angola (UPA), the Democratic party of Angola (CPDA), the National Front for the Liberation of Angola (FNLA), and the National Union for the Total Liberation of Angola (UNITA). The formation of these parties illustrates that for the first time since Portugal established colonies in Africa in 1575, the Portuguese colonial officials were facing an unprecedented test of will. Never before had it been subjected to a national political crisis that would mean its collapse. Moreover, the rise of the African mind was a new phenomenon, widespread in involvement, intense in its character, and clear in its objective. There was no doubt as to what the Africans wanted. Once that objective was identified, it could not be compromised. *Estado Novo* could do nothing to accommodate the aspirations of the Africans within the existing Portuguese colonial institutions.

In Mozambique and Guinea-Bissau, similar developments were taking place with unprecedented speed. In rapid succession, Adelino Gwembe,

Matthew Mwale, and L. M. Malinga exerted the kind of leadership in
Mozambique that enabled the Africans to coordinate their forthcoming
struggle for independence. In 1962 several parties that had been formed
during the past few years decided to merge to form the Frente de Libertaçao
de Mozambique (Frelimo) under the leadership of Eduardo Mondlane
(1920–1969), a former professor of sociology at Syracuse University in
New York. That all of these men were *assimilados* suggests the extent to
which the Africans rejected *Estado Novo*. With a coordinated organization
covering all the Portuguese colonies, there was little the colonial government could do to minimize the effect of the expanding consciousness and
motivation that was all around them. The Portuguese colonial empire in
Africa was on its way to extinction.

With these developments, the final act to liberate the African mind in
Portuguese colonial Africa was about to take place. In 1962 the Africans in
all the Portuguese colonies launched massive coordinated attacks on Portuguese forces and installations. The installations were laid to waste as
massive destruction took place all over the three countries.[49] The Portuguese
military was forced to spread itself thin in a desperate effort to contain the
situation, but was unable to coordinate its strategy. With the assistance given
the revolutionary forces by the newly formed Organization of African Unity
(OAU), the Africans waged an effective guerrilla campaign against the
Portuguese forces. For the next twelve years the wars in the three Portuguese
colonies took a devastating toll on human life and property in both Portugal
and its African colonies. Finally, on April 25, 1974, confused by events they
could no longer control and facing certain defeat, the military forces staged
a coup that removed from office Marcello Caetano, who had succeeded
Salazar in 1968.

A few months earlier the Portuguese military genius, Antonio de Spinola,
who was coordinating Portuguese forces against the African nationalist
guerrillas in all three colonies, had made the painful assessment that
Portugal would not win a military victory against the Africans and that the
only solution lay in the political process. De Spinola published these views
in a controversial book, *Portugal and Its Future*. This admission, from a
man who directed Portuguese military forces against the revolutionary
forces, was a shattering experience for Caetano. Relations between the two
men became seriously strained.

When de Spinola suggested that Caetano convene a conference to discuss
the future of the Portuguese colonies with guerrilla leaders, a major national
crisis developed. Caetano tried to dismiss de Spinola, who in turn dismissed
him by staging a military coup. Caetano went into exile in Brazil where he
died a few years later. As soon as de Spinola assumed the office of president,

he immediately offered a cease-fire and promised to grant independence to all the Portuguese colonies in Africa. When these colonies became independent in 1975, the Portuguese colonial empire came to a close, and the African mind in that region was free at last.

THE ASCENDANCY OF NELSON MANDELA AND THE RISE OF THE AFRICAN MIND IN SOUTH AFRICA

The rise of the African mind caused by the tragedy of apartheid became a major national crisis on February 2, 1990, when F. W. de Klerk announced that Nelson Mandela would be released from prison unconditionally and that the ban on the African National Congress (ANC) would be lifted in order to begin negotiations on the constitutional future of the country, especially on how to share political power. When de Klerk announced in the South African Parliament on June 7 that his government was lifting the state of emergency, it raised a new hope that the solutions to the problems apartheid had been creating since 1948 could now be found. But when de Klerk kept his promise in 1990 to hold talks with members of the ANC, there was a sudden political backlash from conservative Afrikaner elements, especially members of the Conservative party who opposed both lifting the state of emergency and holding talks with ANC members.

By January 1992, as talks with the ANC did not appear to make any progress, de Klerk and his ruling Nationalist party suffered a series of defeats in special elections forcing them to seek the approval of the white voters to continue the talks. In February de Klerk announced that a national referendum would be held on March 17, 1992, to provide an answer to a single question: "Do you support the continuation of the reform process which the State President began on February 2, 1990, and which is aimed at a new constitution through negotiation?" De Klerk considered the referendum so important that his government decided to make arrangements for voters living outside South Africa to cast their ballot on March 11 and 12. The lack of progress in the talks with ANC created a political climate in which some members of both the black and the white communities took extreme positions.

Two examples can be cited to substantiate this conclusion. First, Thami Mcerwa, president of the Azanian Youth Organization, opposed the talks because, he said, "We want total liberation, not cosmetic changes. We may go into civil war struggle, quick fix solutions will not work. As Steve Biko[50] said, 'It is better to die for an idea that will live than to live for an idea that will die.'"[51] The second example is Pieter Rudolph, a member of the neo-Nazi Afrikaner Resistance Movement who considered de Klerk a traitor to Afrikaner interests and emphasized that the Afrikaners had inherited South Africa as a glorious national legacy. Rudolph added, "I received this land as I received my mother's milk. I am a son of Africa."[52] The extreme positions taken by the antagonists placed South Africa at a crossroads until Nelson Mandela's ascendancy in the elections that were held in April 1994. Rudolph and the other extreme Afrikaners were overwhelmed by the rapid pace of events they could not control.

Sadly, de Klerk agreed to be part of a national referendum that allowed only whites to vote on an issue of great national importance. Since de Klerk claimed to be committed to bringing about social reform, what better place for him to start bringing the Africans into his confidence than initiating a process for their involvement in the referendum? On March 12, 1992, seventeen people and on March 13 another twenty-four people were killed in violence related to the forthcoming referendum. Reporting from Johannesburg on March 13, Alan Pizzey put the conflict between the Afrikaner psychology and the rise of the African mind in its proper context: "There is still a belief among the Afrikaners that God has ordained them as the master race of South Africa. But the Africans believed that the future belongs to them."[53] This conflict evinces the tragedy of apartheid.

On March 18, 1992, when the referendum results showed that the "yes" vote had carried the day by a margin of 2:1 out of the total white electorate of 2.8 million voters, de Klerk was euphoric: "Today, we have closed the chapter on apartheid."[54] While generally pleased with the outcome of the referendum, Nelson Mandela had a more somber reaction: "Because I still cannot vote in my country, I cannot say that apartheid is gone."[55] De Klerk also saw the result, coming on his fifty-sixth birthday, as "the real birthday of the real South Africa."[56]

In a similar manner Allister Sparks, the author of *The Mind of South Africa* (1990), recognized the perils of a national crisis in the context of the rise of the African mind, saying,

The danger now is that the right-wing may turn to violence. White South Africa has rejected apartheid and must now embrace a non-racial approach to its problems. The talk of power-sharing is code word for white veto. The mind of the Africans is quite capable of grasping this reality and demands that South Africa move into the realm of a completely non-racial society.[57]

Gary Player, the professional golf player, added, "Change is the price of survival."[58] But seventy-six year-old Pieter W. Botha, whom de Klerk replaced as president in a bitter struggle for power, reacted, "I cannot support a reform process that leads to the suicide of my people."[59] It was too late for the old and tired horse to see things in their proper perspective.

With the referendum over, the task of reconstructing a new South Africa had just begun. But on April 5 violence in black townships broke out on a larger scale than before the referendum. As hundreds were killed, Mandela called for a UN peacekeeping force, arguing that the South African security forces were behind the violence and that that was the only way to contain it. But de Klerk rejected both the call and the charge, arguing that the violence was caused by Africans themselves struggling for power. On April 11, in a strange turn of events, de Klerk tried to campaign in a black neighborhood outside Cape Town in an effort to recruit Africans into the ranks of the Nationalist party. As he tried to make a speech, he was jeered and shouted down, but he managed to say, "Apartheid has been buried and will remain buried. The creation of the new South Africa has begun."[60] One angry African reacted, "We are still discriminated against, we still cannot vote. What is de Klerk campaigning for?"[61]

Unconvinced of his sincerity, ANC called de Klerk's action "a case of political opportunism."[62] De Klerk was forced to cancel the rest of the speech and hurriedly moved out of the neighborhood. The spiral of conflict took an ominous and tragic turn on June 18, 1992, when thirty-nine Africans were massacred in cold blood at Boipatong reportedly by members of Inkatha with what ANC identified as assistance from the government.[63] Although de Klerk denied the charge, "a black mine-security guard told a government-appointed commission that police from a former paramilitary unit had joined in the Boipatong killings."[64] Talks between ANC and the government were suspended as the result of the killings to allow the parties to assess the situation and to determine the next move. Instead of dealing forthrightly with the situation that his government had created, de Klerk threatened to reimpose the notorious state of emergency, an easy strategy the apartheid government had utilized for so many years to control the mind of the Africans.

On August 3, 1992, over a million African workers went on strike for two days in protest against the government's refusal to end apartheid. This action paralyzed major industries and services. On September 18, twenty-eight Africans were massacred in the Bantustan homeland of Ciskei while protesting peacefully against the puppet regime of Brigadier Oupa Gqozo, who was promoted to his position in the government of South Africa for his service against the Africans' demand to dismantle apartheid. According to *Time*, when the 60,000 chanting ANC supporters moved closer to the capital, "trigger-happy troops of the Ciskei army began shooting directly into the crowd. After two prolonged bursts of gunfire, 28 people lay dead in pools of blood, another 400 were wounded,"[65] dragging the country closer to the edge of a major national disaster.

On November 25, Mandela and Mongusatho Buthelezi, the Zulu chief, recognizing that the government was exploiting their differences between them, decided to hold a meeting to resolve the crisis between them. The attack and killing of five whites in a restaurant near Cape Town on December 4, 1992, by an unidentified group of African nationalists added a perilous twist to an already dangerous situation. There is no question that dramatic as they were, these events placed South Africa at the crossroads as a consequence of conflict between the rise of the African mind and the determination of the Afrikaners to maintain apartheid.

The racial confrontation that apartheid has created over many years was destined to intensify with the passage of time. This situation has actually led to one thing, a major racial war that has produced a national tragedy such as the one that occurred in Zimbabwe from 1966 to 1979. Apartheid has been a cancer that has destroyed the delicate tissue of the South African vitality, human resources without which no nation can prosper. Even Brian Nel, an Herstige Nationale party organizer, seemed to agree when he said ironically in 1980, "The cancer of apartheid is spreading and is going to follow you wherever you go."[66]

In the Afrikaner's determination to sustain apartheid at all costs and in the oppressed Africans' determination to rise and envisage the restoration of their mind lie the seeds of the destruction and tragedy of the South African system. Although the world community has exercised its moral duty to help the Afrikaners see the tragic course they have charted for the country, apartheid has extended beyond the boundaries of South Africa. It must therefore be viewed from a global perspective. Indeed, by 1992 the international community came to realize that apartheid's oppression of the black masses of South Africa inescapably enslaved humanity as a whole. This is the reality that de Klerk took into account when he decided to hold serious discussions with the ANC on a new constitution that would bring true democracy to South Africa.

After months of negotiations, the parties agreed to hold free elections on April 26–28, 1994. Immediately, the ANC designed a strategy to "capture at least 67% of the 22.4 million eligible voters."[67] This would mean that the ANC would take 328 of the 490 seats in Parliament. As the election campaign got under way, it was clear that de Klerk was hoping for no more than a respectable showing. He was pleased that he had made it possible to turn over power to the Africans in a way that would ensure the future of the whites in a new country. An African government would not match the brutality of apartheid by utilizing methods that would make life uncomfortable for whites.

As expected, the ANC won the elections with more than the two-thirds majority it had wanted. Nelson Mandela, the man who had spent twenty-seven years in prison for opposing apartheid, emerged as the new man in the incredible saga of the transformation of South Africa. With a sense of duty and humbled by it all, Mandela responded, "It is not the individual that matters, but the group. I come to you as a servant, not a leader above others. We must together begin to mobilize our minds and build a better life for all South Africans. We are here to honor our promise. If we fail we betray the trust placed on us by our people. As we form the government of national unity, we must set the tone for the future."[68]

Conceding defeat, de Klerk pledged the support of his party to the new government that Mandela was about to lead, saying, "After three hundred years all the people of South Africa are now free."[69] When Mandela was inaugurated on May 9, the entire African continent had eliminated the last vestiges of the colonial era, raising the African mind to a new level. But Mandela warned his fellow South Africans not to have too high hopes because the task of rebuilding a country devastated by apartheid was not an easy one. Nonetheless, the transformation of the African continent made possible by the rise of the African mind was now complete.

SUMMARY AND CONCLUSION

The colonial governments thought that they were in Africa to stay for at least a thousand years. Apart from the Portuguese who were in Africa about four hundred years, the rest of the colonial systems lasted less than one hundred years. This shows the delusional miscalculations the Europeans used to plan colonial adventures in Africa. The culture of ignorance had far more severe consequences for the designers of colonial empires than for the objects of their design, the Africans. What went wrong? The colonial governments grossly underestimated the determination of the African mind to survive under severe colonial conditions and to assert itself in extremely oppressive settings when the time was ripe. Regardless of the oppressive nature of the colonial conditions, the Africans refused to give up their own perspective of who they were. This element became crucial in their struggle for self, and the colonial establishments didn't have a clue about it and its potency.

The tragedy of the colonial systems in Africa is not merely that they operated under the myth of the inferiority of the African mind, but that they refused to engage the Africans in dialogue in order to establish bridges of human communication and understanding. If the apartheid system of South Africa had recognized this fact, the country would have been spared the agony it has been enduring for so many years, and efforts would have been directed at building a dynamic society in which race was not a criterion for determining a person's place in society. For this reason, in 1990 F. W. de

Klerk, the leader of the last colonial system in Africa, decided to change tactics and embark on a new direction, holding discussions with the Africans. Another tragic aspect of the colonial governments in Africa is that they refused to accept the fact that the Africans were capable of engaging in the high intellectual and mental processes needed to devise national programs.

This chapter shows that by the time the colonial governments recognized the effect of this tragic reality it was too late. There was no more room for compromise. This situation produced an environment that spelled the end of the colonial governments themselves. The transformation of South Africa in April 1994 shows that Africans all over the continent had become masters of their own destiny because their minds had reached a level of development that was beyond the ability of the colonial governments to control.

NOTES

1. Memmi, *The Colonizer and the Colonized*, p. 119.

2. Ibid., p. 120.

3. Ibid., p. 128.

4. James H. Oldham, *White and Black in Africa* (New York: Green and Co., 1930), p. 3.

5. Ibid., p. 5.

6. Ibid., p. 11.

7. Ibid., p. 13.

8. Donald Fraser, *The Future of Africa* (Westport, Conn.: Negro Universities Press, 1911), p. 115.

9. Ibid., p. 117.

10. Ibid., p. 251.

11. Meredith, *The First Dance of Freedom: Black Africa in the Postwar Era*, p. 82.

12. Ibid., p. 12.

13. Selassie was in office from 1930 to 1974, and Tubman assumed the office of president of Liberia in 1944. Both countries have experienced violence of major proportions.

14. Meredith, *The First Dance of Freedom: Black Africa in the Postwar Era*, p. 91.

15. Ibid., p. 93.

16. Kwame Nkrumah, *Africa Must Unite*, p. 51.

17. Meredith, *The First Dance of Freedom: Black Africa in the Postwar Era*, p. 96.

18. In a similar manner, Botswana, Swaziland, and Lesotho became protectorates rather than colonies of Britain. The status of protectorate meant that Britain was asked to protect these territories from the military action of those who wanted

to take possession of them—in the case of Nigeria from the French and in the case of the other three, from the Boers. Britain gave the Africans of these territories the impression that it was seeking to protect them from other colonial adventurers.

19. Meredith, *The First Dance of Freedom: Black Africa in the Postwar Era*, p. 86.

20. In 1968, Bobby Kennedy (1925–1968), then U.S. senator from New York, during a campaign for president of the United States, made the now famous remarks, "Some people see things as they are and ask why. I dream of things that never were and ask why not." Kennedy was killed in Los Angeles in June of that year.

21. An African graduate student from Kenya attending Northern Arizona University, during an interview with the author in Flagstaff, Arizona, September 3, 1991.

22. Meredith, *The First Dance of Freedom: Black Africa in the Postwar Era*, p. 53.

23. Ibid., p. 54.

24. Embassy of Kenya, in response to the author's request. Memo, Ref. Row/Edu/5/Vol. 25, July 16, 1991.

25. A graduate student from Kenya during an interview with the author in Flagstaff, Arizona, September 3, 1991.

26. Memmi, *The Colonizer and the Colonized*, p. 122.

27. Harold Macmillan, "Commonwealth Independence and Interdependence," an address to the Joint Session of the South African Parliament, Cape Town, February 3, 1960.

28. For a detailed discussion of the argument that Western missionaries operated in Africa in concert with the objectives of the colonial governments, see, for example, Geoffrey Kapenzi, *The Clash of Cultures: Christian Missionaries and the Shona of Rhodesia* (Washington, D.C.: University Press of America, 1979).

29. See Chapter 1 of this study for what Livingstone said on this subject.

30. Mungazi, *Colonial Policy and Conflict in Zimbabwe: A Study of Cultures in Collision, 1890–1979*, p. 10.

31. Ibid., p. 14. The British South Africa Company that ruled Zimbabwe at the time did not release any figures showing the number of deaths among the Africans. Speculation has been that these were considerably higher than thought to be. These figures were not released because they constituted a major atrocity.

32. This structure is discussed in Chapter 2 of this study, and it is not necessary to repeat it here.

33. Mungazi, *To Honor the Sacred Trust of Civilization: History, Politics and Education in Southern Africa*, p. 244.

34. Meredith, *The First Dance of Freedom: Black Africa in the Postwar Era*, p. 105.

35. The subject of political independence and the betrayal of the African mind is discussed in Chapter 7 of this study.

36. Meredith, *The First Dance of Freedom: Black Africa in the Postwar Era*, p. 106.

37. Materials from the Embassy of Malawi in Washington, D.C., July 17, 1991.

38. These four Smiths who served in the Rhodesia Front government from December 1962 to March 1979 were not related by blood but by the political philosophy that, because the Africans were inferior, they must never be allowed to participate in the political affairs of the country.

39. Ian Smith, "Rhodesia's Finest Hour: Unilateral Declaration of Independence, November 11, 1965." Zimbabwe National Archives.

40. Chitepo was assassinated in 1969 in Lusaka, Zambia, by a letter bomb believed to have been sent by the RF. In the same way, Eduardo Mondlane was assassinated in Dar es Salaam in 1969 by a letter bomb sent by Portuguese colonial officials.

41. Herbert Chitepo, president of ZANU, in "Zimbabwe: The Road to Freedom" a documentary film. Zimbabwe National Archives, 1983.

42. Washington Malianga, "We Shall Wage an All-out War," a statement issued following a battle between the African nationalist guerrillas and the RF military forces, April 30, 1966. Zimbabwe National Archives.

43. Mungazi, *To Honor the Sacred Trust of Civilization: History, Politics and Education in Southern Africa*, p. 213.

44. Irving Kaplan, *Zaire: A Country Study* (Washington, D.C.: American University Press, 1979), p. 29.

45. Congolese National Liberation party, *The Question of Zaire* (New York: FLNC, 1978), p. 34.

46. Mungazi, *To Honor the Sacred Trust of Civilization: History, Politics and Education in Southern Africa*, p. 218.

47. Congolese National Liberation party, *The Question for Zaire*, p. 33.

48. Mungazi, *To Honor the Sacred Trust of Civilization: History, Politics and Education in Southern Africa*, p. 31.

49. The author saw evidence of this massive destruction in Mozambique in December 1971.

50. The leader of the Black Consciousness Movement who was murdered in 1977 by the South African police.

51. Scott MacLeod, "South Africa: Extremes in Black and Whites," *Time*, March 9, 1992, p. 38.

52. Ibid., p. 39.

53. Alan Pizzey, reporting for CBS from Johannesburg, March 13, 1992.

54. Alan Pizzey, "South Africa: Day of Decision," March 18, 1992.

55. Ibid.

56. Bruce W. Nolan, "South Africa Says Yes," *Time*, March 30, 1992, p. 34.

57. Allister Sparks, South African journalist, during an interview with Ted Koppel, on ABC's "Nightline," March 18, 1992.

58. Ibid.

59. Ibid.

60. ABC-TV, "South Africa," during "The Evening News," April 11, 1992.

61. Ibid.

62. Ibid.

63. Alan Pizzey, reporting from South Africa for the CBS-TV News Service, June 28, 1992.

64. *Time*, July 6, 1992, p. 19.

65. *Time*, September 21, 1992, p. 16.

66. *New York Times*, December 12, 1980, p. 11.

67. *Time*, February 21, 1994, p. 35.

68. Nelson Mandela, address to South Africa, May 2, 1994, following the ANCs victory in the elections held April 26–28, 1994, as reported by CNN.

69. Ibid.

6

Political Independence and the Betrayal of the African Mind

Africa is in danger of becoming a graveyard of stillborn democracy.
Mark Fritz, 1993

The actual and present condition of Africa is one of deep trouble, a deeper trouble than the worst condition imposed during the colonial years.
Basil Davidson, 1992

NKRUMAH, THE CASTLE, AND THE BETRAYAL OF THE AFRICAN MIND

Political independence in Africa formed a window of opportunity for historical social change, but instead the emerging African leaders used it to betray the mind of their people. This conclusion is not to suggest that political independence was not good in and of itself for Africa, but to argue that the African leaders used it to betray the aspirations of their own people. This chapter discusses four specific examples to substantiate this conclusion: Ghana, Nigeria, Zaire, and the former Portuguese colonies of Angola and Mozambique.

The continental excitement that marked Ghana's independence in 1957 gave way to the somber realities of governing a nation much sooner than Nkrumah and his fellow Africans were prepared to do properly. Nkrumah's decision to make Christianborg Castle his official residence signified two critical factors relative to how the African mind was to respond to the new political conditions. The first is that Christianborg Castle was built in the seventeenth century by Danish slave traders, and successive British colonial governors lived there to conduct the affairs of the colony. It symbolized the power of the white man's dominance. For years Nkrumah had watched with both envy and castigation the operations of a system that oppressed his people, and Christianborg Castle represented it all. Nkrumah used this envy to aspire to political power and castigation to bring the colonial system to an end.

The second factor is that while Nkrumah's move into Christianborg Castle represented the end of one era and the beginning of another, Nkrumah did not refurbish it to signify a change in political direction. While the people of Ghana saw a different occupant, they were struck by the sameness of the castle in its political character. They believed that a change in the occupancy of the castle without change in its physical character denoted a continuation of an imposed system that they hated. Early in his administration, Nkrumah embraced the protocol that the British colonial administrations had put in place. This caused further alienation from the people. Access to the castle was given only to his close friends and associates. In putting these practices into place, Nkrumah was slowly isolating himself from the people who had helped put him there, and the reality of their needs steadily became an illusion visible only to Nkrumah's mind.

Soon after Nkrumah assumed the position of power, Christianborg Castle began to signify a painful contradiction in some important respects. He seemed to neglect the fact that the British colonial governors who had lived at the castle were accountable to the British government which appointed them and that he, unlike them, must answer to the people of Ghana. For Nkrumah residence at Christianborg Castle represented the ultimate power and authority that he felt only he should use as a vehicle to fulfill his destiny and to reach a continental destination. He was not aware that while he regarded his living at the castle as a retaking of the bastion of political power he was also acquiring the remoteness of an absolute despot.[1]

With the protection of Christianborg and his solitude as national leader, Nkrumah felt secure in planning his grandiose schemes. His enormous ego, his immeasurable ambition to attain the level of a continental leader, and his absolute contempt for the colonial system and desire to abolish it in all of Africa combined to lead to his self-delusion that Africa's salvation rested squarely and solely on his shoulders. He had watched the British governors give orders from Christianborg Castle that all had to obey, including himself. He had seen the pomp and circumstance dignify the British colonial system and the officials who operated it. Nkrumah and his fellow Africans had watched from the back alleys of an exclusive system the implementation of a national policy that elevated British nationals to the pedestal of

absolute power over the Africans enshrined in the notion of white supremacy. All that was now history, although the memory and the pain lingered.
Christianborg Castle was the fountain of the power that now rested on his
shoulders. Here he would chart a new course for restoring Africa to the
position of greatness that he believed existed prior to colonization.[2]

To Nkrumah the elimination of colonialism in Africa was all that mattered: he was obsessed with achieving this goal. If accomplished, it would
stand as a shining example of the restoration of the African mind. He
believed that there was no one else in all of Africa with the mind, charisma,
brilliance, influence, determination, and power that he had to lead his
beloved continent to new heights. This would elevate the Africans and place
their continent on a level playing field with the rest of the world whereby
they would receive the respect due to them. He felt that the world could not
show respect for Africa without first showing respect for him. He considered Christianborg Castle the lighthouse for the ships of African endeavors
setting sail into the turbulent oceans of colonial political uncertainty.

All African nationalist leaders who sought to lead their countries from
colonialism to self-actualization and independence were summoned to
Christianborg to gain the inspiration that only Nkrumah could impart.
Indeed, Nkrumah wanted the journey to political independence in all
countries of Africa to begin with a single step from the doorsteps of his new
residence, Christianborg Castle. Nkrumah and all the African nationalists
concluded that without this inspiration and without their journey beginning
at Christianborg Castle, the Africans would never arrive at their political
destination. There was no alternative course of action. The colonial governments were made to understand that once the African nationalists completed
their pilgrimages to Christianborg Castle there was nothing they could do
to stop the advent of independent African governments. Nkrumah was now
playing a powerful psychological game on the colonial mind.

If Christianborg Castle was the hub that turned the wheels of political
independence in Africa, it was Accra, the capital of Ghana, that Nkrumah
wanted as the vehicle that would get them there. Just as London, Paris,
Lisbon, Berlin, Rome, and Madrid had become the undisputed power bases
that European nations used to build vast colonial empires in Africa, so
Nkrumah envisioned Accra as the fountain from which the Africans would
draw the water of inspiration for their cause. It would become the Africans'
major power base for dismantling the entire colonial edifice and rebuilding
their countries into thriving nations led by men of vision.[3] He wanted to
rebuild Accra so that it would become the fitting capital city not only of
Ghana, but also of the United States of Africa, a majestic symbol of the
greatness he believed Africa deserved, worthy of world recognition and

respect. He wanted to see all the countries of Africa achieve political independence so that they would unite with him as their president in efforts to restore the mind of its people, free from any colonial influence, to its historical greatness.

Nkrumah recognized no limits in conceiving new ideas about the future of Africa. He was steadily building for himself a political stature larger than life and making himself a role model for future generations. Slowly, Accra was becoming the Mecca of the African struggle for self, the holy city of their aspirations. In this context Christianborg Castle and Accra became twin shrines that demanded reverence from all of Africa and homage from all African nationalists. Christianborg Castle and Accra had become the Holy Grail from which only the most worthy of politically religious and divine African nationalists could drink in order to attain their sacred crusade, political independence.

Beginning in 1959, Nkrumah's vision of a brave new African world motivated him to bring himself into the inner circle of world leaders who had dedicated themselves to transforming the existing world order and bringing the oppressed masses a respectable and decent standard of living. He was invited to many meetings and conferences that addressed issues of global importance. In 1959 Queen Elizabeth, on the British throne a mere seven years, invited him as her personal guest to the Royal Palace at Balmoral Castle, reinforcing his own image of what Christianborg Castle represented.

From the many visits he made, his participation in conferences and meetings, and the discussions he held with other world leaders, both within and outside Africa, Nkrumah reached the only logical conclusion that Africa had an incredible political potential for greatness. Its resources, both human and natural, were developed in accordance with the distinctive genius of the African mind. With vast raw materials, the continent possessed a potential similar to that of the Soviet Union and the United States of America. But in order to fully tap these resources, African countries had to attain political independence first and then focus on developing the technological skills needed to ensure rapid development. He therefore believed that African nations had no choice but to spend a larger proportion of the national budget on education.

Nkrumah began to believe more strongly than before that the formation of the United States of Africa was the only realistic approach to solving the continent's problems. He then began a continental campaign to promote himself as the only viable and logical candidate for the office of president. He ordered the printing of thousands of copies of pictures taken of him with Queen Elizabeth at Balmoral Castle as part of the campaign.[4] Nkrumah was a man with a mission, a visionary mind, a defined political objective, a clear agenda, unusually high energy, and an obsession to fulfill his destiny.

NKRUMAH, THE OAU, AND THE AFRICAN MIND

The visionary Nkrumah believed in the biblical saying, "Where there is no vision, the people perish." He became the African Isaiah,[5] making predictions of things to come. Although he neglected a cardinal point of vision, that it can err,[6] he was always conceiving new ideas to realize his grandiose plan of creating the United States of Africa. In its selection of Ted Turner, the American entrepreneur who made CNN a dominant news medium, as its 1991 Man of the Year, *Time* described him in a way that would fit the visionary character of Kwame Nkrumah, saying, "Visionaries are possessed creatures, men and women in the thrall of belief so powerful that they ignore all else, even reason, to ensure that reality catches up with their dreams."[7]

Nkrumah became instrumental in founding the Organization of African Unity (OAU) on May 25, 1963. At that time thirty independent countries of Africa participated, and Nkrumah played a leading role in defining the elements of OAU's charter, which exemplified the best of the African mind. OAU's structure and goals stand out as the finest tribute to Nkrumah as a leader of unquestionable qualities. The assembly of the heads of state and governments was the highest authority. OAU met once a year, but the Council of Ministers, consisting of foreign ministers or other government officials, met two or more times a year as conditions warranted.

The main function of the Council of Ministers was to approve the resolutions passed by the assembly. The Commission on Mediation, Conciliation, and Arbitration was designed to settle disputes between member states. A permanent secretariat, headed by a secretary general, was headquartered in Addis Ababa, not Accra, as Nkrumah had hoped. Nkrumah was forced to swallow his pride to allow this momentous continental organization to be based in Ethiopia, a country that was being led by Haile Selassie, an autocratic ruler who was heavily influenced by the ancient Amharic culture that inhibited his ability to see the future and design a national policy and agenda to reflect contemporary trends. Impatient as he was, Nkrumah understood the need for compromise in order to have his agenda accepted. But he was deeply angered, believing that compromise was not the art of diplomacy and democracy, but an erosion of basic principles essential to important accomplishments. Nkrumah would never recover from the disappointment of this experience.

As an organization, the OAU symbolized the best of the African mind when it outlined its goals and objectives. The five goals considered essential to the accomplishment of its agenda were: (1) to promote international cooperation in seeking solutions to many problems of global development; (2) to remove all forms of colonization in Africa, political, economic, and cultural; (3) to defend the sovereignty of independent African states; (4) to promote cooperation among African states in all aspects of development; and (5) to promote the unity and solidarity of African nations. Julius Nyerere of Tanzania spoke for the African nations when he said, "This conference is intended to guide us in our struggle to end the last vestiges of colonialism. Ours is a task to restore our continent from foreign domination and to restore our mind to its proper place."[8] Nkrumah made an impassioned appeal to the delegates to return to their respective countries fully committed and dedicated to the liberation struggle for Africa. He warned that any other course of action would lead to disaster. There was no compromise with the colonial systems.

Thus was born an organization that was destined to alter the present course of development in Africa. The colonial governments and European nations that they represented were alarmed by the OAU's agenda for action. Considering its role in the struggle for independence "imperious and urgent,"[9] the OAU resolved to accelerate the end of the colonial era and the restoration of the African mind in dramatic fashion. Nkrumah succeeded in convincing his fellow Africans that achieving political independence was an essential condition for resolving other continental problems because the colonial conditions were far more oppressive of the African mind than any other aspect of the African life. When the mind was oppressed, argued Nkrumah, no aspect of the African life was free. He also argued that the struggle for political independence was, in effect, the struggle for the freedom of the mind and must take precedence over any other form of struggle. In a manner characteristic of Nkrumah's thought process, the delegates to the inauguration of OAU understood him to say that freedom of the African mind could not be separated from political freedom because these were like love and marriage: one could not have the one without the other.

Twenty years later, in 1983, Robert Mugabe, president of Zimbabwe, who, as nationalist leader, used to make annual pilgrimages to Ghana, echoed a similar line of thinking as his administration grappled with the problems of national development. Launching a national literacy campaign in July, Mugabe acknowledged that the campaign was aimed not merely at illiterate adults, but at all adults outside the formal educational process. He emphasized the value and importance of the individual's mental liberation to the advancement of the nation.

Indeed, Mugabe warned his countrymen that it was impossible to achieve political and economic independence while their thinking was still oppressed by forces such as the lack of freedom to educate themselves. Mugabe argued that the struggle for political independence was meaningless if the African mind was still oppressed, adding, "To set the mind free, to make observation and analysis accurate, to make judgment informed, objective and fair, and to make the imagination creative, are as important a cause of struggle as the struggle for political and economic emancipation. Mental emancipation is both the instrument and modality of political and economic emancipation and cannot be taken for granted."[10]

In order to fulfill its objectives, the OAU worked out a three-dimensional strategy that combined political, diplomatic, and military components. Its major focus was an attack on the core of the colonial establishments in Angola and Mozambique, the extreme right-wing administration of the Rhodesia Front in Zimbabwe, and the entrenched apartheid system in South Africa and Namibia. OAU's logic in initiating this strategy was that if the wall that these colonial governments represented fell under the weight of the African mind, then, indeed, the dismantling of the colonial conditions that had engulfed it for so long would be accomplished much faster.[11] The strategy that the OAU designed was greatly strengthened by the independence of Tanganyika in 1963, altering the political landscape of southern Africa.

When Tanganyika was joined by Zanzibar in 1964 to form Tanzania, this development enabled the OAU to form what has become known as frontline states—black independent countries that have common borders with white-ruled countries. The OAU began to grow from weakness to strength with its ability to formulate objectives and design strategies for effecting them. Hassau Patel and Ali Mazrui maintain that the OAU sought primarily to create conditions in all countries still under colonial domination for the African mind to assert itself. Patel and Mazrui conclude: "In the face of trying problems of seeking independence, OAU used the rallying cry of liberation to maintain a fragile unity among its members."[12]

To reduce the possibility of failure or of limited success in seeking to fulfill its objectives and other endeavors, the OAU created a committee to coordinate its liberation programs. Known as the Liberation Committee, this steering committee demonstrated the ascension of the African mind as evinced by its central objective, "To serve as a vehicle of direct moral, military and territorial support to the African nationalists waging armed struggle in their respective territories."[13] The creation of the OAU and the objectives it set represented a serious threat to the colonial establishments as demonstrated by their response. Hendrik Verwoerd, the prime minister of South Africa from 1958 to 1966, Antonio Salazar, the Portuguese dictator from 1933 to 1958, and Ian Smith, the rebel leader in colonial Zimbabwe from 1964 to 1979, formed a military, economic, and political alliance to counteract the growing peril to their positions from the new power of the collective African mind.

Thus, a colonial "triple alliance" of sorts was formed for the exclusive purpose of sustaining the colonial status quo. But the more the members of the alliance attempted to mobilize their receding forces, the more the Africans became determined to restore their mind. In their respective actions, the members of the alliance and the OAU were drawing the battle lines. With the collapse of the Federation of Rhodesia and Nyasaland, the psychological effect on the ability of the "triple alliance" to offset pressure from OAU was profound. The colonial forces that they once commanded were now in disarray and in retreat, a victim of the prowess of the rising African mind. Times had changed; it was no longer possible to control African cognition in the way colonial conditions had done in the past. It was the Africans' turn to establish terms for interaction between the colonial governments and themselves.

In 1973, on its tenth anniversary, the OAU had become more than a symbol of the rapidly expanding consciousness among the Africans. It represented the reality of the prowess of their mind. It had become "a powerful machinery at the disposal of the oppressed Africans as they yearned to breathe free in a hostile environment."[14] As the struggle for that freedom was reaching a critical stage in Angola, Mozambique, Namibia, South Africa, and Zimbabwe, the OAU fortified the political gains it had made and converted them into a military and diplomatic strategy, placing the "triple alliance" in a defensive posture. The OAU was now playing the psychological game that the colonial governments had conducted with impunity to subdue the Africans.

Hendrik Verwoerd's assassination in 1966 by a white colonist disillusioned with the policy of apartheid created new political conditions that John Vorster, who succeeded him, could not fully understand and control. Recognizing the vulnerable position in which the "triple alliance" found itself, the OAU now directed its efforts toward the struggle in Angola and Mozambique. On May 25, 1974, the Portuguese military led by General Antonio de Spinola, convinced that Portugal was fighting a losing war against the African nationalist guerrillas, staged a military coup that removed Marcello Caetano from office and immediately sued for peace with a promise of independence in 1975.

John Vorster and Ian Smith were desperate, for they knew that the "dual alliance" they maintained was not strong enough to halt the avalanche of African awareness as it slowly began to gain momentum. The snowball was rolling down the hill, and at the bottom stood Rhodesia and South Africa. This success boosted the OAU's morale as it translated its accomplishments into an intensification of the struggle to free the African mind once and for all. The fortunes of the African mind and those of the colonial governments were now reversed. The tables had turned. The process of the transformation of the African mind in South Africa would not be completed until the elections held in April 1994 which brought apartheid to an end.

To add a critical dimension to its strategy, the OAU also successfully persuaded the international community through the UN to design a multi-dimensional plan to terminate the colonial governments in Africa. The success that the OAU scored on this front made it a credible player on the stage of international relationships. The OAU was fast becoming a new rising star in representing and promoting the role that the African mind was destined to play. Nobody could deny the African mind a place in the sun; its fifteen minutes of fame had just begun, thanks to the crucial role that Kwame Nkrumah played as a continental leader who dared to dream of things that never were and to ask why not. That is, as far as his vision would allow him to go, from this point on it was a downhill run. The rise of the African mind was about to suffer a severe setback, betrayed by the African leaders themselves.

NKRUMAH'S DEMISE AND THE BETRAYAL OF THE AFRICAN MIND

The success that Nkrumah achieved in Ghana and throughout Africa was not without cost. By 1966, three years following the founding of the OAU, Nkrumah had become the brightest hope, the beacon light of African political aspirations. In his effort to create new conditions for the self-actualization of the African mind, Nkrumah was trying to build what he thought was a lasting monument to the resurgence of the African mind. His restless mind began to conceive new strategies for accelerating the collapse of the colonial governments and the ascent of the African mind.

Slowly, he became increasingly intolerant of the snail's pace of change in Africa and of differing ideas that were expressed by his fellow Africans. He seemed to forget that they were just as enthusiastic about bringing the end of colonialism as he was. Slowly but surely, Nkrumah became a victim of his enormous power. He began to think that only his ideas were correct and that anyone who expressed ideas or points of view different from his were traitors.

Nkrumah's reputation as a true son of Africa was gradually being converted into a reputation as a callous leader who placed his own interests above those of the people he led. In his desire to end colonialism quickly, Nkrumah adopted methods for dealing with issues that actually entailed dictatorial behavior. He was not aware that power has a way of corrupting those who have and use it. The Nkrumah that had become the *osagyfo*, the George Washington of the continent of Africa in 1957, had by 1966 shown the malevolent side of his humanity. Between 1963 and 1966, when he thought that he was the undisputed *osagyfo* of the continent, Nkrumah appointed men to serve in his government and demanded their absolute loyalty to him personally.

There was nothing unusual about this demand, for all over the world leaders of governments commonly demand loyalty from the people who work in their administrations. But when viewed in the context of the struggle for independence in Africa, this practice acquired questionable elements. For Nkrumah the practice suggested that he wanted to use his associates to promote his own image as a continental leader with an agenda for action that he and he alone could conceive.

Nkrumah's unsavory political behavior began only one year after independence. In 1958 he surprised his countrymen by introducing legislation giving him power to detain without trial for five years any person suspected of opposing his program. The very thought that anyone who opposed Nkrumah's policy and program could go to prison for five years was a frightening reality, totally unbecoming to a leader who claimed to represent all of Africa's political aspirations. What had happened to the ideas he espoused so vehemently during the conference of African nationalists held in London in 1945?

What had happened to his constant criticism of the colonial systems in Africa as undemocratic? What had happened to his belief that anything imposed on man is likely to invoke a negative response that may lead to social conflict?

All important aspects of his education became meaningless as Nkrumah sought to implement his programs and policies in total disregard of the democratic process that had been so vital a part of his campaign against the British. In this kind of setting, the mind of black Africa, both in Ghana and the rest of black Africa, was being betrayed by the action of a man in whom it had placed its total confidence. Nkrumah was out for his own interests.

The colonial governments in Africa had introduced the practice of preventive detention measures to silence political opponents, and in the

Gold Coast Nkrumah had utilized his opposition to it to arouse a new level of consciousness among the Africans. Ironically, now that he was in power, Nkrumah should use the measure he knew the people would not accept. Nkrumah had forgotten that it was not the fulfillment of his objectives and programs that counted, but the method he used, democratic process or dictatorial action. In theory, Nkrumah argued that the detention bills and other measures that he forced through Parliament would be used only in cases of emergency. In practice, he used them all in an arbitrary manner to silence his political adversaries and the critics of his policies and programs.

Between 1958 and 1966 the people of Ghana recognized that in his obsession with the end of colonialism in Africa and his ambition to create the United States of Africa with himself as president, Nkrumah had put his own political interests above those of his people and country. Soon, his power to control society became absolute. The press, radio, and other media were silenced or forced to sing his praises as he converted them into an instrument to advance his argument that the newly independent countries of Africa must have strong governments so as to unite the people, mobilize resources, and demonstrate that, indeed, political change had taken place.[15] In the activities and agenda of Nkrumah's Convention People's party, his control of the country steadily grew to the point where he controlled every aspect of national life. Trade unions, youth organizations, farmers' associations, the civil service, and any other organization that carried national significance came under his direct control. Slowly the *osagyfo* was alienating himself from the people he was there to serve. Christianborg Castle became more than an official residence; it now became a symbol of an oppressive institution and a callous and ruthless administration.

By 1961 Nkrumah had developed such a personality cult that he began to believe that he was bigger than life. He took on such titles as Man of Destiny, Star of Africa, His Dedication, Victor in War. The title of *osagyfo* was no longer sufficient to satisfy his enormous ego. Nkrumah was derailing the course the African mind had charted since 1945. He was not aware that in his action to brighten his own star, he was being disloyal to the African mind that he had dedicated himself to transform. Nkrumah's attempt to compare himself with Vladimir Lenin, Abraham Lincoln, and Mahatma Gandhi accentuated the grotesque and the absurd. Nkrumah's political fortunes were suffering an irreplaceable loss at his own hands.

In Accra *The Evening News*, which, of course, he fully controlled, ran an editorial in 1961, stating that when the history of Africa was written, the name Kwame Nkrumah would be presented as the liberator, the messiah, the Christ of his day, whose mission was to bring political independence to Ghana and to Africa as a whole.[16] As if this was not enough, Nkrumah announced a new political ideology that he appropriately called *Nkrumaism*, which he defined as a political philosophy designed to distinguish himself from all other leaders in Africa and as a semi-supernatural being whose savvy was the ultimate salvation of Africa.

Following a series of assassination attempts from August 1962 to January 1964, Nkrumah removed from office Arku Korsah, chief justice of the Supreme Court, because he had dismissed charges against the accused for lack of evidence. He placed the legal system under his personal direction. By this time there was no opposition, either in Parliament or in the country, to his policies and programs. Nkrumah had turned Ghana into a one-party state with one-man rule. He had, in effect, become a dictator. His betrayal of the African mind was now complete. For the next two years, from 1964 to 1966, only Nkrumah held all the political cards. Ghana's destiny rested squarely in his hands. At last, he thought that he was secure in his position to carry out his programs without any opposition or criticism. But surprise was around the corner for him. On February 24, 1966, while he was on an official visit to Hanoi at the invitation of Ho Chi Minh, the army staged a coup and removed him from office.

Nkrumah went into exile and died in 1972 without achieving his dream of creating the United States of Africa with himself as president. Nkrumah left a legacy that has become a major problem for Africa. His failure to rise above the ordinary human tendency to serve the self set a precedent that in turn has set in motion the betrayal of the African mind from which it has not been able to recover. For the people of Ghana, democracy has remained as elusive as it was under the British colonial government. The curse of Christianborg Castle was to fall on the rest of Africa.

INDEPENDENCE AND THE BETRAYAL OF THE AFRICAN MIND IN NIGERIA

Nkrumah's fall left behind a trail of continental practices that have set Africa on a tragic course. In this regard Nkrumah's legacy is evident in two important aspects of the rise of the African mind and its struggle to restore itself. The first is that in Ghana succeeding administrations have not brought about the true democracy that it enjoyed at the inception of independence. Instead, military dictatorships, coups, and countercoups have been the *modus operandi*. The betrayal of the African mind has been effected in a cruel twist of fate. In essence, apart from the short period following independence, Ghana has never enjoyed a democratic form of government that the Africans fought so hard for after 1945. The second aspect is that nearly all the countries that gained independence in Africa since Ghana have adopted a similar practice having instituted either a one-party or one-man dictatorship.

The curse of Christianborg Castle has been a painful experience for the Africans. In these totalitarian governments lies the tragedy of Nkrumah's legacy. As African countries gained political independence, the governments they formed showed no regard for the needs of the people.[17] The rest of this chapter presents evidence that, in failing to sustain the democratic principles and values of their struggle for self, certain Africans manipulated political independence to betray the mind of their fellow Africans.

To support this conclusion this chapter discusses specific examples, beginning with the brutal civil war in Nigeria and concluding with the tragic civil strife in Angola and Mozambique. When Nigeria gained independence in 1960, three years after Ghana, the British government hoped that the new nation would become a showcase of the democratically run African nation. The reason for this optimism was that Nigeria had more educated people than Ghana. There were other important differences between Ghana and Nigeria that raised hopes that Nigeria was geared to show the perfect example of a model system that Britain was trying to promote as the ideal African state. First, in Ghana, Nkrumah ran a one-man show, dominating the entire scene. Ghana is a small country in which diverse groups of people do not exist.

In contrast, Nigeria is a huge country with a powerful regional leadership system. Second, the federal character of the Nigerian constitution was so designed that power was not concentrated in the hands of one man as in Ghana; rather, it was distributed evenly among several levels of federal authority and regional leadership. In this manner, Nigeria would provide a promising example of carefully structured, balanced, stable parliamentary democracy needed to bring about national development.[18]

Democracy had a better chance in Nigeria than in Ghana because Nigeria had no single individual ruler with megalomanic tendencies and total power as Nkrumah. Obafemi Awolowo, Nnamdi Azikiwe, Abubaker Tafawa Balewa, and Chief Akintola, to name only a few, were men whom the British Colonial Office had tried to educate and groom carefully to assume the reins of a democratic government in a responsible and prudent manner. Respect for constitutional democracy seemed to guide the principles of early national development as several parties began to form in 1963 in preparation for the elections scheduled for 1964, the first since independence was obtained.

These parties included the United Progressive Grand Alliance (UPGA), the Nigerian National Alliance (NNA), and the Nigerian National Democratic party (NNDP). Observers concluded that the creation of these parties was a healthy sign for the political future of Nigeria because they made it difficult for one party or man to emerge to impose a dictatorship as had happened in Ghana. This, in the mind of many, enhanced the prospects for democracy. But in 1965, in spite of this apparent thorough preparation, evidence began to mount that the politicians were coming under the corrupting influence of the political power they possessed.

Within a few months of the formation of these parties, there was an ominous and unsettling turn of events. When the nominations for candidates closed on December 19, 1964, in preparation for balloting, it was discovered that sixty-one candidates, most of them from the North, had been returned unopposed. That most of these seats were held by NNA raised serious questions about the fairness of the elections. Matters came to a head when UPGA accused NNA of violating the constitution. The elections were marred by bribes, threats of violence, arson, and assaults. Thugs were hired to hurt prominent candidates of every opposing party.

Chief Akintola's NNDP made very effort to turn the election results in its favor. Balewa and Azikiwe, two distinguished and seasoned politicians who were trying to lead their country into a sane direction were neutralized by events they did not understand and could not undo. The betrayal of the African mind that had started with Nkrumah was now slowly showing its ugly face in the national malaise in Nigeria as citizens all over Africa were feeling the spreading curse of Christianborg Castle.

During the next two years Nigeria painfully disintegrated, torn apart by individual politicians who were vying for power they did not know how to use for the benefit of the country. These events ultimately led not only to the end of the constitutional government that Britain was hoping would become a model democratic state in Africa, but also to a climax of unprecedented violence. On January 15, 1966, one month before Nkrumah's fall, a group of young military men mounted an assault on the entire political system. In the early hours of the morning they seized the federal prime minister, Abubaker Tafawa Balewa, dragged him outside the city limits, executed him, and threw his body into a ditch. They also killed Akintola following a brief battle between rival military units. For several days Nigeria was subjected to plunder and murder on a scale that had never been seen in the past, not even during the tribal conflicts that periodically broke out prior to colonization in the nineteenth century.

As various military units tried to gain an upper hand, they created a carnage that reduced the country to rubble. Anarchy and chaos ruled supreme as government functions came to a halt and installations were destroyed. There was death in the street, death in the homes, death everywhere. City after city was the target of military units that did not know why they were killing. Men, women, and children were subjected to extreme brutality by a system that had gone berserk. The rise of the African mind that had become a hallmark of African ability to rationalize its action was being betrayed in traumatic ways.

In Lagos, trying to make sense of what was happening, Major-General Aguyi-Ironzi, alerted by the wife of one of his murdered officers, attempted to rally loyal troops in an effort to bring about a semblance of law and order. In Kaduna, where the Sardauna of Sokoto, the premier of Northern Region, was brutally murdered, Major Chukwuma Nzeogwu declared martial law and dissolved the regional assembly, placed its members under arrest, and ordered their execution without trial. Realizing that the country was in the throes of a painful death, Ironzi proclaimed himself head of state of the national government, but his inability to bring about peace and stability quickly eroded his credibility.

Nigeria had entered a new phase, a self-destructive and violent civil war. Ironzi, an Ibo from the Eastern Region, was viewed by the Hausas, a tribe from the North, as a self-seeking individual bent on revenge for the poor treatment of his people. Hausas and other ethnic groups believed that Ironzi's regime was going much further than getting rid of corrupted politicians and restoring national stability, as he claimed in justifying his action. In this setting, Ironzi was handicapped by fear, suspicion, and resentment from the Northern Region.

Ironzi's effort to govern was sabotaged by his own actions. Wishing to protect the Ibos from attack by the Hausas, he filled key military positions with Ibo appointments. By May 1967, Ironzi issued a national proclamation abolishing the federal system and concentrating all power in his hands. All tribal and political organizations were banned. Nigeria, like Ghana, was now a one-man dictatorship. Reaction to Ironzi's measures came quickly from all over the country. In all regions civil servants were joined by students and huge crowds in demonstrating against his decrees. Hundreds of demonstrators went on a rampage of terror, attacking Ibos wherever they could find them and killing 30,000 within a few weeks.[19] In July 1967, junior military officers from the Northern Region staged a countercoup that caught Ironzi by complete surprise. They seized and quickly executed him. For nearly a decade Nigeria was without a properly constituted government. The betrayal of the African mind had taken a heavy toll, for no individual wanted to risk his life by appearing to want to take control of events, to influence the direction things were moving, or to try to bring stability to a rapidly deteriorating situation. The African mind was experiencing an all-time low, and its self-esteem was severely affected.

In the chaos and confusion that followed Ironzi's execution, new elements came into play that would have a profound impact on the national character of Nigeria. In the chess game of political power and grandstanding, Colonel Yakuba Gowon emerged as a new player, trying to bring the country to its senses. Fearing new reprisals from the North, represented by Gowon, Lieutenant Colonel Emeka Ojukwu, a thirty-four-year-old Ibo officer educated at Oxford University in Britain, flatly refused to accept Gowon as a new national leader. Ojukwu, seeking to exercise political power, rallied the Ibos behind him.[20]

With this show of political power, Ojukwu severed all ties with the federal government that Gowon now claimed to lead and tried to restructure the nation following nearly five years of national chaos and anarchy since Ironzi's demise. In October 1967 Ojukwu ordered the expulsion of everyone who was not Ibo from the eastern region. He also refused to send delegates to the constitutional conference that Gowon had convened in Lagos and to travel there himself to discuss the future of the country.

When Ojukwu issued decrees appropriating all federal revenues collected in the eastern region, Gowon thought that he had gone too far. In his effort to restore the credibility of the federal government that he was now leading, Gowon created an even more explosive situation. He and Ojukwu entered into a dangerous phase of national conflict and reached a new height in the betrayal of the African mind. Instead of accepting Gowon's move as an effort to restore the integrity of the country, Ojukwu saw it as a move designed to oppress the Ibos. On May 30, 1967, Ojukwu proclaimed the independence of Iboland as the independent state of Biafra, with himself as president. In July, after futile efforts to persuade Ojukwu to rescind the proclamation, Gowon moved troops into the region to assert his claimed authority.

Thus began one of Africa's bitterest and bloodiest civil wars. For the next three years the hatred and killing recognized no limits as Ojukwu's forces and Gowon's army clashed with such ferocity that it defied comprehension. More than a million people, most of them civilians, were killed by both sides. On January 10, 1970, tired and demoralized, Ojukwu found himself on the losing side of the conflict as he fled the country and went into exile in the Ivory Coast. Still defiant, he warned that Gowon intended to carry out the genocide of the Ibos. But to Ojukwu's surprise Gowon vigorously pursued a policy of clemency, general amnesty, and reconstruction.

Of course, the country had been laid to ruin. Gowon also reabsorbed Biafran military units into the federal army, and the process of restoring the Nigerian African mind now began in earnest. These efforts, however, would yield only minimal results. From that time to the present, Nigeria, like

Ghana, has enjoyed brief periods of democratic experiments, but these experiments have not resulted in the restoration of the African mind as it was originally envisaged by the delegates to the London conference in 1945 and by the British government at the time of independence in 1960.

Since the end of the civil war in 1970, Nigeria has been struggling to find itself again. The task has not been easy. Although it has experienced brief periods of democratic administration, it has been ruled by ruthless military men who seek to sustain power for its own sake. Like post-Nkrumah Ghana, Nigeria has experienced one military dictatorship after another, with no clear-cut lines of national development. In this setting, the political independence in both countries has brought about a betrayal of the African mind in tragic and painful ways. Indeed, the African mind has been left in the twilight zone of national programs. In 1990 Ibrahim Babangida, then military ruler of Nigeria, recognized the disastrous course that his nation had taken and its cost in betraying the African mind: "We in Africa must quickly learn to give full reins to our inborn adaptive and creative technological capabilities. We must strive towards the minimization of income differentials among our people through an efficient system of publicly accountable bureaucracy through the promotion and sustenance of our own cultural identity."[21]

As a military man, Babangida seemed to ignore a key consideration, not only for Nigeria, but also for Africa as a whole—that is, whatever the government attempts to do in the name of national leadership is bound to fail if its effort is not anchored in the educated mind of the people. In order to generate this level of confidence, retapping these intellectual resources requires a fundamental recognition that observing democratic principles is a prerequisite of any national endeavor. In concluding, "Our dream of tomorrow's Africa must nurture a new national spirit. We must discover new bearings. To succeed we need imagination and vision,"[22] Babangida missed a very important point in not acknowledging that imagination and vision cannot be promoted under military dictatorship. Babangida seems to dismiss the philosophy of collective wisdom that must be embedded in democratic behavior.

To place undue emphasis on national leadership, most of which is military in Africa, is to neglect the powerful potential that is found in abundance in the people. Failure to recognize this basic truth has led Nigeria to endure the price of underdevelopment. A critical component of the tragedy of Africa is that the African leadership must recognize that the betrayal of the African mind carries a costly national and continental price tag. There is no escape. Instead of emphasizing leadership per se, Babangida should have stressed how his nation must endeavor to return the country to its proper democratic foundations to allow proper and full utilization of the African mind.

On August 26, 1993, Babangida handed over power to a civilian administration headed by Chief Ernest Shanekan but which he fully controlled. The 250 tribes in Nigeria knew that the struggle for democracy was not over. Since July 5, 1993, when hundreds of people clashed with the police, Nigeria has been moving toward a major national disaster. After ten years of military rule, the country was in debt to the tune of 220 million pounds sterling.[23] Corruption by government officials has become an accepted way of conducting official business. Didi Adodo, a labor leader, concluded: "The colonists did not do as much damage to the Nigerians' psyche as Babangida has done."[24] Femi Adefope, owner of a travel agency in Lagos, added, "If you do business honestly, no one will do business with you."[25]

In discussing the betrayal of the African mind in Nigeria, *Time* concluded: "For some, the shame of being Nigerian has cut so deep that they are willing to contemplate what almost everyone in this fiercely proud country would have previously dismissed as unthinkable: inviting outside interference. The Campaign for Democracy has called for any international boycott of Nigerian oil until a democratic government takes office, even though that would push the economy into an even deeper slough."[26] In December 1993 *Our World* added that Nigeria ranked "as the third largest supplier of oil to the United States and oil production accounted for 80 percent of the government's revenue and 90 percent of the nation's foreign exchange. But mismanagement and corruption by government officials resulted in a $27.5 billion foreign debt."[27] If Shanekan hopes to succeed in his claimed mission to restore the mind of his fellow Nigerians to its proper place, he must demonstrate that he has a formula for applying a set of new ideas to do more than "to restructure the economy away from dependence on petroleum by diversifying it.,"[28]

In 1989 an educator in Zimbabwe shared with me his view that African leaders have used political independence to betray their own people:

It is sad but true that political independence in Africa has betrayed the African mind. I am not suggesting that political independence has been a bad thing for Africa; rather, I am saying that the African leaders have exploited political independence to betray the African mind in some painful ways, such as gross corruption by government officials, the imposition of military or one-party or one-man system of government, and the absence of frequent free and fair elections. Creative and imaginative mind cannot be utilized in the climate of the absence of democracy. Real leadership requires recognition of these critical elements of national life.[29]

That Babangida failed to recognize these elements is typical of the collective failure of just about all African leaders, black or white, to understand the real meaning of the African mind. There is no question that Babangida and other military dictators in Africa are the primary problem the continent has experienced in its endeavor to elevate its mind to its appropriate level, and the sooner they realize and accept it, the better.

Writing in November 1993 with special reference to the betrayal of the African mind in Nigeria, Associated Press writer Mark Fritz observed, "Nigeria's descent into raw dictatorship is only the biggest of many shattered dreams on this continent. Africa is in danger of becoming a graveyard of stillborn democracies. African nations have seen almost every bright hope impeded or derailed by power-thirsty rulers or ethnic animosities."[30] Fritz went on to discuss the degenerating conditions of life in Africa as examples to show that most national leaders in Africa have betrayed the mind of their own people. These include the action of Pascal Lissouba of the Congo who has become increasingly dictatorial, General Gnassingbe Eyadema who has ruled Togo for twenty-six years, and many other countries where the dream of democracy has turned into a nightmare.

INDEPENDENCE, ANARCHY, AND THE BETRAYAL OF THE AFRICAN MIND IN ZAIRE

As shown in Chapter 5, Zaire's attainment of political independence on June 30, 1960, came as a result of the resoluteness of the African mind and its unwavering resistance to subject itself to the colonial status quo any longer. Although the Africans of Zaire had been fighting for it, the announcement of impending independence in 1959 caught them by complete surprise. Many did not think that the Belgian government would grant independence within the time frame that it actually did. What the Africans did not know is that the Belgian government had come to the end of the road in seeking to resubject the African mind to the colonial conditions similar to those Leopold II used at the time he established the Congo Free State in 1878. The African mind was moving so fast that the colonial mind could not comprehend it or the events that it was generating.

Amidst the fanfare and excitement of impending freedom came a sad irony to the colonial legacy. As a condition for sovereignty, the Belgian government, in accordance with the practice established by other colonial powers, demanded that elections be held to determine what party should assume power at the inception of independence. Ironically, the colonial governments demanded elections as a prerequisite for independence but never provided the electoral experience in which Africans participated, so the confusion was immense as Zaireans were asked to do something they had never done before.

This act by the colonial establishments proved to be an inhibiting component of the retreating colonial systems in Africa. Differences of views and political philosophy quickly began to form and divide the Africans into a political quagmire of alliances; ultimately, at least a hundred political parties were formed, centered around ethnic groupings.[31] In this manner, the Africans were heading for a deadly confrontation that became the manifestation of the betrayal of the African mind. Although the election campaign in Zaire was relatively peaceful and was marked by an impressive absence of violence, the competition was actually between two men, Patrice Lumumba and Joseph Kasavubu.

When the elections did not produce a clear winner, Lumumba and Kasavubu engaged in political horse-trading in which Lumumba became prime minister and Kasavubu president as stipulated by the new constitution. The Africans of Zaire thought that their country had found a solution to the political problems that had handicapped the democratic development of other countries. With the end of colonial rule, the people's euphoria now translated into a new hope of building a nation. It would be one of the best independent countries in Africa because Zaire had vast mineral resources that had barely been tapped. They thought that this was a millennium for Zaire, for no country in Africa was quite comparable in its potential for development and greatness. Unaware of the curse of Christianborg Castle,[32] the people of Zaire thought that their country would be a model state in Africa, a showcase of the African mind unmarred by the bitter political feuding that became the typical miserable lot of many other African countries.

But as soon as the politicians tried to begin the task of governing a huge and bustling nation,[33] Lumumba and Kasavubu realized that it was much easier to demand independence than to lead a restive nation by democratic process. The orderly process, the logic and the reasoning that became the hallmark of Lumumba's political behavior as evidence of his brilliant mind, and the promise of greatness that compelled Belgium to grant independence sooner than it wanted to, quickly gave way to political histrionics and immaturity. The political savvy that the two leaders had utilized to bring the African mind out of its intellectual coma now failed to measure up to expectation.

The nationalistic rhetoric that had yielded good political dividends against the colonial government failed to convert an effective national policy into needed action. The charisma and brilliance that had elevated both Lumumba and Kasavubu to positions of influence and leadership simply disappeared in the wake of their lack of will to make decisions in the interests of the people. Only two months following independence, Lumumba's government was confronted by formidable problems it could not resolve. With no financial resources to run the country, he presented his program agenda to Kasavubu who refused to accept it because it did not include items he considered important. This political stalemate was the beginning of the parting of the ways, spelling disaster for both men and their country.

With no national program, Lumumba's administration had no budget. The democratic process that he and Kasavubu had promised to respect quickly gave way to the struggle for personal interests and ambition. In this degenerating action, the two leaders were betraying the African mind in malevolent ways as they allowed anarchy to take hold. On July 5, 1960, the notorious Force Publique, the national army that Leopold had utilized to implement his policy, mutinied because its members had not been paid since independence. Army units did not like what Lumumba and Kasavubu were doing, betraying the trust the people had placed in them. A week later, on July 11, Moise Tshombe, the strongman of the mineral-rich Katanga Province, announced that he was seceding from the Congo Federation. In this manner Tshombe was the Emeka Ojukwu of Zaire. Tshombe's action was supported by Belgian nationals who wished to protect their investment in the copper mining industry; thus, an all too familiar twist of fate was added to the colonial postscript. Tshombe had betrayed the African mind in his own way, just as profoundly and painfully as others had done.

A month later, on August 8, Albert Kalonji, the leader of the resource-wealthy South Kasai Province and an implacable political foe of Lumumba, proclaimed his mining state independent. While this was happening, Lumumba was having problems of his own with members of his administration. His cabinet included highly influential individuals who had nothing in common philosophically. This made it virtually impossible to pool their resources to structure an administration. It also made it impossible for them to provide an effective government, with confidence, and to confront the country's problems.

The people's needs could not be met. Constant bickering and disagreement made it unfeasible for Lumumba to mediate between such diverse positions and to advocate for one common one. Lumumba was placed in a role in which he was completely powerless and was unable to provide an effective national leadership. On the one hand, a powerful radical wing was being established and led by Antoine Gizenga and Abiciet Kashamura, men who were dominating most cabinet discussions and decisions. During the height of the crisis in 1961, Gizenga told UN Secretary-General Dag Hammarskjold (1905–1961) quite bluntly:

The people of the Congo do not understand that we, against whom aggression has been committed, we who are in our land, we who have made an appeal to international armed forces are systematically and methodically disarmed, while the aggressor, the Belgians, who are here in a conquered territory, still have their arms and the power of death and are simply being asked to go to certain parts of the Congo which some dare call Belgian bases.[34]

This was the wing that demanded immediate expulsion of all Belgian nationals because it believed that they were causing the country's problems as evinced by its support of Tshombe and Kalonji. On the other hand, Joseph Ileo, the brilliant, popular editor of the influential *Conscience Africaine*, and Jen Bolikongo, formed an equally strong opposition group to the Gizenga–Kashamura wing. Lumumba, presiding over a badly divided cabinet, was unable to solve national problems.

Lumumba was caught in the middle as he tried desperately to bring some unity to his cabinet who held widely different and conflicting views about national directions. The African mind was being reduced to a level even lower than it had been under colonial conditions. It was virtually impossible for Lumumba to formulate and implement a set of policies that would give meaning and purpose to independence. Lumumba was indeed beleaguered and embattled. The vitality of his mind that first surfaced in 1952 was brought to the ultimate test of wills that proved to be its own tragic betrayal. It had fallen far below the level of mediocrity. With it the country was falling apart. It seemed that no one could reach consensus out of competing regional interests, chronic mistrust, and personal ambition.

Finding himself president of an explosive nation and having an impotent prime minister at his side, Kasavubu took an action that proved a further betrayal of the African mind. He ordered Lumumba to decisively end the secession of both Katanga and South Kasai and to restore the country's unity. As the first step toward achieving this goal, Kasavubu ordered Lumumba to restore the integrity of his government so that it could focus on the problems the country was facing.

When Kasavubu threatened to dismiss Lumumba and his government if he failed to act along the lines he defined, the crisis surrounding the African mind in Zaire relative to independence took a perilous twist. Kasavubu now accused Lumumba of a lack of political maturity, and Lumumba accused Kasavubu of being an agent of Belgian colonial interests. Indeed, the future of Belgian nationals who were still in Zaire had become a source of conflict between Lumumba and Kasavubu. Kasavubu believed that Belgian nationals should be allowed to stay and contribute to the development of the country. Lumumba held exactly the opposite position, arguing that Belgium had previously made fortunes by exploiting the Africans and the resources of the country, and that as long as they remained, the Africans would never have any meaningful opportunity to run their own affairs independent of their influence. This was Gizenga's position, and although it brought him and Lumumba closer, it did not help solve the larger policy issues the government was facing. Nor did it persuade Kasavubu to see things from Lumumba's perspective.

With the two men unable to resolve their differences, their relationship rapidly moved toward the breaking point. With government operations paralyzed, the army in mutiny, Katanga and South Kasai seceding, and Lumumba's government in disarray, chaos and anarchy substituted for the potential of the Zairean African mind. Suddenly, in September 1960, Kasavubu announced that he was dismissing Lumumba as prime minister and Lumumba immediately announced that he was dismissing Kasavubu as president. The betrayal of the African mind had reached its lowest level in Zaire as the two major camps, those supporting Lumumba and those supporting Kasavubu, were unable to mend their political differences in the interest of the country.

The two camps were poised for a new wave of political violence. Fearing for his political life, Kasavubu ordered Joseph Mobuto, his chief-of-staff, to arrest Lumumba. Mobuto secretly handed him over to his bitter political foe, Moise Tshombe, who in turn ordered his soldiers to murder him. In an action that further suppressed the Zairean African mind, Kasavubu named Cyrille Adoula new prime minister, not Antoine Gizenga, the radical who had served as Lumumba's deputy prime minister. The betrayal of the Zairean African mind did not end with these developments. On the contrary, chaos and anarchy intensified to the extent that in August 1961 Dag Hammarskjold, the UN secretary-general, was forced to undertake a peace mission to help restore the African mind. He never completed his mission because he was killed in a plane crash in Zambia. The rumors were that the plane he was traveling in was sabotaged by members of Roy Welensky's ill-fated Federation of Rhodesia and Nyasaland, who were desperately trying to maintain the colonial status quo. In 1962 U Thant, the new UN secretary-general, presented a plan for restoring the Zairean African mind but with little success. Zaire was degenerating into a bitter civil war, and there was no solution in sight.

On June 30, 1964, on the fourth anniversary of Zaire's independence, Adoula, frustrated by his inability to restore his country and unable to provide the kind of leadership needed to reunify the country, resigned as a new wave of fighting erupted. Kasavubu's political fate was sealed as he invited Moise Tshombe and Evariste Kimba to take center stage in the current national disaster. Kasavubu, Kimba, and Tshombe all failed to cooperate in seeking a formula to resolve national problems. They also accentuated the environment of conflict by expressing disagreement in public and accusing each other of corruption and political ineptitude. The betrayal of the Zairean African mind was getting deeper.

Suddenly, on November 24, 1965, there was a new tragic turn of events in Zaire. On that day Joseph Mobuto, who, under Kasavubu, had assumed the rank of general, decided that the politicians had inflicted enough damage on the country and its future. He therefore staged a coup that sent Adoula to the gallows and Kasavubu, Tshombe, and Kimba to prison. Mobuto threw the ineffective legislature into the round file cabinet of political oblivion. He outlawed all political parties and activity. Thus, Mobuto instituted a new era of terror among the people by designing and pursuing a set of policies that set the country back to conditions worse than those prevailing under Leopold.

Under Mobuto, the Zairean African mind has been controlled in excruciating ways. He has become an absolute despot with only one purpose: to institute his own power and impose it with ruthless determination. He has become a new strongman, a little warlord, a small village tyrant whose whims are carried out without question. To this day, Mobuto's regime remains more oppressive than any the Africans have ever experienced. His slogan "Retroussons les manches" (Let us roll up the sleeves) was intended to make his treason of the African mind permanent.

The people of Zaire have never experienced the joy of living in a free society. Since 1965 Mobuto has depended on the French and Belgian Foreign Legion, a ruthless mercenary force, to keep him in power. In return, he has given both France and Belgium a free hand in exploiting the Africans, a charge that Gizenga and Lumumba had made earlier. Mobuto's reign of terror is the worst insult to date of the African mind. No African country had endured so much sorrow under a native African leader.

From time to time, since 1965, the Africans of Zaire have tried under very difficult conditions to resuscitate their suffocating mind by seeking to get rid of Mobuto. But Mobuto always uses a heavy hand to suppress them. The latest and most serious of these efforts were made in September 1991, when military units that Mobuto depended on for protection, joined civilian demonstrators in Kinshasa to demand an end to his brutal dictatorship and the restoration of the Zairean potential. The strength of the demonstration forced Mobuto to request French and Belgian assistance.

Robert Caputo, writing for *The National Geographic* in November 1991, decries the hardships that Mobuto has placed on Zaire, "While I was in Zaire, there was daily erosion of the currency and daily inflation. In one two-week period, the money in my pocket lost almost half its value. For workers in the towns the nightmare of frozen wages and skyrocketing food prices means few can survive on their salaries. Money had become virtually irrelevant in the economy that has turned to one of almost pure barter."[35] At the same time, reports have widely circulated that since 1965 Mobuto has stashed billions of dollars in European banks and has bought costly property there, while he has subjected his people to unbearable suffering. Indeed, Mobuto has become the Ferdinand Marcos of Zaire.

Using Mobuto as an example to show that African leaders have used their political power to betray the African mind and so have lost the will to provide adequate leadership needed to build a future different from the past, Adam Zagorin, writing to *Time* in February 1993, observed:

In Zaire shortages of food and gasoline are severe; road and rail links between major cities have been virtually swallowed by the encroaching jungle. Even in the capital's Mama Yemo hospital—named for Mobuto's deceased mother—children suffer without medication, and hundreds of victims of the AIDS epidemic die untreated. In the trackless bush, where millions of peasants and tribesmen still lived, the scourge of leprosy, trypanosomiasis and malaria are again pandemic. With inflation of 7,000%, banks are closed and people clutching sacks full of almost useless paper currency. Zaire's central monetary authority, which Mobuto has in the past treated as a personal piggy bank, is virtually bankrupt.[36]

The question now is: How long will the European nations allow themselves to be used by an African leader who openly starves the minds and bodies of his own people? How long will the people themselves continue to let a callous dictator continue his plundering ways? And how long will the international community continue to watch from the sidelines the unfolding tragedy that will have such severe consequences?

INDEPENDENCE AND BETRAYAL OF THE AFRICAN
MIND IN ANGOLA AND MOZAMBIQUE

Tragic events began to unfold in Angola and Mozambique following their attainment of independence in 1975. As shown in Chapter 5, the new Portuguese military government led by Antonio de Spinola, who replaced Marcello Caetano on April 25, 1974, was a cause of celebration for the Africans of this region because it meant the demise of the Portuguese colonial system as they knew it. De Spinola, the ruthless genius who had masterminded military operations against the ascending East African mind, deduced that Portugal would not win a military victory over the East Africans. He was at last convinced that the mind of the people could no longer be colonized. In 1973, de Spinola had experienced a change of mind regarding his earlier obsession to squash any African effort to achieve independence. That year he published his controversial book *Portugal and Its Future*. In it he argued for a diplomatic and political solution to the African struggle for independence. He postulated that it was in Portugal's best interest to allow the African colonies to exercise self-determination.

Caetano was infuriated by the suggestion, and conflict between the two men reached a crisis that led to the military coup that removed Caetano from office. This action paved the way for a truce that finally led to independence for Angola and Mozambique in 1975. The Africans had been waiting for this day nearly four hundred years. As soon as he assumed the office of president, de Spinola dispatched his foreign secretary, Mario Soares, to Angola and Mozambique to begin negotiations with the Africans about independence. On October 22, 1974, Portugal and the Africans under their domination reached agreements that would bring independence to both countries in 1975.

At this shining moment in the history of both Angola and Mozambique, there was an unexpected and cruel turn of events. In Mozambique the arrangements for independence were less complicated than in Angola. In 1962 the various nationalist organizations voluntarily decided to merge and form Frelimo with Eduardo Mondlane as president. When June 25, 1975, was set as the date for independence, Portugal simply handed over the reins of power to Frente de Libertaçao de Mozambique (Frelimo). He found it easy to assume power because it was the only political party in the country. Portugal, having satisfied itself that proper arrangements had been made, was happy to transfer power to a government led by Samora Machel. This means that the people of Mozambique were never given an opportunity to elect their own government, a slap in the face to the Mozambiquean-African mind. Angola presented a different problem. The three major liberation organizations that had been fighting for the restoration of the Angolan-African mind, UNITA, MPLA, and FNLA, signed a cease-fire agreement and began immediately working toward a constitution that would grant independence in accordance with de Spinola's ideas.

In January 1975 Agostinho Neto, Jonas Savimbi, and Holden Roberto met in Mombasa, Kenya, and reached an agreement on a set of conditions that they would want Portugal to respect in order to hold discussions about independence. On January 15, 1975, the three Angolan leaders and Portuguese officials met at Alver in Portugal and signed an agreement, setting November 11, 1975 as the date for independence. There were four conditions that they had stipulated. The first was that each nationalist group would contribute 8,000 men toward a national army. The second was that each leader was to be part of a transitional presidential triumvirate, with each man taking turns in the chairmanship of it. The third condition was that elections for a constitutional assembly would be held before independence, and the assembly in turn would elect the first national president.

In other words, the voters would elect members of the assembly, and the assembly would elect the president. One does not have to go far to see that this was a subtle but effective way to betray the mind of the populace. The fourth condition was that as soon as the national assembly was seated its first order of business was to elect the president and Portugal would immediately confer independence on Angola. That Portugal readily agreed to all four conditions suggests the strength of the Angolan-African mind at this juncture.

The election campaign in Angola immediately turned into a contest for personal power by the three leaders. The campaign was marred by violence, with each leader accusing the other two of gross irregularities. Portuguese officials were completely helpless. Two weeks into the campaign, political violence broke into a bitter struggle for domination. The parties now turned loose their forces against each other. As a result, the elections for the assembly were never held, so that there was no constitutional assembly to elect the first national president. As November 11, 1975, steadily approached, Portugal faced two choices: to postpone independence until the fighting had stopped so they could resume the election campaign, or simply to hand over power to a man or party that seemed to have control of the situation. After a period of indecisive agony, de Spinola instructed Admiral Leonel Cardoso, Portuguese high commissioner, not to ask the parties to postpone the date for independence.

Portugal clearly wanted to get out of its African colonies as quickly as possible. After four hundred years of colonial rule, no one could blame them. The three African leaders and their parties were intensifying the fighting with no hope of holding the scheduled elections. Soon after midnight on November 10, 1975, Cardoso simply lowered the Portuguese flag at the assembly building in Luanda, read a brief statement officially granting independence to Angola, and without handing the credentials of transferred power to a specific person or party, hurriedly left for Portugal during the night. Angola had been plunged into a vicious betrayal of the Angolan-African mind. Soon after midnight the MPLA, a socialist group, declared itself the government of Angola, and Neto assumed the office of president.

Within a few days Jonas Savimbi, UNITA leader, launched a campaign of massive destruction killing and laying waste to anything that lay in his path. Using the financial assistance he received from the United States during the Reagan administration, Savimbi and UNITA brought death and suffering to the people of Angola that was far more extensive than the

Africans had endured under four centuries of Portuguese colonial rule. Savimbi ignored appeals from the UN and the OAU to use peaceful means to solve the enormous problems Angola was facing. Arguing that MPLA was a communist agent, Savimbi refused to listen to the appeals and continued to pillage and plunder. Simple village people were subjected to the wrath of a man whose own mind was betrayed by both the conditions he had lived under and his own failure to come to terms with new situations.

The brutality, rage, and destruction reduced the mind of black Africa in Angola to the lowest point in all its history. As 1991 came to a close, the betrayal of the Angolan-African mind had spread to Mozambique, where a rebel force financed by South Africa was carrying out a campaign of violence with major ramifications. The killing in both countries had reached alarming proportions with no end in sight. I saw this senseless brutality and campaign during a study trip to Africa in May 1994. The summit conference of African leaders met in Harare to consider ways of ending the carnage in both Rwanda and Angola. Savimbi was as defiant as ever, refusing to accept the outcome of the elections that had been monitored by international observers because his party had done very poorly.

This dark side of the betrayal of the African mind had a bright side when Hastings Banda, who had ruled Malawi with an iron hand since October 1964, was defeated by Bakili Muluzi in the elections that were held on May 19, 1994. Recognizing the betrayal that Banda's rule had been to Malawi, Muluzi observed: "The outcome of this election is the real freedom we have been waiting for for thirty years. We have finally shown Banda the exit door. We face a major task of ending poverty as a way of restoring dignity to our people. Once again Malawians have an opportunity to enjoy their freedom as human beings."[37] Muluzi's recognition that for thirty years Banda had betrayed the Malawian African mind suggests the need to initiate a process that would restore it in all aspects of national life.

SUMMARY AND CONCLUSION

We can make two disturbing conclusions about the attainment of political independence and the betrayal of the African mind. The first is that the colonial governments never gave the people electoral experience, so that their first experience with it was bound to be confusing and clumsy. When the colonial governments discerned what this inexperience was leading to and the Africans wrestled with democratic procedures, they failed to step in and facilitate the proper growth that only guided experience can provide. They washed their hands clean of the disastrous results of their granting independence to a people who for generations had no experience with it. In order to save their own political face, they hurriedly made quasi-constitutional arrangements, bringing the Africans into the electoral process as a condition for independence. Thus, when things went wrong, as they always did, they could blame the inferior African mind for failing to sustain the democratic values they had put in place for themselves during the colonial period. Thus, the granting of independence under these conditions was a betrayal of not only the African mind but the universal mind as well.

The second conclusion is that amidst all the excitement over independence, the Africans invariably failed to understand two fundamental principles as they assumed responsibility for governing: (1) The need to ensure that constitutional provisions had to be respected even if they were inadequate: this inadequacy could later be removed by constitutional amendments and would prevent the practice of resorting to violence; and (2) the idea that the government belonged to the people and that it was first and foremost for the people. Failure to uphold these two basic principles constituted the ultimate betrayal of the African mind. The colonial governments cannot be blamed for the failure of the Africans to uphold these principles. It is up to them to refine the poorly structured constitutional arrangements made by the colonial governments in order to serve the needs of their people and countries. One-man, one-party, or military systems of government that have become the order of things in Africa constitute a case of fools rushing in where angels fear to tread.

Basil Davidson captured the meaning of the betrayal of the African mind when he wrote in 1992:

The actual and present condition of Africa is one of deep trouble, a deeper trouble than the worst imposed during the colonial years. Some time now, deserts have widened year by year. Broad savannahs and their communities have lost all means of existence. Tropical forests such as the world will never see again have fed the export materials. Cities that barely deserve the name have spawned plagues of poverty on a scale never known in earlier times. Harsh governments or dictatorships rule over people who distrust them to the point of hatred. All too often one dismal tyranny gives way to a worse one. Despair rots civil society, the state becomes an enemy, bandits flourish.[38]

This critical situation suggests that Africa has a moral obligation and duty to restore the mind of its people to the level where it can help resolve the enormous problems the continent is facing. If it does not, the nightmare in Somalia in 1993 and the carnage in Rwanda in 1994 may well be a hint of things to come. With future so-called rescue missions looming on the horizon from Western nations, such as France initiated in Rwanda in June

1994, will Africa experience a new face on the old body of colonialism? Where does a continent in disarray fit into the so-called New World Order?

NOTES

1. Meredith, *The First Dance of Freedom: Black Africa in the Postwar Era*, p. 187.

2. Curtin, *Africa South of the Sahara*, p. 82.

3. Hapgood, *Africa in Today's World Focus*, p. 82.

4. Meredith, *The First Dance of Freedom: Black Africa in the Postwar Era*, p. 188.

5. Isaiah 1:1.

6. For example, in the wake of the demise of the Soviet Union in December 1991, Western experts concluded that the road to socialist utopia that the country had been trying to build since the revolution of 1917 was based on the vision of Vladimir Lenin and that this vision had taken seventy years to prove itself wrong.

7. *Time*, January 6, 1992, p. 22.

8. William E. Smith, *Nyerere of Tanzania* (Harare: Zimbabwe Publishing House, 1981), p. 147.

9. Christian Patholm, *Southern Africa in Perspective* (New York: Free Press, 1972), p. 243.

10. Robert Mugabe, "Literacy for All in Five Years," speech given in launching National Adult Literacy Campaign, July 18, 1983. Zimbabwe Ministry of Information.

11. Mungazi, *The Struggle for Social Change in Southern Africa: Visions of Liberty*, p. 85.

12. Hasu Patel and Ali Mazrui, *Africa in World Affairs: The Next Thirty Years* (New York: Third World Press, 1973), p. 38.

13. Yassin El-Ayouty, *The Organization of African Unity After Ten Years: Comparative Perspective* (New York: Praeger, 1975), p. 118.

14. Mungazi, *The Struggle for Social Change in Southern Africa: Visions of Liberty*, p. 87.

15. Meredith, *The First Dance of Freedom: Black Africa in the Postwar Era*, p. 188.

16. Ibid., p. 189.

17. The author does not take the position that political independence was a bad thing for Africa, but that the Africans were so excited about independence that they actually abused it.

18. Meredith, *The First Dance of Freedom: Black Africa in the Postwar Era*, p. 199.

19. Hapgood, *Africa in Today's World Focus*, p. 74.

20. Meredith, *The First Dance of Freedom: Black Africa in the Postwar Era*, p. 211.

21. Ibrahim Babangida, "The Challenge of Leadership," in Olusegun Obasanjo and Hans d'Orville (eds.), *Challenges of Leadership in African Development* (New York: Taylor and Francis, 1990), p. 20.

22. Ibid., p. 22.

23. *Time,* September 6, 1993, p. 41.

24. Ibid., p. 36.

25. Ibid., p. 41.

26. Ibid., p. 41.

27. *The U.S. Today*, "Our World: Nigeria," December 14, 1993, p. 1.

28. Ibid.

29. An educator, during an interview with the author in Harare, Zimbabwe, July 27, 1989. The educator declined to be identified because, he said, "I do not wish to appear to criticize my own government."

30. Mark Fritz, "African Democracy Takes a Backward Leap," *Arizona Daily Sun*, Flagstaff, November 21, 1993, p. 16.

31. Mungazi, *To Honor the Sacred Trust of Civilization: History, Politics and Education in Southern Africa*, p. 223.

32. Lumumba visited Ghana and held talks with Nkrumah in August 1960. The two men signed a secret agreement to form a Union of Ghana and the Congo.

33. Zaire is the second largest country in Africa after the Sudan.

34. *Great Lives: Patrice Lumumba* (London: Panaf Books, 1978), p. 139.

35. Robert Caputo, "Lifeline for a Nation: Zaire River," *National Geographic*, Vol. 180, No. 5, (November 1991), p. 24.

36. Adam Zagorin, "Leaving in His Wake: As Anarchy Grows Around Him Mobuto Sese Seko of Zaire Serenely Enjoys Lobster and Champagne in His Jungle Paradise," *Time*, February 22, 1993, p. 56.

37. Zimbabwe, *The Herald*, Harare, May 20, 1994, p. 1.

38. Basil Davidson, *The Black Man's Burden: Africa and the Curse of the Nation State* (New York: Times Books, 1992), p. 9.

7

The Mind of Black Africa: Past, Present, and Future

Colonized society is a diseased society in which internal dynamics no longer succeed in creating new structures.

Albert Memmi, 1965

Africa has become the basket case of the planet, the Third World of the Third World, a vast continent in free fall.

Time, September 7, 1992

THE MIND OF BLACK AFRICA IN PERSPECTIVE

This study has presented facts concerning the mind of black Africa in four areas of its development. The first area pertains to European perceptions about African cognition; the second is the African perception of itself; the third is how the African mind struggled to free itself from colonial oppression only to find the oppression continued by the African governments which they installed; and the fourth area is concerned with how the African mind is currently struggling to free itself from the repression imposed by present African governments.

Differences of perception between Europeans and Africans about the mind of black Africa were so great that as the two racial groups came into contact with each other, especially in the nineteenth-century era of colonization, they created a cultural chasm that grossly inhibited their ability to establish dialogue based on mutual respect and understanding. The study also discusses how important it was for the African mind to make necessary adaptations to survive under oppressive conditions once colonial governments were fully established.

The critical factor that later played a decisive role in the drama of conflict between the African mind and the colonial governments is that the colonialists erroneously concluded that in seeking to adapt to the new order of things the Africans accepted their domination. But colonial governments ignored two very important facts. The first is that no group of people in human history has willingly accepted conquest by another. This means that as long as colonial conditions exist, the colonized will always find ways to end them. The second fact is that colonialism is not destined to last forever because sooner than later the oppressed will rise up against their oppressor. In the context of colonization of Africa, the third focus area in this study indicates a sober irony of human relationships: people of one culture invariably assume they are superior and use the notion of their superiority to impose their will on the people of another culture.

By the same reasoning, the people whose culture is invaded take it upon themselves to restore their sense of self. In Africa this inevitable action constituted the context in which colonial governments were not destined to last forever. The rise of the African mind led to the conflict between the Africans and the colonial governments, which culminated in a restoration of political independence. Once the Africans became determined to rid themselves of colonialism, there was nothing that the colonial establishments could do to stop it from attaining its objective.

This study has also shown that Africa experienced the tragic betrayal of its aspirations by fellow Africans. The excitement that came with political independence derailed the success achieved by the African mind. During colonialism in Africa, the Africans never had an opportunity to participate in the affairs of their countries except in service as laborers and other menial tasks. On assuming the political power that came with independence, the African leaders made two cardinal errors that would cost them dearly in their efforts to carve out a new national character. The first is that they ignored the valued traditions that sustained African social institutions for hundreds of years before the Europeans came to Africa.

Among these traditions was the observance of democratic principles. European colonial governments' argument that Africans did not practice democracy is completely erroneous. It was the colonial systems that left the legacy of dictatorial behavior that the African leaders used as role models following the end of colonialism. The second error is that the leaders of the newly independent countries of Africa also adopted the methods that the colonial governments used in dealing with the people. As was the case during the colonial period, the leaders of the independent countries of Africa sought political office to maximize personal gain, not to serve the needs of their people.

The combination of these two errors resulted in the tragic betrayal of the African mind, a depressing irony to the end of the colonial systems. Instead of resurrecting the systems of democracy that existed long before the Europeans came to Africa, the African leaders imposed new forms of oppression that were just as vile and inhibiting as that of the colonial governments. This is why, beginning in 1990, the Africans entered into a new phase in asserting their individual and collective rights, demanding an end to any form of oppression as imposed by the African leaders. Clearly, the African leaders who imposed dictatorial systems on their people were unable to understand this dimension of the phenomenon of the rise of the African mind. They mistakenly thought that their people would accept their form of oppression but would reject that of the colonial systems.

How does one explain the incongruity that emerged between the European and African perception of the African mind? One answer we can make is to relate events to theoretical considerations. This chapter puts together the points made in the preceding chapters and succinctly presents the factors that have shaped African history. We begin with European perceptions of Africans and themselves.

RACE AND COLONIAL RACISM: SOME THEORETICAL CONSIDERATIONS

Many Europeans who came into contact with Africans, especially in the nineteenth and twentieth centuries, based their perceptions of them on the myth of their intellectual inferiority. This illusion was based on race and racism. Hermann Bleibtreu and John Meany discuss this myth, saying, "Racism is, by definition, a belief that individual's capacities are predetermined and limited and that their behavior is dictated by genetic membership in a group identifiable as a race. A racist sorts individuals into preexisting pigeonholes ascribing to the individuals the characteristics attributed to his race."[1] Bleibtreu and Meany conclude that racial characteristics are not fixed and can only be modified by the influence of environmental factors such as motivation, nutrition, education, culture, and the extent of human interaction.[2]

Two major problems arise from racism, one for the victim and the other for the victimizer. For the victim his performance in any line of human endeavor is always inadequate, no matter how hard he tries; his efforts are always regarded as flawed. In the eyes of the colonizer, this judgment is often based on prejudice, which dictates the conclusion that the colonized are inferior because they belong to an inferior race. For the colonized, racism inhibits his ability to rise above the level of cultural and racial prejudice to structure human relationships on the basis of mutual respect. The loss of respect for one group of people is the result of a cultural perception of their presumed inferiority. In this context, emphasizing cultural differences creates an assumption that one's own culture is superior.

Once the judgmental perception influences relationships between the people of two cultural groups, it becomes virtually impossible to develop respect because the notion of cultural and racial superiority stands in the way of understanding those who are different. This superiority complex has a devastating effect on the formation of attitudes from which policy ensues. Once prejudice becomes the *modus operandi*, it permeates every aspect of human thinking and behavior. The people whose culture is presumed to be inferior can do nothing to correct or influence the change in attitude. Bleibtreu and Meany also conclude that this kind of social climate creates a situation in which human relationships are permanently marred and eventually lead to conflict between the two cultural groups.[3]

Bleibtreu and Meany state that "Racist reasoning is the product of topological thinking which in turn is due to an ignorance of the process of evolution. The need to rationalize injustice and to assure his own superiority gives rise to the attributes with which a racist endows race."[4] In this kind of social setting, the racist uses his or her assumed superiority to promote his or her own culture and demean that of the people he or she considers inferior. Once he does this, he can freely castigate the people whose culture he considers inferior as lacking in basic intellectual potential and human endeavor. When cultural variation is cast in an educational setting, the racist is forced to conclude that only he has the necessary intellect to determine proper relationships between people of different races. When the behavior of the colonial governments in Africa is examined, one can easily see the application of these basic theoretical concepts to the reality of the kind of relationships that evolved between the Africans and the colonial systems.

The assumption of the European entrepreneurs that the Africans were inferior, fit only to supply cheap labor, was their principal justification for colonizing Africa and introducing forced labor. Their superiority complex had an adverse effect on both themselves and the Africans. When viewed in these cultural, racial, and intellectual settings, colonial conditions became increasingly oppressive with the passage of time. All the Africans could do was to try to adapt to those conditions in order to ensure their survival. It was also this strategy for survival that later led to the Africans' demand that colonial conditions be ended.

Oscar Lewis states that the *culture of poverty* is a critical dimension of racism as practiced by the racist. Lewis defines the culture of poverty as a thinking/acting dyad aimed at distorting the cultural values of a group of people so that the racist reaches the inevitable conclusion that they are void of any real potential, behaviorally and cognitively. By approaching the question of human relationships from this perspective, the racist denies himself or herself an opportunity to appreciate the positive attributes of the people considered inferior. He or she wants nothing to do with them because they have nothing of value to offer in human interaction.

The racist's intellectual poverty robs both cultural groups of an opportunity to know each other as human beings. Lewis concludes:

The culture of poverty, however, is not only an adaptation to a set of objectives but also shows inhibition of the larger society. Once it comes into existence it leads to perpetuate itself from one generation to another because of its effect on the children. By the time children are old enough to see the damage that has been done to them they have already observed the basic values and attitudes of their culture and are not psychologically geared to take full advantage of changing conditions or increased opportunity which may accrue in their life time.[5]

According to Lewis, the racist either pretends he does not know about the cultural values of the people presumed to be inferior or he simply does not want to know. This is precisely why colonial officials in Africa did not want to learn about the important cultural values of the Africans, including their languages. They assumed that learning these values would not help them gain basic components of human relationships so essential to understanding.

In denying themselves an opportunity to appreciate the African culture, the colonial governments perpetuated their ignorance, or the culture of poverty, that became the root cause of conflict after the Second World War when the African mind began to assert itself. In this self-deception, evident in their inability to comprehend the dynamics of the mind of black Africa, the colonial governments forgot the wisdom that Rabindranath Tagore so eloquently expressed in 1916, saying, "A mind all logic is like a knife all blade. It makes the hand bleed that uses it."[6] Indeed, Tagore's proverbial knife, represented by the rise of the mind of black Africa, later cut the colonial hand when the time was right. The intellectual culture of poverty often controls the mind of the racist so that his or her own rationality, rather than that of the colonized, affects relationships. It also inhibits the ability to see all people as possessing those qualities that are uniquely human, including an ability to perceive what is real. Rather, their limited potential is used to promote the belief that one has to function in a stratified political and socioeconomic system that was created to serve his or her own interests. In this context, racists live on borrowed time as they begin to live in a world of fantasy. Lewis argues that as in the case of the social system that existed during the feudal period, the modern-day racist uses "results from imperial conquest in which the native social and economic structures are smashed and the natives are maintained in a sterile colonial status for many generations."[7]

In this kind of setting, institutional structures and functions across cultures are rendered meaningless as the racist imposes on them his or her own definition of their purpose. Once put into effect under these conditions, the outcomes of institutional operations invariably oppress both the racist and the victims, the colonized. The mind of the colonizer is thus unable to function beyond the peripherals of a social order designed to sustain the myth of colonial cultural superiority and the assumed inferiority of the colonized. This situation oppresses both.

We can see the clear implications of these theoretical concepts in Africa. The formulation and application of the various forms of colonial policy show that Lewis offers an accurate explanation of why the colonial governments were never quite free in their interactions with the Africans. The application of the German policy of *Deutsche Kolonialbund*, the Portuguese *Estado Novo*, and the Afrikaner *apartheid* did not take into account the importance of promoting human understanding and institutional and cultural values because they were designed to sustain the myth of the racial superiority of Europeans. But in doing so these policies entrenched the reality of the cultural and intellectual poverty that Lewis concludes victimizes both the colonizer and the colonized. This is why the colonial officials never quite came to know the Africans as people capable of contributing to the general good of humanity. A leading educator in Zimbabwe shares this line of thinking:

One of the great tragedies of colonialism in Africa is that the white man never came to understand the mind of the African. Either he pretended he did not know or he simply did not want to know in order to form a justification for his conclusion that the Africans were inferior because they belonged to an inferior culture. The white man should have known that at some point in time, the mind of the African would rise to the occasion and demand fundamental change both in the attitudes and policies of the colonial governments. Their refusal to see things from this perspective inevitably created a climate of conflict and struggle for the restoration of the African mind.[8]

The result was that colonialism was doomed. This is why the colonial governments lasted far less than the thousand years that colonial enthusiasts such as Cecil John Rhodes had predicted they would. Rhodes made this arrogant prediction at the height of his power in 1896. Memmi presents a logical argument on the effect of race and racism on the mind of the colonized: "The economic meaning of colonial adventure, even if it is realized after arrival, thrusts itself upon the colonized no less strongly and quickly. But the discomfort of the knowledge that at some point in time the mind of the colonized will rise to demand change offers no advantages of colonization."[9]

Memmi argues that ignorance of the culture of the colonized is not bliss when the wisdom of folly demands knowledge. He adds that what makes colonial adventure a reasonable substitute for the comfort of the colonizer's own country is that he engages in psychological games to convince the colonized that he is inferior and that he must be grateful to his colonizer for bringing him the benefits of his civilization. The colonizer also uses this strategy to strengthen his racist attitude toward the colonized and proceed to exploit him politically, socially, and economically.[10] In doing so the colonizer systematically destroys the culture and institutional values of the colonized and forces him or her to develop a dependency complex.

Memmi also discusses the effect of racism on both the colonizer and the colonized. For him, colonial racism always symbolizes the nature of the relationship they are forced to have, dictating how the colonized must function and behave. In this process, this relationship invokes in the mind of the colonized a clear understanding of his own sense of self. He also understands that, although he is colonized physically, he must not allow his mind to be colonized as well. This knowledge becomes his salvation.[11] But to the extent that this relationship has only one object—to bond the colonized to the wishes and interests of the colonizer it imposes a condition of oppression that victimizes both. Whereas the colonized loses his proper sense of his social values and begins to doubt the true meaning of existence, the colonizer lives and operates under illusions cast in the infallibility of both thinking and behaving.

Memmi utilizes this context to conclude that this social environment, harmful as it is to both the colonizer and the colonized, helps spontaneously incorporate colonial racism in even the most trivial acts and words to the extent that it constitutes a fundamental pattern that forms the colonizer's personality.[12] In this unavoidable situation, the colonized cannot envision himself as a human being except in the meaningless imitation of the colonizer. In seeking to convince himself that manipulating the colonized's mind yields tangible results, the colonizer justifies his strategy of control based on the notion that he has a divine responsibility to salvage the colonized from the condemnation of his primitive culture. In this manner, both the colonized and the colonizer are trapped by a mental process that offers no escape.

Memmi suggests that colonial racism is built on three major ideological components: (1) the gulf that is forced to exist between the culture of the colonizer and that of the colonized; (2) the inevitable exploitation of the cultural differences for the sole benefit of the colonizer; and (3) the utilization of these differences to reinforce the notion that the colonized are inferior because they belong to an inferior culture. In this context, the colonizer thinks that the colonized must be grateful for bringing civilization to him. This forced condition brings out paternalism as a new *modus operandi*.[13] Therefore, the colonial governments considered race an absolute fact of irreconcilable differences in mental capacities and intellectual potential. For anyone in the nineteenth century to suggest that the Africans had a mind and an intellect capable of high achievement was to run head into a myth that had been accepted as fact. In seeking to maintain this myth to ensure their own survival, the colonial governments became prisoners of their own actions. They were never able to overcome their prejudice against Africans and get to know them as equal human beings. This was the social climate that created an environment of conflict.

Paulo Freire adds yet another dimension of thought relative to colonial racism. He argues that when taken to its full extent, colonial racism creates a confused duality of existence for the colonized and "establishes itself in their innermost being."[14] The important aspect of this concept is that the colonizer designs this duality of existence to impress on the colonized the idea that it is in their own best interest to accept his cultural values and, at the same time, the colonized must continue to function in his own cultural settings. What Freire considers disturbing about this duality of existence is that the colonizer has no respect for the culture of the colonized, and he does not really want him to be fully operative in his own culture.

This situation suggests the reality that the colonized is placed between a rock and a hard place. Freire concludes that this duality of existence can have two outcomes. The first is that it inhibits the colonizer's ability to see the viability and authenticity of the colonized's culture. Once this attitude sets in, he no longer sees the colonized as people, but rather as an object, an instrument for fulfilling the colonizer's purposes. The second outcome is that while it gives the colonizer a false sense of security, it enables the colonized to retain an unquestionable understanding of its manipulative intent. This understanding becomes a silver lining in the cloud of the colonizer's existence cast in the colonizer's racism.[15] Because racism is a social illness, colonial society is an unhealthy environment. Sooner than later, such a society dies from the inside. Racism brings about societal implosion.

"Colonial society," Memmi states, "is a diseased society in which internal dynamics no longer succeed in creating new structures. Its century-hardened face has become nothing more than a mask under which it slowly smothers and dies."[16] He suggests that the hard reality that the colonizer either refuses or fails to see is that a diseased society cannot perceive the future beyond itself. It is therefore unable to envisage the need for innovative ideas to benefit its people because it is preoccupied with maintaining the status quo, and the colonizer cannot maintain the status quo without losing the opportunity to obtain something new that can be utilized to heal the sick society. The problem is that the cognitive virus that afflicts the colonial society cannot be healed.

Whether or not the colonizer wants it, then, colonial society will die, and with its death the demise of the colonizer becomes inevitable. One must conceptualize it this way. Colonialism and the ancillary racism is analogous to HIV and AIDS in that the carrier/host eventually dies from an inability to heal itself. In this situation, the colonizer is unable to see that the institutions he created cannot be saved until it is too late. This study has shown that the colonial governments did not realize how much danger they were in until it was too late. South Africa traveled this road until 1990 when it was almost too late to save the country from disaster.

This discourse on theoretical considerations relative to the behavior of the colonial governments and the response of the Africans to it leads to two basic conclusions. The first is that no matter how much they wanted to assure the security of the colonial institutions they established, the colonial governments were not able to do so simply because they did not understand the African mind. Their declared intent of making profit out of both the Africans and the raw materials they went to Africa to obtain was so callously pursued that the Africans quickly became aware of what was happening and took necessary measures to preserve their integrity. The second conclusion is that, although the colonial systems oppressed the Africans physically, they did not oppress their mind as they would have liked. One of the major redeeming features of the African mind is its ability to retain its distinctive quality under severe conditions. This led ultimately to its salvation. The culture of poverty eventually proved to be the demise of the colonial governments.

THE CULTURE OF VIOLENCE AND THE CHARACTER
OF COLONIAL SOCIETY

The culture of poverty became the basis of the colonial governments' justification to engage in colonial adventure. The decision not to seek functional knowledge of African cognition was the main reason why the colonial governments concluded, without any evidence, that colonization was a blessing to the Africans because it was benevolently intended to rescue them from the imprisonment of their primitive culture.

Based on this delusion, the European nations vigorously pursued the colonization of Africa following the conclusion of the Berlin Conference. As colonization proceeded, the culture of poverty that had become its foundation now turned into the culture of violence. Memmi graphically describes how the colonial culture of poverty translated into the culture of violence. In this context, the colonized's traditions are eliminated or rendered meaningless, and his culture is forced to lose its meaning. This forces him to lose his language and the symbols of his values, his technical knowledge, his very existence and rights. He is then forced to give up everything that he holds dear as the conditions that govern his life become more oppressive. His hope for a better future for himself and his children is dashed as the colonial culture of violence becomes legalized and is converted into an instrument of oppression.[17]

The reality of the colonial culture of violence in Africa was not limited to the subjection of the African mind to oppressive conditions; it also manifested itself in physical and legal violence. The random cutting off of hands that Leopold initiated as a form of punishment for those laborers who failed to meet their daily rubber production quotas in the Congo Free State[18] symbolized the malevolence of the colonial culture of violence. The practice of forced labor that British colonial Africa introduced under the notorious Orders-in-Council in 1894[19] is yet another example of how the colonial culture of poverty translated into the culture of violence.

In 1964 Herbert Chitepo, president of the Zimbabwe African National Union, convinced his fellow Africans to recognize colonial conditions for what they were, "a situation of violence"[20] that only they could eliminate. Another example of colonial violence is imprisonment for failing to obey the infamous passbook laws. This combined both the legal and the physical forms of the colonial culture of violence. During the last twenty years of its existence, the government of South Africa acquired the status of an international pariah because it refused to discontinue this form of violence. The tragic part of the colonial utilization of the culture of violence is that the colonial governments used the culture of poverty to argue that this was good for the Africans.

All over Africa, the colonial culture of violence started with the blatant use of military force to subject the Africans to colonial rule. In every country of Africa, the colonial system was established by using brute military force, and the first viable evidence of the establishment of the colonial governments was the creation of a military police that actually terrorized the people they had colonized. Any action by the Africans to register a protest was dealt with swiftly and forcefully. The colonial culture of violence had been institutionalized as the absolute law that had to be obeyed. The Africans could not question this absolute power without expecting severe reprisals, a definite form of colonial frontier justice. To the colonial governments the gun became the majestic symbol of their power over the Africans and the only means for their security. In the hands of the colonial military force, the gun became the most visible symbol of the culture of violence.

Muted by conditions they could not control, the Africans understood the language of the gun, even though they would not speak to it in the same way it spoke to them. Their only response was to obey the orders issued by the colonial governments, and so the gun became a visible instrument of enforcement. There was no escape from the wrath and violence of this lethal weapon. In the end, the gun became synonymous with colonial violence. Freire argues that, regardless of the form of violence, the cause for the colonized is not lost as they must realize that "To surmount the situation of oppression, the oppressed must first critically recognize its causes so that through transforming action they can create a new situation, one which makes possible the pursuit of a fuller humanity."[21] This is the reality that the Africans took into account when they designed a strategy to confront the power represented by the gun in its manifestation of colonial culture violence. Matched against the power of the human mind and determination, the gun eventually became silent and so lost the power of its language.

Another component of the colonial culture of violence concerns the laws that the colonial governments enacted. According to Memmi, the fundamental purpose of the colonizer's law, as it related to the colonized, was to create pervasive fear and to force the emergence of a dependency complex. It is also designed to turn the colonized into cheap labor because colonial society does not have any need for trained technicians from among the colonized[22] because it depends on the colonized cheap laborer who becomes indispensable to the sustenance of the colonizer's socioeconomic privilege. Everything else contributes to this system of exploitation.

In this setting, the colonizer's law gives legitimacy to the culture of violence. Even the Africans' education constituted another important dimension of the colonial culture of violence. Two examples from colonial Zimbabwe illustrate the accuracy of this conclusion. The first is Ethel Tawse Jollie (1874–1950), speaking in 1927 in the colonial legislature in colonial Zimbabwe. One of the first women to sit in the legislature in colonial Africa, Jollie was quite blunt in expressing her support of a bill designed to reduce the Africans to the position no higher than that of laborers. "We do not intend to hand over this country to the Natives or to admit them to the same social and political position that we ourselves are enjoying. Let us make no pretense of educating them in the same way we educate whites."[23] Here again, the culture of poverty did not enable Jollie and other colonial officials to see that they did not have to hand over the countries they governed to the Africans; they would take back what was rightfully theirs.

The second example is from a high-ranking colonial official who argued in 1912, "I do not think that we should educate the Native in any way that will unfit him for service. The Native is and should always be the drawer of water and the hewer of wood for his white master."[24] Indeed, on July 19, 1912, the colonial legislature passed Ordinance Number 7: To Control Native Schools exactly along the lines that the official had suggested. Only the Africans were treated in this manner. When one understands the intent of the colonial legislature, the colonial culture of violence becomes evident.[25] These two examples clearly show that the colonial legislatures in Africa institutionalized the culture of violence as an important instrument of controlling the African mind. It is hard to believe that in enacting legislation to accomplish this objective the sole purpose was to reduce the Africans to a level where they would function only as laborers. Without question, one can also conclude that the colonial governments institutionalized the educational process as a form of the culture of violence. Here the innate character of the Africans manifested itself when it was forced to adapt to the colonial conditions in order to survive.

Just as the colonial governments had instituted the culture of poverty, they also designed legislation to make the colonial culture of violence legal so that the Africans would not question it. This gave the colonial governments power to deal ruthlessly with any Africans who felt compelled to react negatively in order to ease the suffering to which they were subjected. One does not need Galileo's genius to see that the colonial governments refused to acknowledge the extent of the suffering the colonial culture of violence had inflicted on the Africans. This is what Freire has in mind when he argues that the relationships between the oppressor and the oppressed create a situation in which the oppressed are "thwarted by injustice, exploitation, oppression, and violence from the oppressor."[26]

Albert Schweitzer (1875–1965), the famous German missionary to nine-teenth-century Africa, fully recognized the extent of this colonial culture of violence when he wrote toward the end of his life, "Who can describe the misery, the injustice, and the cruelty which the Africans have suffered at the hands of Europeans? If a record would be compiled, it would make a book containing pages which the reader would have to turn unread because their contents would be too horrible."[27] In fact, colonial governments survived by imposing the culture of violence; this violence could not be eased and still enable them to justify their policies. The survival of the African mind was ensured in the rejection of the argument that colonization was a civilizing act. Therefore, powerful as it was, the colonial culture of violence did not accomplish its intended objective–to subject the African mind to colonial control.

RABINDRANATH TAGORE ON THE COLONIAL CULTURE OF VIOLENCE

One prominent thinker who has articulated the effect of the colonial culture of violence is Rabindranath Tagore (1861–1941). Tagore was born and lived all his life under colonial conditions in India and he was a mentor to Mahatma Gandhi (1869–1948). Because Tagore's ideas are relevant to colonial conditions in Africa, this part of the study briefly discusses the salient aspects of these ideas. Recipient of the 1913 Nobel Prize for literature, Tagore understood the impact of the colonial culture of violence perhaps better than other individuals whose lives were controlled by colonial conditions. In his *The Unity of Education* written in 1921, Tagore concluded that because Western nations utilized their education to engage in empirical thinking consistent with Western cultural values, they came to believe that the fate of the world and the people in it could easily come under their political control just as it had been during the height of the Roman Empire.

Tagore argued that the inherent weakness of Western cultures is its negative perception of other cultures and their inability to recognize that other societies have the capacity to contribute to the general good of humankind.[28] This low regard of non-Western cultures was evident in the behavior of European nations toward people in their colonial empires.[29] Tagore's conclusion that the inability of Western nations to recognize the viability of other cultures threatened the fundamental concept of human understanding that was evident in the behavior of the British colonial government in India. The practice among European colonial governments of creating horizontal relationships with the people they ruled precluded the possibility of building bridges to human understanding. Under these practices, colonial officials operated under the assumption that the colonized people were inferior.

The culture of violence had its origins in this line of thinking. Once the colonial governments placed themselves under the influence of this thinking, their mind became as much a victim of their action as the people in the colonial empires who were under their political control. Tagore concludes that after the colonial governments instituted the culture of violence, it was virtually impossible to see it as violence. It is in this context that conflict between the colonial governments and the colonized becomes inevitable.

Tagore further concludes that the net result of this colonial pattern of behavior is that it inhibits the ability of the colonizer and the colonized to the extent that the colonizer is totally unable or unwilling to understand and appreciate the plight of the colonized as the two groups become strangers to each other. For this reason, Western nations needed a new form of education to free them from the oppression of their own negative attitudes and action. New forms of education would help them appreciate the potential of the people they controlled and their ability to engage in meaningful human interactions in order to find common ground on which to initiate the search for solutions to universal human conflict.

Taking this line of thinking, Tagore observed,

I find much that is deeply disturbing in modern conditions. I am more conscious of the inevitable and inescapable moral links that hold together the fabric of human civilization. I cannot afford to lose my faith in the inner spirit of man, not in the sureness of human progress. We have seen Europe spread slavery over the face of the earth. Exploitation and social violence become easier if we can succeed in denying educational creativity and generate a callous attitude towards those who are their victims.[30]

Tagore's notion that the negative attitudes of European nations toward other cultures constitute the beginning of colonial culture of violence is quite consistent with the evidence presented in this study. The ideas expressed by S. T. von Soemmering and Charles White can be viewed as the basis of the culture of violence, which later translated into a set of actions designed to control the Africans. The essential thrust of Tagore's argument is that, while the attitudes of European nations toward the people in the colonies they ruled had a negative impact on human relationships, it was their refusal to place human values on a level that demanded an understanding of the worth and potential of human life.

This refusal was a major component of the colonial culture of violence. This is why Tagore argued: "In human greed for political power we are apt to ascribe the fact that human tendency towards separateness to accidental circumstances in the creation of new relationships between all people."[31] He also maintained that the failure and unwillingness of colonial powers to see human relationships from this perspective led inevitably to conflict. Tagore further concluded that this situation demanded of them a new approach to their own education so that they would start anew to study and understand the dynamics of human relationships. The first outcome of this approach would be that the colonial governments would seek to eliminate the scourge of the culture of ignorance as a condition of seeking to eliminate the culture of violence. Unless the colonial governments summoned all the courage needed to muster the essential nature of this strategy in order to remove the specter of human conflict, they were destined to live with their inescapable limitations as imposed by their own faulty thinking.

In Africa, the continuation of colonial tyrannical governments, the denial of civil liberties to the colonized people and the repression and violence associated with colonial conditions always translated into the cultural decadence that pervaded colonial society itself. This adversely affected its basic functions, depriving the people's lives of any real meaning. In the end, the culture of violence and the colonial decadence "combined to betray the mind and the consciousness of man of his inescapable responsibility,"[32] destroying the delicate fiber that must facilitate human communication. This fiber is commonly referred to as the Golden Rule—treat others as you would want them to treat you. It is threaded with respect for and acceptance of others. The violence of apartheid in South Africa serves as a clear example of how contemporary Africa has endured the agony of this social malfunction when this fiber is missing.

According to Tagore, when seen in the context of colonial conditions in Africa, these elements created a shadowy social environment that engulfed the mind of both colonial officials and the Africans in one continuous maze walled in by the colonial culture of violence. This took on various forms such as in the political and economic spheres of colonial society. The colonial notion that the Africans were valuable only insofar as they could provide labor and that they were inferior to whites represented one of the worst features of the colonial culture of violence.

Memmi sees the impact of this form of violence from another perspective: not being allowed to vote, the colonized were forced to endure the burden of colonial violence, making them less than human.[33] In discussing the effect of this colonial culture of violence to concur with Tagore, Memmi suggests that in not being allowed to consider himself an equal citizen, the colonized was forced to lose all hope of improvement in his social condition or in that of his son. For future generations there would be nothing to suggest improvement in conditions unless the colonized could act to end the prohibitions imposed by colonial conditions. In its existence and application, the colonial culture of violence has a devastating effect on the mind of the colonized.[34]

Based on Tagore's argument and Memmi's concurrence, we can conclude that the colonial culture of violence operates like the tentacles of an old octopus: it reaches out in all directions to place the colonized in an inescapable grip—social, political, educational, interactional, and economic—so that they are sentenced to a continual prison of silence. In Africa the Africans were left with no recourse but to appeal to the colonial governments themselves, a situation similar to that of a patient who has been treated by Dr. Jekyll seeking a second opinion from Mr. Hyde. The critical point that these two thinkers from the Third World make is that, in spite of the various forms of colonial violence, the African mind remained untarnished by it all. Its struggle for self is a fascinating tale of human courage and determination. Against all odds the African mind resurrected itself.

COLONIAL VIOLENCE, THE RISE OF THE AFRICAN MIND, AND THE STRUGGLE FOR INDEPENDENCE

The combination and application of the colonial culture of violence leads to the conclusion that colonial governments were not destined to last the thousand years that colonial enthusiasts had predicted in the nineteenth century. How, then, does one explain the fact most colonial governments in Africa lasted less than one hundred years? Bernard J. Siegel seems to provide a logical theoretical answer:

Civil violence is a product of social change in the physical and social circumstances to which people have to make more or less workable cultural adaptation.

There is an increase in conflict and violence as a direct response to new environmental stress which creates tensions within a society, and erodes the means of resolving disputes, and so loses their effectiveness. In this manner conflict between people of different cultural backgrounds is accentuated as the oppressed feel they have to get rid of their oppression.[35]

Siegel continues that when a group of people imposes its own value system on another group on the assumption that its people are inferior, then it must expect that at some point in time those people will demand an improvement in the conditions that control their lives and then demand an end to them entirely.[36]

Siegel, like Tagore and Memmi, believes that once the mind of the people whose culture has been invaded asserts itself, the invaders can no longer control it. Instead, they proceed to design a strategy to end the culture of violence that has been part of their existence. As the saying goes, the colonized know that they must use fire to fight fire. The Africans, having been subjected to the colonial culture of violence for so long, resorted to the same type of violence to end it. For example, in 1964, when the colonial government in Zimbabwe threatened to use violent and unconstitutional means to seize power in order to perpetuate itself, the Africans responded by indicating that they would use political violence to stop it and to restore their rights. Robert Mugabe, now president of Zimbabwe, warned the colonial government: "If the government takes illegal action or resorts to violence to continue to oppress us, then we will confront it with illegal action and respond with violence. We shall fight fire with fire to the bitterest end to regain our rights."[37]

Indeed, on November 11, 1965, when the colonial government took that illegal action declaring Zimbabwe independent unilaterally, the Africans resorted to the same form of violence by declaring war on the colonial forces, setting the stage for one of the harshest conflicts between the Africans and the colonial government. The conflict ended only when the colonial forces decided to lay down their arms and agree to turn over the government to the Africans. The power of the gun had been supplanted by the power of the African mind. A veteran nationalist who was part of these events stated in July 1989:

The action of the Rhodesia Front government that Ian Smith led left us with no alternative but to utilize the same form of violence that the colonial government had been using to oppress us. Our response to the RF's violence was not a response to the principle of an eye for an eye, or a tooth for a tooth, but a recognition that we had to use violence to end violence. We had no other option. We had come to the end of the road and the RF must have known that we were now in a position to exercise the potential of our mind. It was a renaissance of a new order.[38]

This pattern of behavior was characteristically how the colonies in Africa gained their independence. Zaire, Angola, Mozambique, Zimbabwe, Namibia, Algeria, and Kenya all achieved independence in this manner. It is a pattern that began to unfold in South Africa in response to the violence of apartheid. The culture of silence to which the Africans had been subjected for many years now began to give way to a new reality, a response to end it. Among the Africans who endured the suffering imposed by the colonial culture of violence was Robert Mugabe. In 1990 Patricia Cheney, an

American resident who was born and raised in Zimbabwe, seemed to understand the effect of this form of colonial violence when applied to Africans.

When the prisoners at the Sikombela political prison heard in 1964 that Robert Mugabe was to be imprisoned there, they built him a thatched hut and painstakingly wove reeds together to make a door. When he arrived many were surprised. They had expected to see a powerful, charismatic figure, but instead they found a short, reserved bespectacled man who looked more like the schoolteacher that he had been. Mugabe has changed little since those days. He is a thinker thrust before the glaring footlights of the world stage. To Ian Smith he is "an apostle of Satan," but to most black Zimbabweans he is a revered liberator. His teacher, Father O'Hea, described him as having an exceptional mind.[39]

Smith's comment on Mugabe is a classic example of the colonial culture of ignorance and poverty. It is not surprising that the colonial mind and the African mind could not reach a common ground. Mugabe is also among the countless African leaders who endured the colonial culture of violence. Albert Luthuli and Nelson Mandela of South Africa, Jomo Kenyatta of Kenya, Patrice Lumumba of Zaire, Kenneth Kaunda of Zambia, Sam Nujoma of Namibia, Eduardo Mondlane of Mozambique, and Agostinho Neto of Angola are only a few of the many Africans who were subjected to the colonial culture of violence.

That Mandela spent twenty-seven years in prison for his opposition to apartheid demonstrates the malevolent nature of the colonial systems. All these examples illustrate that in spite of their suffering the Africans did not allow the colonial governments to own their minds as well. With independence, however, the Africans entered a new phase: their oppression by their very own leaders.

INDEPENDENCE AND THE BETRAYAL OF THE AFRICAN MIND: THE TRAGEDY IN UGANDA

As discussed in Chapter 6, attainment of political independence set the stage for the betrayal of the African mind. The five specific examples given are the military coups in Ghana and Nigeria, the anarchy and dictatorship of Mobutu Sese Seko in Zaire, the tragic civil war in Angola, and the savage and senseless brutality in Mozambique. This betrayal from within resulted partly from the colonial governments and partly from the gross failure of the African leaders themselves to understand how to govern.

The people living in these countries have never known freedom and democracy. They have never had an opportunity to participate in fair elections in which they were asked to determine the character of their government and shape new directions in economic development. All they have experienced are military coups, countercoups, or perpetual civil wars that have destroyed their countries and have left a trail of destruction and confusion about the future. To these five examples must be added a sixth, the tragedy that gripped Uganda soon after its independence.

The prospect of independence brought great expectations for the Ugandans. The problems that had arisen concerning the status of Buganda had amicably been resolved. Under a federal constitution designed to recognize the rights of all the people, the kingdom of Buganda was allowed a high degree of autonomy. It was permitted its own legislative structure, the Lukiiko, which empowered democratic principles. In making elaborate plans for independence, Britain hoped that Uganda would join Nigeria as a showcase for the African nations.

Preparations for independence were made with the idea that Uganda would follow Ghana and Nigeria as stellar examples of the Africans' ability to rise above the level of function placed by colonial conditions. It was the best of times for the African mind, totally unaware of the nightmare to come.

As this study has shown, as a condition of independence elections were to be held to determine which political party would have power at the inception of independence. The colonial powers, including Britain, had never previously involved the Africans in the electoral process beyond the peripherals because it was thought that Western politics and the electoral process were too complicated for the Africans to understand. Why then did the colonial powers fail to initiate a process that would gradually bring the Africans into the mainstream of the political process?

The answer is very clear: preparation would have made it possible for the Africans to demand independence much sooner than they actually did. However, since the Africans had no opportunity to learn the dynamics of the electoral process, three political parties began to position themselves to contest the elections in 1961. As was the case in other countries of Africa, the election campaign and the candidates for national office heavily reflected tribal groupings that had little interest in developing a new national identity demanded by independence. The quest was for clan power, not national independence.

As the elections drew closer, two major parties appeared to have a reasonable chance of winning. The first party was the Uganda People's Congress (UPC), which was composed of several tribal groups from the north, the Acholi and Laugi. It was led by the flamboyant Milton Obote, himself a Laugi. The second party that had a reasonable chance of winning the elections was the Democratic party (DP), which consisted of several

tribes from the south and had the blessing of the Kabaka, Sir Edward
Mutesa. The election campaign was marked with gross corruption, as
became typical of elections in postcolonial Africa.

The practice of corruption at the outset in the independence of the country
spelled disaster for Uganda. Slowly, the Africans were being robbed of their
rightful opportunity to participate in an important national process to
determine the future of their country and to set an example for their African
brothers and sisters.

As in other countries of Africa, Uganda has never known honest and fair
elections. Abandoning the stated constitutional provisions made to protect
the integrity of the country, politicians began instead to manipulate the
process to gain maximum political advantage. The governor, Sir Walter
Coutts, appeared either unable or unwilling to put things back on course. In
his impotence, Coutts became an indirect participant in the conspiracy to
betray the African mind. If the elections had been held to determine the
future of the colonial government, Coutts would certainly have ensured that
the election campaign was held under proper conditions and that candidates
respected constitutional provisions. But he was apparently not interested in
such a guarantee. This, then, became the ultimate betrayal from within by
the British colonial government.

The Ugandans participated in the elections with full understanding of
their responsibility and their meaning to the future of the country. When the
election results were known, no party had gained an absolute majority to
establish the first independent administration on its own, although Obote's
UPC had gained more seats than the other parties. Therefore, the first
independent government of Uganda consisted of a coalition between UPC
and the Buganda royalist party, known as the Kabaka Yekka. The publicly
exhibited spirit of cooperation between the two parties led to Sir Edward
Mutesa's endorsement of the coalition government in 1963. He believed
that this was necessary to give the country a sense of political unity and
stability.

Unfortunately, it soon became evident that Obote had secret plans to
subvert the constitutional arrangements in order to wrest sole power. First,
the coalition set out to neutralize the Democratic party, which had made a
strong showing in the elections, in order to remove the threat to Obote's
future plans. Second, Obote secretly began to lure members of the DP and
of the Kabaka Yekka with bribes and promises of positions in the government in order to destroy the party. He began to speak in favor of a one-party
system of government, arguing that opposition against the government was
a typical capitalist practice that should not be allowed in Africa.[40] Obote
was on his way to betraying his own people.

In his determination to thwart the aspirations of his people, Obote quite candidly admitted that "tribal and factional groupings tend to threaten the stability of the country and that one-party state is needed to forge a sense of national unity."[41] Having tried to eradicate the DP and having manipulated the Kabaka Yekka, Obote now positioned himself for the final power play.

Recognizing that Obote was selling out the people through his ruthless methods, a crisis developed within the coalition over confidence in his leadership. Grace Ibingira, a high government official, broke ranks with the coalition and openly opposed the one-party state under Obote's dictatorship. In response, Obote turned to the army and the police to strengthen his political hold. He then disregarded the delicate democratic system that had been put in place at the inception of independence and began to rule by decree.

By the end of 1963, hardly a year after independence, Uganda had become a one-man dictatorship. Ibingira and members of the DP who refused to be bribed were all on Obote's list of undesirable people who would vanish into the night. Obote appointed to his administration only those who swore absolute loyalty to him. Divergent views were not allowed and cabinet meetings were to be held for only one purpose—to carry out Obote's instructions without question.

Obote's decision to use the army and the police to impose a one-man dictatorship led to a tragic twist of fate for both himself and Uganda. He began to form a close personal relationship with a junior army officer named Idi Amin Dada. During the waning years of the British colonial government, Amin had risen rapidly to the top of the military hierarchy through his loyalty to his superiors. Amin, a virtual illiterate, impressed his superiors as a soldier of loyalty, stamina, and leadership ability, and so the British colonial officials promoted him to the rank of colonel within the British colonial army itself.[42]

But Amin had ambitions of his own and was slowly positioning himself to make a quick and decisive move against Obote when the time was right. During the Mau Mau uprising in Kenya, Amin was secretly sent there to help the colonial forces crush it, indiscriminately killing innocent civilians from the Turkana tribe. Amin later claimed that he was only obeying orders and had no regrets for his action.

Amin was totally devoted to his Muslim faith. His hatred of non-Muslims can be compared to Adolf Hitler's hatred of the Jews. Later, when in full power, Amin pursued a systematic elimination of non-Muslims in exactly the same way that Hitler sought to exterminate the Jews. In this African holocaust, Obote's hands were covered in blood.

When Amin's savagery against the Turkana tribe became fully known, the colonial authorities in Kenya requested that Coutts hand him over for trial. Coutts argued that to put him on trial six months before independence for Uganda would damage the national morale. Did Coutts really care about the national morale of a colony about to gain independence? Coutts's action in this matter is yet another example of the colonial governments' betrayal of the African mind.

Coutts convinced the colonial authorities in Kenya to have Amin face a court martial instead of putting him on trial. In one last act of gross negligence against the African mind, Coutts left Amin's fate in Obote's hands. Obote recommended that Amin receive only a reprimand.

In 1964, when British colonial military forces were being withdrawn from Uganda, Obote promoted Amin to the rank of lieutenant-colonel. Obote was not required by any constitutional provision to consult with anyone to make sure that his appointments were made within the guidelines of how national interests would be served. On February 4, 1966, the nightmare intensified when Daudi Ocheng, a member of the now defunct legislature, accused Amin and Obote of gross corruption in handling national affairs.

Instead of facing those charges as a national leader should, Obote secretly arranged with Amin and the police to put a quick end to this uncomfortable situation. Obote arranged a fake meeting to be held on February 22, supposedly to answer the charges Ocheng and other critics had made against them. He made sure that those who had made the charges against him and Amin were present, including Ibingira, Ocheng, and three others. As the fake meeting was just about to begin, the police burst into the cabinet room and arrested all five. Two days later Obote suspended the last vestiges of the now ineffective constitution and dissolved the legislature, making these his final acts in betraying the African mind. Obote and Amin formed a new "dual alliance" that they thought was absolute in every way. There was nothing that the African mind could do once it was betrayed by its own leaders.

Believing that Uganda was his for the taking, Obote began to build a secret and elaborate informer system that most Ugandans came to fear and resent. He appointed his own cousin, Akena Adoko, as its commander and director.[43] Obote would take no chances. He trusted no one, not even the people he ruled, except his close associates and members of his own family. He made most of his appointments from his own Laugi tribe. Under Obote, the government of Uganda had become a family affair, a private business designed to benefit only the inner circle.

In this situation, the interests of the people were ignored completely, while Obote began to harbor a false sense of security, until the events of

January 11, 1971. On that date, Obote left Uganda to attend the annual meeting of the British Commonwealth Conference to be held in Singapore.[44] During the past six years, Obote and Amin had been slowly drifting apart, because each wanted absolute power for himself. By the end of 1970 the two men had serious suspicions about the intentions of the other.

Obote had made secret plans with units of the army to arrest Amin while he was in Singapore in order to provide an excuse that he was not involved in the plot against Amin. As soon as he arrived in Singapore, Obote ordered Amin's arrest. On January 24 a loyal junior army officer warned Amin of his impending arrest, and Amin quickly moved to announce that Obote had been removed from office. Amin proclaimed himself president of Uganda for life and announced his intention to become king of all of Africa. Thus began a perilous phase in the history of Uganda, that became known all over the world as one of the most brutal dictatorships Africa has ever known. "The Butcher of Kampala," as Amin became known throughout Africa and the world, betrayed the African mind in a way that has rarely been known.

For a brief period of time following Obote's overthrow, Amin became a folk hero among the people of Uganda for his action in removing Obote from the seat of power. They hoped that as a military man Amin had no interest in politics and that he would soon return the country to a civilian administration popularly elected by the populace. They did not believe him when he said that he wanted to be president of Uganda and king of Africa for life. They were wrong. Although he did not achieve this objective, the damage he inflicted on the Ugandan people was heart-wrenching. Amin's regime did not last a millennium, but in a short time it inflicted a thousand years worth of pain and sorrow.

From the moment he assumed the office of president to his overthrow in 1979, Amin inflicted incalculable damage on Uganda. By the time he fled to Saudi Arabia, Uganda had become a wasteland destroyed by a man who cared little for the lives of the people. The destruction was so extensive that it could not be measured. Amin established what he called the State Research Bureau, which, in effect, was the incinerating chamber for those who opposed him.

Amin especially singled out those non-Muslims. Martin Meredith described the ultimate betrayal of the African mind in Uganda under Amin when he suggested that Amin's rule had, in effect, left Uganda lawless, ravaged, and bankrupt. There was to be no respite from the carnage. Tragically, as soon as exiled politicians returned to Kampala to set up a new national administration, old rivalries reemerged in more powerful ways.[45] Today Uganda has still not recovered from this violation by one of its own. What the future holds is a matter of speculation. But it is clear that the people are as confused and uncertain now as they were during the Obote–Amin conspiracy.

MILITARY COUPS, DICTATORSHIP, CORRUPTION, AND BETRAYAL OF THE AFRICAN MIND

The African mind faces three major problems that have to be resolved if the future is to be better: military coups, one-man or one-party dictatorship, and pervasive corruption. The military's coup against Nkrumah was the beginning of a new phenomenon in the betrayal of the African mind. Many African military leaders were trained in the European tradition to believe that political intervention was not a military function. They were taught to understand that their responsibility was to defend their countries against foreign aggression and to leave politics to the politicians.

But as politicians proved incapable of providing ethical governments unmarred by dictatorial behavior, the military began to believe that it would provide a viable alternative to serve the interests of their people and so found it hard to remain uninvolved in the political arena. For the Africans trained in the traditions of Sandhurst and similar military schools in Europe, their decision to overthrow civilian governments triggered a situation that proved to be the demise of the countries they tried to rescue. This is why Colonel Afrifa, one of the military leaders who plotted to overthrow Nkrumah in 1966, observed, "I have always felt it painful to associate myself with a coup to overthrow a constitutional government however perverted that constitution may be. But it was equally painful to come to the conclusion that the coup was necessary to save our country and our people."[46]

Two disturbing phenomena are part of military action in African politics. First, whenever a coup takes place, military leaders are quick to portray the civilian leaders they have overthrown as a callous group of self-serving professional political criminals who had to be stopped before they brought the country to the brink of collapse and ruin. This is exactly what Colonel Afrifa had in mind when he explained the military takeover in Ghana. Then they immediately announce that the coup is a temporary measure and that return to civilian rule will be initiated when new constitutional arrangements have been completed.

But as the military men develop a taste for the political power they never had before, the promise of a temporary takeover of the government becomes meaningless as they suspend the constitution and dissolve the legislature. With no opposition, they rule by decree and deal severely with dissidents. In this setting, the overthrow of civilian governments is immediately followed by the dictatorship of the military. In this climate the betrayal of the African mind enters a new realm. This is precisely what has happened in Ghana, Nigeria, the Central African Republic, Zaire, Togo, Niger, Ethiopia, Liberia, and many other African countries.

The military juntas that have ruled these countries have inflicted more suffering on the people than the civilian governments they replaced, and so the vicious circle of the betrayal of the African mind is never broken. The hopes and aspirations that were central to the people's struggle have become distant dreams realized only by the powerful and the uncaring. The African populations become unwelcomed guests in a home in which they are not wanted. How much more can they take?

The second disturbing phenomenon is that once a military coup takes place, even if the promise to return to civilian rule is kept, the military establishments closely watch and monitor both the election process and the behavior of the new civilian governments to assure that they are operating according to their dictates. Then any civilian government that appears to operate outside these demands is immediately removed from office. For example, in 1969, three years after Nkrumah's fall, the military allowed elections to choose a new civilian government. When Kofi Busia, Nkrumah's persistent critic and opponent, was elected to the presidency, the people of Ghana were excited about the prospects of a new era of democracy. Busia was believed to be a man of democratic principles who would be true to his beliefs.

For the African mind this was the dawn of a new era, a starting point for a new national endeavor launched to give the people that motivation called hope and a sense of great national expectation. The eyes of Africa and the world were once more on Ghana to determine whether it could utilize this rare second chance to reclaim its rightful leadership role to revitalize democracy on the continent. It was a new day for Africa, the sunrise of the aspirations of the masses.

But this flickering ray of hope soon turned into the worst of times when once more the people of Ghana came face to face with the reality that neither the military nor Busia had anticipated. At that point Ghana was burdened with the debt it had incurred for the programs Nkrumah had initiated. As the economy continued to decline, Busia was forced to introduce austerity measures that only aggravated the situation. Production of goods continued to decline, essential services came to a halt, unemployment rose, and foreign debts increased as the unfavorable balance of payment crippled industrial production.

Desperate in his efforts to turn this situation around, Busia tried new measures that only compounded the problems. First, he tried to introduce liberal economic policies to encourage trade. But the unfavorable balance of payments plunged Ghana deeper into debt. Second, without waiting to see the results of his new economic policies, Busia reversed himself and began to impose new trade regulations. As a result, foreign trade was hurt, and industrial production was reduced to a point where the economy was weakened. This situation caused a decline in the price of cocoa on the world market. By 1971 economic conditions were even worse than they had been during the years of Nkrumah's programs.

The new Ghana military regime led by General Acheampong attempted to assure the people that it had the power and the will to turn things around and that the people should anticipate a better future under its leadership than under past civilian administrations. But the hope of improved conditions soon turned into despair when a power struggle erupted within the ranks of the military. With this new crisis, the country's problems were ignored. In 1978, fearing the erosion of public confidence, senior military officers led by General Akuffo staged a countercoup that removed Acheampong from office.

Within one year, on June 4, 1979, Akuffo had proved so ineffective that another coup was staged, this time led by Flight Lieutenant Jerry Rawlings, who assumed the office of president. This comedy of errors was taking a heavy toll on Ghana. Eight senior army officers, including Afrifa, Acheampong, and Akuffo, were executed by firing squad without benefit of trial. In September 1979 Rawlings found the task of running a country so difficult that he turned the government over to a civilian administration led by Hilla Limann, a career diplomat. By January 1982, Limann's government collapsed under pressure from the military to do something dramatic to turn things around. Rawlings quickly returned to power. The comedy of errors had turned into a tragedy of errors.

These sad developments have created a tidal wave of problems that African countries have not been able to resolve. The example of military coups and countercoups in Ghana has been duplicated many times over in countries all over Africa. For example, Amin's fall in 1979 was not a cause for celebration for Uganda. Yusufu Lule, the first civilian leader the people chose, lasted no more than sixty-eight days, and his successor, Godfrey Binaisa, a lawyer trained in Britain, was overthrown within a year. This has left the people of Africa completely paralyzed and unsure about the future.

The reality of this situation is that military dictatorships rob the African mind of its legitimate expectations. Corruption has become the routine way of doing government business, and the people are left with no course of action to redress the gross injustice inflicted on their countries. This pattern has become the accepted way of life. The September 7, 1992, issue of *Time* discussed how these developments had combined to constitute the ultimate betrayal of the African mind:

Africa has begun to look like an immense illustration of chaos theory. Much of the continent has turned into a battleground of contending dooms: AIDS and overpopulation, poverty, starvation, illiteracy, corruption, social breakdown, vanishing resources, overcrowded cities, drought, war and the homelessness [and the hopelessness] of the war's refugees. Africa has become the basket case of the planet, the Third World of the Third World, a vast continent in free fall.[47]

In *The Mind of the South* (1941), Wilbur Joseph Cash (1901–1941) listed some of the characteristics that constituted the mind of the South:

Violence, intolerance, aversion and suspicion toward new ideas, an incapacity for analysis, an inclination to act from feeling rather than from thought, an exaggerated individualism and a too narrow concept of social responsibility, attachment to racial values and a tendency to justify cruelty and injustice in the name of those values, sentimentality and a lack of realism have been its characteristic vices in the past. Despite changes for the better, they remain its characteristic today.[48]

In *The Mind of South Africa* (1990), Allister Sparks concluded:

Eighty years ago,[49] as South Africa stood on the brink of independence from Britain, Olive Schreiner wrote of the kind of leadership needed to weld a nation out of such a heterogeneous society. South Africa needed a leader, she said, who while loving his own people intensely, was able to place the interests of the whole above their interests. He did not have to be brilliant, not a Cavour[50] or a Talleyrand,[51] but he had to be someone of human breadth, an inclusionist, a reconciliator, who could draw everyone together.[52]

That is, the tragic developments that have unfolded in both the southern United States and South Africa were an outcome of a mind that refused to see things from their proper perspective.

In discussing implications for the future of Africa, a white South African told the author in December 1994:

The transformation of South Africa from an oppressive white minority rule to a black majority government raises a hope for a better future. But the government of Nelson Mandela must learn to avoid the errors that other leaders of black Africa have made. They have only been mere substitutes for the colonial governments. Corruption, economic decline, dictatorship, intolerance to new ideas, insensitivity to the needs of the people, inability to perceive the future in terms of the past and the present, have led Africa to what Charles Dickens called the worst of times. Both the government and the people must utilize their minds to confront the problems that have been created since 1910. If they fail a new situation will arise that will derail the hopes and aspirations of the people and will betray their trust. The people of South Africa, both black and white, cannot reject the betrayal of their mind by the apartheid government only to be betrayed by an African government. Mandela and his government have to succeed in the restoration of the African mind where the apartheid government failed.[53]

Mandela himself seems to have been aware of this reality and the implications of rising to the occasion. Speaking at a White House dinner held in his honor on October 4, 1994, he said, "Although in its infancy in our country, a system of democracy is a reality we must protect for all our citizens. However, many of our people face ignorance, hunger, and disease on an unprecedented scale. We must find solutions to these problems if the future must be different from the past."[54] Although this hope is rooted in the African spirit of courage and determination, it must be tempered with the reality of the enormous problems that South Africa, like the rest of Africa, is facing. This is the challenge that black Africa faces today, and its leaders must alter its mindset and see the tragic situation they have created from its proper perspective.

THE AFRICAN MIND AND THE FUTURE: SOME IMPLICATIONS

What does the future hold for black Africa? The action of the military forces in Zaire in October 1991, in which they went on a rampage of terror, destruction, and looting because they had not been paid, was a sad reminiscence of the anarchy that occurred in 1961 following the attainment of their independence in 1960. The tragic part of the nightmare in Zaire is that Mobutu Sese Seko staged the coup that deposed the civilian government of Patrice Lumumba and Joseph Kasavubu in 1965 because he claimed that he wanted to restore democratic government. But, as has been shown in this study, conditions have deteriorated so badly under Seko that the African mind has been robbed of its expectations and potential.

In 1989 this author wrote about conditions in Southern Africa with special reference to how Seko has brought Zaire to the brink of a major national disaster: "It is important to understand that in terms of the situation in Southern Africa the concept of paradigm shift acquires elements of violence because the parties to the conflict are in disagreement about the form it must take to make change possible. This is the perspective from which one must view the attempt to remove Sese Seko of Zaire from office."[55]

The problems that Zaire is facing have, of course, been caused by Seko himself. Since 1965 he has imposed an iron grip on Zaire. He has taken creativity away from the people and has ruled as a dictator with little care for the conditions of the people. In November 1991 *Time* wrote:

The latest unrest in Zaire was prompted by Mobuto Sese Seko's ouster of his new prime minister, Elienne Tshekedi, a leader of the opposition coalition, who had angered him by refusing to swear allegiance to him. Mobuto named a lesser opposition figure, Bernardin Mungul Diaka, as replacement. But Tshekedi refused to step down. Instead he rallied opposition support and the stand-off continued. What had started as an experiment in multi-party democracy has become a murderous farce.[56]

Seko has no intention of letting up the iron grip he has imposed on Zaire since 1965. While this has been happening, he has reportedly plundered Zaire and deposited the loot in Swiss banks, estimated in the billions of dollars.

The defeat of Kenneth Kaunda of Zambia in the presidential elections held in 1991 and of Hastings Banda of Malawi in 1994 was one of the very few good things that have ever happened to Zambia and Malawi since gaining independence in October 1964. Kaunda and Banda were forced to agree to free elections by the events that began to unfold in 1990 when an attempted military coup nearly removed them from office. From that time the people themselves decided to do something to restore their rights, which have been violently betrayed by the application of one-party system.

Although Kaunda and Banda merit great respect as persons and for some of their ideas, their action in turning their countries into a one-party state and their own dictatorship cannot be condoned. The action that the people of Zambia and Malawi took to demand democracy is the kind of action the people of Zaire, and for that matter, all countries of Africa, must demand to restore their individual and collective mind. This is what Africans in South Africa began to do in 1991. If the people themselves do not take action, Seko will entrench himself deeper. This simply cannot be allowed to continue without bringing Zaire to the brink of disaster.

The betrayal of the African mind by the self-seeking politicians and military leaders will one day end with its restoration. What must the African mind do to restore its legitimate place? For that to happen, the Africans must demand an unconditional end to dictatorship, both military and individual. They must understand that there is no such thing as benevolent dictatorship, whether it comes from Jerry Rawlings, Mobutu Sese Seko, Kamuzu Hastings Banda, Idi Amin, or Jean-Bedel Bokassa. Far too many dictators have emerged in postcolonial Africa. It is a sad truth that all African dictators seek to survive by denying their people the basic freedom of self-expression, which is the very essence of creative and critical thinking that nations need to generate a pool of new ideas to ensure national development.

Any manner of betrayal of the African mind carries a heavy national and continental price tag. The African leaders who ignore basic democratic principles decide to dismiss a very important point—that is, in assuming dictatorial powers, they neglect the fact that the colonial administrations were appointed by governments in Europe and that they represented these governments, but that leaders in Africa must respect the wishes of the people to whom they are accountable. The Africans must evaluate the behavior of their governments by a set of criteria different from the one they used to assess the colonial governments. Anything less than an effort to create a national climate in which freedom of self-expression is fully recognized is a dictatorship and an abomination.

The African mind must understand that the idea of one-party or one-man rule is an insult as great as colonialism and must never be allowed to take root. This study has concluded that Africans like Milton Obote, Mobutu Sese Seko, and Kamuzu Hastings Banda, who argue that this form of government is necessary to bring about national unity, ignore the fact that military takeover or bloody coups destroy the very essence of the national unity they claim they want to promote. The military juntas justify their action by claiming that civilian governments are corrupt. The juntas promise to resolve democracy and to hold free elections by a given date. But when that time comes, the juntas give one excuse after another to justify why the promise of elections cannot be kept.

Meanwhile, the juntas institute new forms of totalitarianism worse than those of the civilian governments they have deposed. The function of removing the government from office must be left to the people by recall elections or by some other constitutional means of due process. Democracy is a system of checks and balances. It must be given a chance to reach adulthood, and not be killed in infancy.

The question that the African mind must ask in the interest of its restoration is: What elements must be present to ensure democracy? To be truly democratic, a two-party system must be preserved at all times. The people must demand the right to exercise a clear choice between candidates of two opposing parties with differing views on issues. The voters must demand that the candidates discuss issues freely and fully. Free press coverage of the speeches and related matters must form an integral component of the democratic process. The people must ask candidates to reveal their financial resources and sources of income to make sure that there is no conflict of interest between their seeking public responsibility and their private business practices. The press must always have the right to disclose any practices of corruption by those who seek public office, from candidates for the office of national president to the junior member of the local legislature. Candidates for all local government offices must submit to the same press scrutiny. Party leaders, supporters, assistants, secretaries, and any other workers, must allow background checks as well.

Once in office, the government must at all times tolerate opposition to any and all national programs. All parliamentary procedures must be strictly followed. The leaders of the government must not make the government their personal property, and they must always be mindful that the government belongs to the people. Frequent elections must be held to ensure that the government carries out its functions in accordance with the constitutional provisions and the wishes of the people. The policies and programs of the party in power must be subject to public scrutiny at all times. There is another important consideration: many presidents of postcolonial Africa have held office since their countries gained independence from European nations. Some, such as Kamuzu Hastings Banda of Malawi (who lost to alik Bakili in the elections held in June 1994), have proclaimed themselves president for life. Others, such as Jean-Bedel Bokassa of the Central African Republic, have proclaimed themselves emperors. Still others, such as Idi Amin Dada of Uganda, have tried to be kings of all of Africa. Many have ordered stadiums, squares, streets, and buildings named after them. Some have demanded that their portraits be conspicuously placed in prominent positions in public buildings as reminders of their power. Others have forced the people to become party members against their will and to pay annual dues in order to keep their jobs. Some have amassed personal fortunes by corrupt practices, subjecting the people to conditions of unbearable poverty. There is only one possible solution for this sad situation: the term of office of the president must be limited beyond which he cannot by constitutional provision seek another term.

If this practice were instituted, it would mean that no person would have a monopoly of political power and that all citizens would have an equal opportunity to serve their country. It would also mean that the best minds would be constantly searched for in the service of the country. The African mind must constantly remember one universal principle, and that is, no matter how good a leader may be, the longer he stays in office, the more his sense of virtue is corrupted by the power he holds. Sooner than later he begins to think that he is both indispensable and infallible. He begins to regard those who disagree with him on national policy and programs as enemies of the state because he now thinks that they are wrong and that he is always right. That is the beginning of the road to dictatorship.

There is yet another important consideration. All over the world, including Africa, some individuals seek public office because they believe they have a contribution to make to their countries. Unfortunately, however, far too many people seek office to gain personal power, fame, and fortune. Africa has had more than its fair share of this kind of leader. The result has been an erosion of public confidence in politicians.

Thus, the African mind must be ever vigilant to determine whether an individual seeking public office is genuinely seeking public office to serve his country or to serve his own personal interests. Once in public office, officials must be reminded of their responsibility to behave in accordance with a properly constructed constitutional code of ethics and conduct. Any public official who attempts to put a distance between his public and private conduct must not remain in office.

In connection with this practice, an independent body subject to the scrutiny of its operations by the free press must be instituted to work closely with the public to assure compliance with properly instituted law. This would ensure that public officials who violate their charge would be subject to criminal action, removal from office, and imprisonment. If any wrongdoing is proven, and if, as is the case in Africa, financial criminal conduct is disclosed, the public officials concerned must be required to make financial restitutions.

The era of Kamuzu Hastings Banda, Idi Amin Dada, and Mobutu Seso Seko must come to a close. In addition, any criminal action brought against public officials must be done in an open court of law. Recall elections must form an integral part of this process and will provide a balance between the legal action and the political action against a public official who violates his public trust. This would spare the African countries the agony that they have endured for so long.

Finally, it is important that the African mind remember that public officials who bribe citizens or receive bribes from citizens for services hurt the country in more ways than one. Any citizen who fails to take appropriate action when he has reason to believe that public officials have violated their public trust is himself in violation of his responsibility to both self and country. Any citizen who knowingly becomes an accessory to public official misconduct must become subject to criminal charges. To reduce the chances of this tragic development, the African mind must demand that all government appointments go through a confirmation process by an appropriate constitutional national body. This will allow scrutiny and serve as a reminder to the appointees of their responsibility and accountability to the people.

This process will caution them that if they abuse their position they will be removed when the citizens are convinced of their wrongdoing. In turn, the people must take notice of all activities of public officials to preserve the integrity of their nation. As Thomas Jefferson (1743–1826), president of the United States from 1801 to 1809, advised his fellow Americans, the salvation of their nation was assured by their watchfulness. The turn of events in Malawi and South Africa in 1994 must serve as an example of the need for this watchfulness. The mind of black Africa, be well advised and be wise!

NOTES

1. Hermann Bleibtreu and John Meany, "Race and Racism," in Thomas Weaver (ed.), *To See Ourselves: Anthropology and Modern Social Issues* (Glenview, Ill.: Scott Foresman & Co., 1973), p. 184.

2. Ibid., p. 185.

3. Ibid., p. 186.

4. Ibid., p. 185.

5. Oscar Lewis, "The Culture of Poverty," in Thomas Weaver (ed.), *To See Ourselves: Anthropology and Modern Social Issues*, p. 234.

6. Quoted in Frank S. Pepper (ed.), *Wit and Wisdom of the 20th Century* (New York: Peter Bedrick Books, 1987), p. 230.

7. Ibid., p. 235.

8. An African educator during an interview with the author in Harare, Zimbabwe, August 14, 1989.

9. Memmi, *The Colonizer and the Colonized*, p. 4.

10. Ibid., p. 5.

11. Ibid., p. 11.

12. Ibid., p. 69.

13. Ibid., p. 71.

14. Freire, *Pedagogy of the Oppressed*, p. 32.

15. Ibid., p. 34.

16. Memmi, *The Colonizer and the Colonized*, p. 98.

17. Ibid., p. 128.

18. Congolese National Liberation Front, *The Question of Zaire* (New York: FLNC, 1978), p. 8.

19. For a more detailed discussion of this practice, see, for example, Dickson A. Mungazi, "The Change of Black Attitudes Towards Education in Rhodesia, 1900–1975," Ph.D. diss. (Lincoln: University of Nebraska, 1977), p. 52.

20. Zimbabwe, "The Road to Freedom," a documentary film. Zimbabwe Ministry of Information, 1983.

21. Freire, *Pedagogy of the Oppressed*, p. 31.

22. Memmi, *The Colonizer and the Colonized*, p. 116.

23. Ethel Tawse Jollie, in *Rhodesia: Legislative Debates*, 1927.

24. A colonial official quoted in *The Rhodesia Herald*, June 28, 1912.

25. For a detailed discussion of colonial policy, including education, see Dickson A. Mungazi, *Colonial Policy and Conflict in Zimbabwe: A Study of Cultures in Collision, 1890–1979* (New York: Taylor and Francis, 1992).

26. Freire, *Pedagogy of the Oppressed*, p. 28.

27. *The Christian Century,* October 1975.

28. Rabindranath Tagore, "The Unity of Education," in Robert Ulich (ed.), *Education and the Idea of Mankind* (Chicago: University of Chicago Press, 1964), p. 2.

29. Ibid., p. 5.

30. Rabindranath Tagore, in a letter dated September 16, 1934, addressed to Professor Albert Murray of Britain. Courtesy of the United Nations.

31. Ibid.

32. Ibid.

33. Memmi, *The Colonizer and the Colonized*, p. 96.

34. Ibid., p. 97.

35. Bernard J. Siegel, "Violence and Social Change," in Thomas Weaver (ed.), *To See Ourselves: Anthropology and Modern Social Issues*, p. 379.

36. Ibid., p. 380.

37. Robert Mugabe, "The Road to Majority Rule," speech delivered at Munomutapa Hall, Gweru, March 14, 1964. Zimbabwe National Archives.

38. An African nationalist during an interview with the author in Harare, July 30, 1989.

39. Patricia Cheney, *The Land and People of Zimbabwe* (New York: J. B. Lippincott, 1990), p. 131.

40. Meredith, *The First Dance of Freedom: Black Africa in the Postwar Era*, p. 219.

41. Ibid., p. 220.

42. Ibid., p. 221.

43. Ibid., p. 225.

44. This annual conference consists of former British colonies and Britain itself. In August 1991, the conference was held in Harare, Zimbabwe. Forming the background to this conference was Zimbabwe's rapidly deteriorating economy. In January 1992, President George Bush was in Singapore during a visit to Australia and Japan in an effort to revive the U.S. economy.

45. Meredith, *The First Dance of Freedom: Black Africa in the Postwar Era*, p. 234.

46. Ibid., p. 235.

47. "Africa: The Scramble for Existence," *Time*, September 7, 1992, p. 40.

48. Wilbur Joseph Cash, *The Mind of the South* (New York: Alfred A. Knopf, 1941), p. 429.

49. South Africa gained political independence in 1910 and began to formulate the notorious policy of apartheid which remained in force until April 1994.

50. Camillo Benso Cavour (1810–1861), an Italian statesman who helped unite the people of Italy under a single kingdom.

51. Charles-Maurice de Talleyrand (1754–1838), a French statesman who became famous for his diplomatic achievement under Napoleon I.

52. Allister Sparks, *The Mind of South Africa* (New York: Alfred A. Knopf, 1990), p. 399.

53. A white South African during a conversation with the author in Johannesburg, December 19, 1994.

54. Nelson Mandela speaking at the White House during a state dinner hosted by President and Mrs. Bill Clinton, October 4, 1994, as reported by C-SPAN 2.

55. Mungazi, *The Struggle for Social Change in Southern Africa: Visions of Liberty*, p. viii.

56. *Time*, November 4, 1991.

Selected Bibliography

BOOKS

Anglin, Douglas (ed.). *Conflict And Change in Southern Africa. Papers from a Scandinavian Conference.* Washington, D.C.: University Press of America, 1978.

Banana, Canaan. *Theology of Promise: The Dynamics of Self-reliance.* Harare: College Press, 1982.

Battle, M., and Charles Lyons. *Essays in African Education.* New York: Teachers College Press, 1970.

Berens, Denis, and Albert B. Planger (eds.). *A Concise Encyclopedia of Zimbabwe.* Gweru: Mambo Press, 1988.

Bond-Stewart, Kathy. *Education.* Gweru: Mambo Press, 1986.

Carter, G. *Southern Africa: The Continuing Crisis.* Bloomington: Indiana University, 1982.

Cash, Wilbur Joseph. *The Mind of the South.* New York: Alfred A. Knopf, 1941.

Chidzero, B. T. *Education and the Challenge of Independence.* Geneva: IEUP, 1977.

Christie, Ian. *Samora Machel: A Biography.* London: Panof Books, 1989.

Cohen, Robin (ed.). *Democracy and Socialism in Africa.* Boulder, Colo.: Westview Press, 1991.

Cory, Robert, and Dianna Mitchell, (eds.). *African Nationalist Leaders in Rhodesia's Who's Who.* Bulawayo: Books of Rhodesia, 1977.

Cox, Cortland. *African Liberation.* New York: Black Education Press, 1972.

Curle, Adam. *Education for Liberation.* New York: John Wiley and Sons, 1973.

Curtin, Philip. *The Images of Africa: British Ideas and Action.* Madison: University of Wisconsin Press, 1964.

Curtin, Philip. *Africa South of the Sahara.* Morristown, N.J.: Silver Burdett, 1970.

Davidson, Basil. *The Black Man's Burden: Africa and the Curse of the Nation State.* New York: Times Books, 1992.

Demon, Donald, and Balam Nyeko. *Southern Africa Since 1800.* London: Longman, 1984.

Dewey, John. *Experience and Education* New York: Collier Books, 1938.

Diffendorfer, Ralph E. [ed.]. *The World Service of the Methodist Episcopal Church.* Chicago: Methodist Council on Benevolences, 1923.

Dugard, John. *The Southwest Africa/Namibia Dispute.* Berkeley: University of California Press, 1973.

Eicher, J. C. *Educational Costing and Financing in Developing Countries.* Washington, D.C.: World Bank, 1984.

El-Ayouty, Yassin. *The Organization of African Unity. Ten Years After: Comparative Perspective.* New York: Praeger, 1975.

Fafunwa, Babs. *History of Education in Nigeria.* London: George Allen and Unwin, 1974.

Fraser, Donald. *The Future of Africa.* Westport, Conn.: Negro Universities Press, 1911.

Freire, Paulo. *Pedagogy of the Oppressed.* New York: Continuum, 1983.

Fritz, Mark. "African Democracy Takes a Backward Leap." *Arizona Daily Sun* (Flagstaff), November 21, 1993.

Gelfand, Michael. *African Background.* Cape Town, South Africa: Juta and Co., 1965.

Gelfand, Michael. *Diet and Tradition in African Culture.* London: E. and S. Livingstone, 1971.

Gelfand, Michael. *Growing Up in Shona Society.* Gweru: Mambo Press, 1979.

Gibbs, Peter. *Flag for the Matabele: An Entertainment in African History.* New York: Vanguard Press, 1956.

Gordon, Robert. *The Bushman Myth: The Making of a Namibian Underclass.* Boulder, Colo.: Westview Press, 1991.

Grundy, Kenneth. *South Africa: Domestic Crisis and Global Challenge.* Boulder, Colo.: Westview Press, 1991.

Hapgood, David. *Africa in Today's World Focus.* Boston: Ginn and Co., 1971.

Harden, Blaine. *Africa: Dispatches from the Fragile Continent.* New York: W. W. Norton, 1990.

Henderson, Lawrence. *Angola: Five Centuries of Conflict.* Ithaca, N.Y.: Cornell University Press, 1979.

Herbstein, Dennis. *White Man, We Want to Talk to You.* London: Oxford University Press, 1979.

Hirst, Paul. *Knowledge and the Curriculum: A Collection of Philosophical Papers.* London: Routledge and Kegan Paul, 1974.

Holeman, J. F. *Shona Customary Law.* New York: Oxford University Press, 1952.

Houtandji, Paulin. *African Philosophy: Myth and Reality.* Bloomington: Indiana University Press, 1982.

Huddleston, Trevor. *Naught for Your Comfort.* New York. Oxford University Press, 1956.

Irvine, Sanders. *Cultural Adaptations within Modern Africa.* New York; Teachers College Press, 1987.

Jaster, Robert. *The Defence of White Power: South African Foreign Policy under Pressure.* New York: St. Martin's Press, 1989.

July, Robert. *A History of the African People.* New York: Scribner and Sons, 1974.

Kaplan Irving, Zaire: *A Country Study.* Washington, D.C.: American University Press, 1979.

Kaunda, Kenneth. *Zambia Shall Be Free.* New York: Frederick Praeger, 1963.

Kimble, H. T. *Emerging Africa.* New York: Scholastic Books, 1963.

Knorr, Kenneth. *British Colonial Theories.* Toronto: University of Toronto Press, 1974.

La Guma, Alex (ed.). *Apartheid: Collection of Writings of South Africa by South Africans.* New York: International Publishers, 1971.

Lovejoy, Paul (ed.). *African Modernization and Development.* Boulder, Colo.: Westview Press, 1991.

Lyons, Charles H. *To Wash an Aethiop White: British Ideas about Black African Educability, 1530–1960,* New York: Teachers College Press, 1975.

Machel, Somara. *Mozambique: Sowing the Seeds of Revolution.* Harare: Zimbabwe Publishing House, 1981.

Marquard, Leo. *The Peoples and Policies of South Africa.* London: Oxford University Press. 1960.

Mason, Philip. *The Birth of a Dilemma: Conquest and Settlement of Rhodesia.* London, 1956.

McIntyre, W. *Colonies into Commonwealth.* New York: Walker and Co., 1966.

Memmi, Albert. *The Colonizer and the Colonized.* Boston: Beacon Press, 1965.

Meredith, Martin. *The First Dance of Freedom: Black Africa in the Postwar Era.* New York: Harper and Row, 1984.

Mondlane, Eduardo. *The Struggle for Mozambique.* Baltimore: Penguin Books, 1969.

Moore, Clark D., and Ann Dunbar. *Africa Yesterday and Today.* New York: Bantam Books, 1968.

Msabaha, Ibrahim, and Timothy Shaw. *Confrontation and Liberation in Southern Africa: Regional Directions After the Nkomati Accord.* Boulder, Colo.: Westview Press, 1987.

Mungazi, Dickson A. *The Cross Between Rhodesia and Zimbabwe: Racial Conflict in Rhodesia, 1962–1979.* New York: Vantage Press, 1981.

Mungazi, Dickson A. *The Underdevelopment of African Education.* Washington, D.C.: University Press of America, 1982.

Mungazi, Dickson A. *To Honor the Sacred Trust of Civilization: History, Politics, and Education in Southern Africa.* Cambridge, Mass.: Schenkman Publishers, 1983.

Mungazi, Dickson A. *The Struggle for Social Change in Southern Africa: Visions of Liberty.* New York: Taylor and Francis, 1989.

Mungazi, Dickson A. *Education and Government Control in Zimbabwe: A Study of the Commissions of Inquiry, 1908–1974.* New York: Praeger Publishers, 1990.

Mungazi, Dickson A. *The Challenge of Educational Innovation and National Development in Southern Africa.* New York: Peter Lang, 1991.

Mungazi, Dickson A. *Colonial Education for Africans: George Stark's Policy in Zimbabwe.* New York: Praeger, 1991.

Mungazi, Dickson A. *The Honored Crusade: Ralph Dodge's Theology of Liberation and Initiative for Social Change in Zimbabwe.* Gweru: Mambo Press, 1991.

Mungazi, Dickson A. "Africa in Light of the Columbus Controversy." Documentary film, Ref. NAU/CEE, July, 1992.

Mungazi, Dickson A. *Colonial Policy and Conflict in Zimbabwe: A Study of Cultures in Collision, 1890–1979.* New York: Taylor and Francis, 1992.

Mungazi, Dickson A. *Educational Policy and National Character: Africa, Japan, the United States, and the Soviet Union.* Westport, Conn.: Praeger, 1993.

Mungazi, Dickson A. *The Fall of the Mantle: The Educational Policy of the Rhodesia Front Government and Conflict in Zimbabwe.* New York: Peter Lang Publishing, 1993.

Naylor, W. S. *Daybreak in the Dark Continent.* New York: Young Peoples' Missionary Movement, 1905.

O'Callaghan, Marion. *Namibia: The Effects of Apartheid on Culture and Education.* Paris: Unesco, 1979.

O'Callaghan, Marion. *Rhodesia: The Effects of Apartheid on Culture and Education.* Paris: Unesco, 1979.

Obasamjo, Olusegun, and Hans d'Orville (eds.). *Challenges of Leadership in African Development.* New York: Taylor and Francis, 1990.

Oldham, James. *White and Black in Africa.* New York: Green and Co., 1930.

Omari, C. K. *The Family in Africa.* Geneva: World Council of Churches, 1974.

Panof Books. *Great Lives: Patrice Lumumba.* London, 1978.

Panof Books. *Great Lives: Sekou Toure.* London, 1978.

Parker, Franklin. *African Development and Education in Southern Rhodesia.* Columbus: Ohio State University Press, 1960.

Patel, Hasu, and Ali Mazrui, *Africa in World Affairs. The Next Thirty Years.* New York: Third World Press, 1973.

Patholm, William. *Southern Africa in Perspective.* New York: Free Press, 1972.

Piper, Alan. *South Africa in the American Mind.* New York: Carnegie, 1981.

Powers, B. A. *Religion in Tswana Chiefdom.* London: Oxford University Press, 1961.

Psacharopoulos, George, and Maureen Woodhall. *Education for Development: An Analysis of Investment Choices.* New York: Oxford University Press, 1985.

Ranger, Terrence. *Revolt in Southern Rhodesia, 1896–1897*. Evanston, Ill.: North-western University Press, 1967.

Raphaeli, Nimroid. *Public Sector Management in Botswana*. Washington, D.C.: World Bank, 1984.

Raynor, William. *Tribe and Its Successors: An Account of African Traditional Life after European Settlement in Southern Rhodesia*. New York: Frederick Praeger, 1962.

Riddell, Roger. *From Rhodesia to Zimbabwe: Education for Employment*. Gweru: Mambo Press, 1980.

Rolin, Henri. *Les Los at l'Administration de la Rhodesie*. Bruxelles: l'Etablissment Emil Bruylant, 1913.

Samkange, Stanlake. *What Rhodes Really Said about Africa*. Harare: Harare Publishing House, 1982.

Segai, Ronald, and Ruth First. *Southwest Africa: Travesty of Trust*. London: Deutsch, 1967.

Shillingtom, Kevin. *History of Southern Africa.* Essex (Britain): Longman, 1987.

Smith, William. *Nyerere of Tanzania*. Harare: Zimbabwe Publishing House, 1981.

Smuts, J. C. *The League of Nations: A Practical Suggestion*. New York: UN, 1918.

Southall, Aiden. *The Illusion of Tribe*. R. J. Brill, 1970.

Sparks, Allister. *The Mind of South Africa*. New York: Alfred Knopf, 1990.

Sparrow, George. *The Rhodesian Rebellion*. London: Brighton, 1966.

Sylvester, Christine. *Zimbabwe: The Terrain of Contradictory Development*. Boulder, Colo.: Westview Press, 1991.

Thompson, A. R. *Education and Development in Africa*. New York: St. Martin's Press, 1981.

Tumin, Melvin (ed.). *Race and Intelligence: A Scientific Evaluation*. New York: Anti Defamation League of B'nai B'rith, 1963.

Turner, V. W. *Schism and Continuity in an African Society*. Manchester: Manchester University Press, 1957.

Tutu, Desmond. *Crying in the Wilderness: The Struggle for Justice in South Africa*. Grand Rapids, Mich.: William Eerdmans Publishers, 1982.

Ulich, Robert (ed.). *Education and the Idea of Mankind*. Chicago: University of Chicago Press, 1964.

Vaillant, Janet G. *Black, French, and African: A Life of Leopold Sedar Senghor*. Cambridge, Mass.: Harvard University Press, 1990.

Vambe, Lawrence. *The Ill-Fated People: Zimbabwe Before and After Rhodes*. Pittsburgh: Pittsburgh University Press, 1957.

Van Til, William. *Education: A Beginning*. Boston: Houghton Mifflin Co., 1974.

Watson, George. *Change in School System*. Washington, D.C. National Training Laboratories, NEA, 1967.

Weaver, Thomas (ed.). *To See Ourselves: Anthropology and Modern Social Issues*. Glenview, Ill.: Scott Foresman & Co., 1973.

Wills, A. J. *An Introduction to the History of Central Africa*. London: Oxford University Press, 1964.
Winterbottom, Thomas. *An Account of the Native Africans*. London: Richard Brooks, 1803.
Wirendu, Kwanisi. *Philosophy and the African Culture*. Cambridge: Cambridge University Press, 1980.

GOVERNMENT DOCUMENTS AND MATERIALS

Botswana. *Ten Years of Independence*. Gaberone, 1976.
Botswana. *Botswana Update*. Gaberone, 1982.
Botswana. *Education for Kagisano: Supplementary Report of the National Commission on Education*. Gaberone, July 1979.
Botswana. *Education Statistics*. Gaberone: Government Printer, 1979.
Botswana. *Report of the National Commission on Education*. Gaberone, April 1977.
British South Africa Company Records. Earl Grey, 1896–1898: Folio: AV/1/11/1/11:547–548. Zimbabwe National Archives.
Edwards, Eppie D. Letter dated January 30, 1992, addressed to the author about Edward Long.
Huggins, Godfrey (Prime Minister of Colonial Zimbabwe, 1933–1952, and of the Federation of Rhodesia and Nyasaland, 1953–1956). *Education Policy in Southern Rhodesia: Notes on Certain Features*, 1939.
Huggins, Godfrey. "Partnership in Building a Country." Political speech, December 21, 1950.
Huggins, Godfrey. "Partnership in Rhodesia and Nyasaland." Speech given during a campaign for the establishment of the Federation of Rhodesia and Nyasaland, May 1950.
Huggins, Godfrey. "Rhodesia Leads the Way: Education for Europeans in Southern Rhodesia." *Times Educational Supplement*, February 14, 1931.
Huggins, Godfrey. "Taking Stock of African Education." Address to the Southern Rhodesia Missionary Conference, Goromonzi, August 26, 1954.
Mozambique, Samora Machel, "Leadership in Collective, Responsibility Is Collective." Speech given to the Joint Meeting of Frelimo Instructors, February 2, 1972.
Mozambique, Samora Machel. "Educate Men to Win the War, Create a New Society, and Develop a Country. Speech given at the Second Conference on Education and Culture, September 1970.
Mozambique, Samora Machel. "The Liberation of Women as a Fundamental Necessity for Revolution." Address given at the opening of the First Conference of Mozambique Women, March 4, 1973.
Mozambique. Ministry of Information. *Education in Mozambique*. 1982.
Mozambique. Ministry of Information. *Education in Mozambique*. Maputo, 1982.
Rhodesia. *African Education*. Ref. 738, 1973.

Rhodesia. *Parliamentary Debates*. August 26, 1974, August 27, 1974, August 30, 1974.

Rhodesia. *Report of the Commission of Inquiry into Racial Discrimination* [Vincent Quenet, Chairman] Ref. 27015/36050, April 23, 1976.

Rhodesia. *Education: An Act*, No. 8, 1979.

South Africa. *South Africa Broadcasting Corporation on Political Rights*. Ref. SABC/TV, 1/90, February 2, 1990.

South Africa. *Proclamation over Southwest Africa*. November 27, 1918.

Southern Rhodesia. *Annual Reports of the Director of Native Education*, 1927–1960.

Southern Rhodesia. *Annual Reports of the Secretary for African Education*, 1962–1979.

Southern Rhodesia. *Education Ordinance Number 18: The Appointment of Inspector of Schools*, 1899.

Southern Rhodesia. *Legislative Debates*, 1923–1961.

Southern Rhodesia. *Ordinance Number 1*. 1903.

Tanzania. *Education for Self-Reliance*. Dar es Salaam: Government Printer, 1967.

Zambia Information Service. *Zambia in Brief*. Lusaka, 1975.

Zambia. *Educational Reform: Proposals and Recommendations*. October 1977.

Zambia. K. D. Kaunda. *Blueprint for Economic Development: A Guide on How to Clear Obstacles*. October 8, 1979.

Zimbabwe-Rhodesia. *Report of the Constitutional Conference*. Ref. R2R3, London. Lancaster House. December 21, 1979.

Zimbabwe. *Annual Digest of Statistics*. Harare: Government Printer, 1988.

Zimbabwe. *Annual Report of the Secretary for Education*, 1980–1989. Harare: Government Printer, 1989.

Zimbabwe. B. T. Chidzero, Minister of Finance and Planning. *Budget Statement*, July 27, 1989.

Zimbabwe. *Constitutional Amendment* No. 23, 1987.

Zimbabwe. Mugabe, Robert. "Literacy for All in Five Years." Speech given in launching a national literacy campaign, July 18, 1983.

Zimbabwe. "Not in a Thousand Years: From Rhodesia to Zimbabwe." Documentary film, PBS, 1981.

Zimbabwe. *Prime Minister Opens Economic Conference*. September 5, 1980.

Zimbabwe. Prime Minister [Robert Mugabe, *Address to the Organization of African Unity*]. Document No. 2. Freetown, Sierra Leone, July 4, 1980.

Zimbabwe. *Prime Minister's New Year's Message to the Nation*. December 31, 1980.

Zimbabwe. *The Constitution of Zimbabwe*. Harare: Government Printer, 1985.

Zimbabwe. *The Prime Minister Opens an Economic Symposium*. September 11, 1980.

Zimbabwe. ZAPU. *Primary School Syllabus*, August 1978.

NEWSPAPERS, JOURNALS, AND MAGAZINES

The Chicago Tribune, October 1, 1981.

The Economist. September 30, 1989.

National Geographic Magazine. Vol. 180, No. 5, November 1991.

Time. March 31, 1961.

Zimbabwe. *The Herald:*

> July 10, 1989, "Apartheid Cannot be Condoned."
>
> July 15, 1989, "Secondary Schools Hit by Shortage of Qualified Teachers."
>
> July 17, 1989, "Worry over Schools Zoning."
>
> July 20, 1989, "Mozambique Peace Drive a Concern."
>
> July 24, 1989, "Concept of Education with Production Explained."
>
> July 28, 1989, "Nkomo's Economic Objectives Are a Priority in Resettlement."
>
> July 28, 1989, "University of Zimbabwe Gets $400 Million from Federal Republic of Germany for Developing Equipment."
>
> April 13, 1989, "Mozambique Looks to the World for $450 Million Aid."
>
> August 11, 1989, "Nkomo Lectures University Students."
>
> August 11, 1989, "Sanctions That Would Bite."
>
> August 12, 1989, "President Calls for Revolutionary Land Reform Programs."
>
> August 17, 1989, "Compensation for Teachers Who Joined Freedom Struggle."
>
> May 20, 1994, "Muluzi Takes over from Banda as Malawi's Leader."

ZIMBABWE: MINISTRY OF INFORMATION

Chung, Faye, Minister of Primary and Secondary Education. "Pre-school Training Graduates." Ref. 317/88/GB/SD/BJ, July 25, 1988.

Chung, Faye. "The Importance of Local Production of Science Textbooks." Ref. 80/89/CB/MA. March 9, 1989.

Chung, Faye. "The Role of Booksellers in Educational Development." Ref. 223/89/CB/EM/SM, July 13, 1989.

Chung, Faye. "Women Are Educated Less Than Men." Ref. 230/89/CB/SM/SR, July 25, 1989.

Culverwell, Joseph, Minister of State for National Scholarship. "Take Education Seriously." Ref. 59/88/SL/BC, February 23, 1989.

Culverwell, Joseph. "U.S. Sponsored Students Graduate." Ref. 78/89/CB/MA, March 1, 1989.

Hughes, Aminia, Deputy Minister of Transport. "Be Selfless and Dedicated Teachers." Ref. 482/88/SM, October 28, 1988.

Karimanzira, David, Minister of Social Services. "Educate the People on the Dangers of Agrochemicals." Ref. 399/88/EMM/CB, September 14, 1988.

Karimanzira, David. "Educate Farmers on Better Livestock Production." Ref. 472/88/EMM/SM, October 25, 1988.

Karimanzira, David. "Government to Provide More Extension Staff." Ref. 235/89/EMM/SM/SK, July 25, 1989.

Kay, Jack, Deputy Minister of Lands, Agriculture, and Rural Settlement. "Zimbabwe Is SADDC's Breadbasket." Ref. 384/EMM/SG, August 29, 1988.

Ministry of Higher Education. "Learner-Tutor Course Applications." Ref. 459/88/CB/SM, October 17, 1988.

Ministry of Information. "Vacancies for Zimbabwe-Cuba Teacher Education Course." Ref. 460/88/CB/SM, October 17, 1988.

Ministry of Public Construction and National Housing. "Three Hundred Million Dollars Boost Rural Housing," Ref. 19/89/BC/SK, January 23, 1989.

Moto. Gweru. August 1983–August 1989.

Muchemwa, Felix, Minister of Health. "State Certificated Nurses Graduate in Masvingo." Ref. 29/80/RN/SD/BJ, July 21, 1988.

Mujuru, Joyce, Minister of Community and Cooperative Development. "Women's Role in Nation Building." Ref. 4/1/89/SG/SM, June 6, 1989.

Mutumbuka, Dzingai, Minister of Higher Education. "Marymount Teachers Graduate." Ref. 365/88/03/MM, August 20, 1988.

Mutumbuka, Dzingai. "The Importance of Revising History." Ref. 15/89/CB/SK, January 23, 1989.

Mutumbuka, Dzingai. "The Role of Professional Bodies in National Development." Ref. 427/88/CB/EMM, September 22, 1988.

Mutumbuka, Dzingai. "The University of Zimbabwe Staff Development." Ref. 405/88/CB/ME, September 14, 1988.

Mutumbuka, Dzingai. "Training Institutions Play Vital Role in National Development." Ref. 447/88/CC/ES, October 7, 1988.

National Geographic. Vol. 180, No. 5, November, 1991.

Nkomo, John, Minister of Labor. "A Call for Educational Program." Ref. 356/88/SK/EM/SG, August 17, 1988.

Nyagumbo, Maurice, Minister of Political Affairs. "Zimbabwe Objects to Education of U.N. Transitional Assistance Group." Ref. 7/89/BC/SM, January 13, 1988.

OTHER MATERIALS AND DOCUMENTS

The Chicago Tribune. October 1, 1981.

The Christian Science Monitor, September 7, 1989. "Future Leaders Learn Nextdoor: Namibians Study at U.N. School in Zambia."

The Economist. September 30, 1989.

The Los Angeles Times. "Africa's Future Riding the Train to Nowhere." July 17, 1990.

The New York Times. "Higher Controls Seen in Zimbabwe." December 10, 1989.

The New York Times. "Students Fail Zimbabwe and Pay Heavy Price." November 16, 1989.

The New York Times. "The Old Men versus the Public: Africa's Iron Hands
    Struggle to Hang on." July 15, 1990.
South Africa Scan. *Facts and Reports*. 1989.
Time. July 9, 1990.
Time. March 5, 1990.
The Washington Post. August 1, 1989.
The World Almanac and Book of Facts. 1990.

UN MATERIALS ON AFRICA

The League of Nations Covenant. Article 22, January 20, 1920.
The League of Nations. *The Mandate for Southwest Africa*. May 7, 1920.
UNESCO. *International Conference in Support of the Struggle of the Namibian
    People for Independence*. Paris, April 25–29, 1983.
UNESCO. "Education in Africa in the Light of the Lagos Conference." Paper
    Number 25, 1976.
United Nations Council for Namibia. *Meetings held in Panama City*, June 2–5,
    1981.
United Nations Council for Namibia. *Meetings held in Algeria*, May 28–June 1,
    1980.
United Nations Council on Namibia. *Arusha Declaration and Program of Action
    on Namibia*. May 14, 1982.
United Nations. *A Trust Betrayed: Namibia*. New York, 1974.
United Nations. Decree Number 1. *For the Protection of the Natural Resources of
    Namibia*. New York, September 1974.
United Nations. *Namibia: A Unique UN Responsibility*. New York, December 1981.
United Nations. *Nationhood Program for Namibia*. New York, 1981.
United Nations. *Objective: Justice: Walvis Bay, an Integral Part of Namibia*. A
    statement on the future of Namibia, April 24, 1978.
United Nations. *Plunder of Namibian Uranium*. New York, September 1974.
United Nations. *United Nations Council for Namibia: What It Is, What It Does,
    How It Works*. New York, March 1983.
United Nations. *A Crime Against Humanity: Questions and Answers on Apart-
    heid*. New York, 1984.

MATERIALS ON AFRICA IN GENERAL

The Anglo-Rhodesian Relations: Proposals for a Settlement. Ref. Cmd/RR/46/71,
    November 25, 1971.
ABC-TV. "20/20: *The Agony of Mozambique*." March 2, 1990.
Africa Action Committee. *Uhuru for Southern Africa*. Kinshasa, December 15,
    1984.
Afro-American and African Studies. *Africana*. College Park, Md., Vol. 2, No. 1,
    1985.

Anad, Mohamed. *Apartheid: A Form of Slavery.* New York: U.N. No. 37/71, 1971.

Ayittey, George. "In Africa Independence Is a Far Cry from Freedom." *The Wall Street Journal*, March 28, 1990.

Basson, S.P.N. Administrative Secretary to President F. W. de Klerk. Letter dated March 12, 1990, addressed to Dickson A. Mungazi, Northern Arizona University, Flagstaff, in response to his dated February 15, 1990, addressed to President de Klerk.

British Council of Missionary Society. "Violence in Southern Africa: A Christian Assessment." Statement of policy on Southern Africa, October 28, 1970.

British Methodist Church in Zimbabwe. *The Waddilove Manifesto: The Educational Policy of the Methodist Church.* Statement of policy and principles, February 9, 1946.

Carlson, Brian. "American Education: A South African Perspective in the Process of Desegregation." *Kappa Delta Phi*, Summer 1988.

Center for Applied Research. *Social Implications of the Lagos Plan of Action for Economic Development in Africa, 1980–2000.* Geneva, November 1981.

Central Committee for SWAPO. *Swapo: Political Program of the Southwest Africa People's Organization, Lusaka, July 28–August 1, 1976.*

Churchill, Winston, and Franklin Roosevelt. *The Atlantic Charter*, August 14, 1941.

Congolese National Liberation Front (CNLF). *The Struggle for Liberation.* New York, 1975.

Davidson, Basil. *Africa: New Nations and Problems.* Documentary film, Arts and Entertainment, 1988.

Dodge, Ralph E. A Political Community. Unpublished essay, May 1964.

Dodge, Ralph. The Church and Political Community. Unpublished essay, 1963.

Evans, M. *The Front-Line State, South Africa and Southern African Security: Military Prospects and Perspectives.* Harare. University of Zimbabwe, 1989.

Gordimer, Nadine. *Gold and the Gun: Crisis in Mozambique and South Africa.* Documentary film, Arts and Entertainment, 1990.

Landis, Elizabeth. "Apartheid and the Disabilities of Women in South Africa." New York: United Nations Unit on Apartheid, 1975.

Loveridge, F. G., Senior Education Officer in the Ministry of African Education, Zimbabwe. "Disturbing Realities of Western Education in Southern Africa." Address to the Rotary Club International, Harare, March 13, 1963.

M'Bow, Amadou-Mahtar. "Unesco Director-General, Unesco and the Promotion of Education for International Understanding." Address to the New York African Studies Association Conference, Albany, New York, October 29, 1982.

Macmillan, Harold. "Commonwealth Independence and Interdependence." Address to the Joint Session of the South African Parliament, Cape Town, February 3, 1960.

Maier, Karl. "Opponent May Thwart Mugabe's Bid for a One-party System." *The Washington Post*, March 29, 1990.

Malianga, Morton, a spokesman for ZANU. "We Shall Wage an All Out War to Liberate Ourselves." Statement issued on April 30, 1966, following a battle between the colonial forces and the African nationalist guerrillas on April 29.

Mandela, Nelson. "A Statement Made in Cape Town Soon After His Release from Victor Verster Prison." SABC, February 11, 1990.

Mandela, Nelson. "Speech Given in Soweto During a Reception Held in His Honor." February 12, 1990.

McHarg, James. "Influences Contributing to Education and Culture of Native People in Southern Rhodesia." Ph.D. diss., Duke University, 1962.

McNamara, Robert. "The Challenge of Sub-Sahara Africa." In John Crawford Lectures, Washington, D.C., November 1, 1985.

Mnegi wa Dikgang. *Education with Production* 5, No. 2, Gaberone, June 1987.

Molotsi, Peter, Fordham University. "Educational Policies and the South African Bantustans." Paper presented at the New York Association of African Studies, Albany, New York, October 29–30, 1982.

Morton, Donald. "Partners in Apartheid." New York Center for Social Action; United Church of Christ, 1973.

Mozambique. "Documento Informativo." Ref. Doc/Inf.01/11, Maputo, 1979.

Mungazi, Dickson A. "A Strategy for Power: Commissions of Inquiry into Education and Government Control in Zimbabwe." *The International Journal of African Historical Studies* 22, No. 2 (1989).

Mungazi, Dickson A. "Apartheid in South Africa: Origin, Meaning, and Effect." Documentary film, Audio-Visual Services, Education, Northern Arizona University. Ref. AC/ECC/2/90, February 22, 1990.

Mungazi, Dickson A. "Educational Innovation in Zimbabwe: Possibilities and Problems." *Journal of Negro Education* 54, No. 2 (1985).

Mungazi, Dickson A. "The Application of Memmi's Theory of the Colonizer and the Colonized." *The Journal of Negro Education 55, No. 4 (1986)*.

Mungazi, Dickson A. "To Bind Ties Between the School and Tribal Life: Educational Policy for Africans under George Stark in Zimbabwe. *The Journal of Negro Education* 58, No. 4 (1989).

Mungazi, Dickson A. Letter dated February 15, 1990, addressed to President F. W. de Klerk of South Africa, on the effect of apartheid on Southern Africa.

Mungazi, Dickson A. "Educational Policy for Africans and Church-State Conflict During the Rhodesia Front Government in Zimbabwe." *The National Social Science Journal* 2, No. 3 (June 1990).

Mutumbuka, Dzingai. "Zimbabwe's Educational Challenge." Paper read at the World University Services Conference, London, December 1979.

New York Friends Group, Inc. *South Africa: Is Peaceful Change Possible?* New York, 1984.

OAU. "A Communique on Mozambique," Nairobi, Kenya, August 8, 1989.

Office on Africa Educational Fund. *The Struggle for Justice in South Africa.* Washington, D.C., February 1984.

PBS. "Not in a Thousand Years: From Rhodesia to Zimbabwe." Documentary film, 1982.

"Prospects of a Settlement in Angola and Namibia." Statement by the Parties [Representatives of the U.S.A., Angola, SWAPO, Cuba].

Rhodesia Front Government. *The Dynamic Expansion in African Education.* Policy Statement. Ref. INF/NE/Acc.40/2710, April 20, 1966.

Riddell, Roger. *From Rhodesia to Zimbabwe: Alternatives to Poverty.* A position paper. Gweru: Mambo Press, 1978.

Rubin, Leslie. "Bantustan Policy: A Fantasy and a Fraud." New York: United Nations Unit on Apartheid, Number 12/71, 1971.

Smith, Arthur, Minister of Education in Rhodesia. An Interview with Geoffrey Atkins of the Rhodesia Broadcasting Service on educational Policy for Africans, January 31, 1968.

Smuts, J. C. *The League of Nations: A Practical Suggestion.* 1918.

South African Ministry of Information. "South Africa Stops Native Students from Territories from Attending Its Schools." Press release, November 2, 1950.

Southern Rhodesia. United Federal Party. *Information Statement.* Ref. UFP/SR/9, 1961.

Sullivan, Leon. "Meeting the Mandate for Change: A Progress Report on the Application of the Sullivan Principles on U.S. Companies in South Africa." New York, 1984

Tanzania. *Basic Facts about Education.* Dar es Salaam: Government Printer, 1984.

Tanzania. *Education for Self-reliance.* Dar es Salaam: Government Printer, 1967.

Thompson Publications. *Parade.* Harare, August 1989.

TransAfrica. *Namibia: The Crisis in U.S. Policy Toward Southern Africa.* Washington, D.C., 1983.

United Methodist Church. *Resolution Warning the Government of Southern Rhodesia against Continued Policy of Discrimination.* Harare, 1963.

United Methodist Church. *Southern Africa.* New York: Board of Global Ministries, 1986.

University of Cape Town. "A Call for Postdoctoral Research Fellows, 1991." *The Chronicle of Higher Education*, March 16, 1990.

Washington Office on Africa. *Resources on Namibia.* Washington, D.C., March 1982.

Watson, P. *The Struggle for Democracy.* Documentary film, PBS, 1988.

World Bank, "Alternatives to Formal Education: Unesco Conference on Education." Harare, June 28–July 3, 1982.

World Bank. *Accelerate Development in Sub-Sahara Africa: An Agenda for Action.* Washington, D.C.: World Bank, 1983.

World Council of Churches, Involvement in the Struggles Against Oppression in Southern Africa, 1966–1980.

ZANU. *Liberation Through Participation: Women in the Zimbabwean Revolution.* Harare: ZANU, 1981.

ZANU. *Zimbabwe: Election Manifesto*, 1979.

Zimbabwe Conference of Catholic Bishops. *Our Mission to Teach: A Pastoral Statement on Education.* Gweru: Mambo Press, 1987.

Zimbabwe Ministry of Education. *School Library News* (Harare) 6, No. 60 (July 1986).

Zimbabwe. Ministry of Information. Press Statements, Speeches by Government Officials on Education.

Zimbabwe. *The Herald.* July 4, 1983; August 8, 1989.

Zimbabwe. *The Sunday Mail.* August 1989, "Teachers Form Union."

Index

Kenya African Union (KAU), 139
Kenyatta, Jomo, xxix, 77, 100, 101,
125, 218; *On Facing Mount
Kenya*, 135; and Kenyan inde-
pendence, 134–41
Kerr Commission, 114
Kikuyu, 137–38
Kimathi, Dedan, 140
Kimba, Evariste, 191–92
Kimbangu, Simon, 154–55
King, Martin Luther, Jr., 2
kings, 44, 56 n.20
Kipling, Rudyard, 135, 150
Knorr, Kenneth, 26
Korsah, Arku, 180
Kublai Khan, 6
Kunze, Neil, xvii

labor, 105, 106, 122 n.28, 127, 204,
210
Labour party, 118
Lagos Island, 132–33
land, stewardship of, 47–48
Land Commission, 76
Laugi, 219
Lenin, Vladimir, 179, 198 n.6
Lennox-Boyd, Allan, 145, 146, 147
Leopold II, 151, 152–53, 154, 210
Lesotho, 164–65 n.18
Lewis, Oscar, 205, 206
Liberation Committee, 175
Liberia, xxv, 128, 225
Libya, 128
Limann, Hilla, 226
Lincoln, Abraham, 179
Lissouba, Pascal, 187
literacy, 68; need for, 69–72, 73, 74–
75, 174–75
Livingstone, David, 23–24, 36, 141–
42, 151–52
Lobengula, King Khumalo, 35–36,
42, 50, 67, 90 n.20, 142–43; nego-
tiation with, 36–39

London Anthropological Society, 20–
21
London Missionary Society, 23, 36,
141
Long, Edward, xviii, 21
Lule, Yusufu, 226
Lumumba, Patrice, xxix, 125, 132,
155–56, 199 n.32, 218; leadership
of, 188–91
Luthuli, Albert, xxix, 28, 82, 218
Lyons, Charles, 1, 16

Machel, Samora, 63, 194
Macmillan, Harold, 132, 141, 148
Maguire, Rochfort, 36
Makonnen, Ras, 100
Malawi, xv, xvi, xxxii, 148, 149, 196,
229, 231, 233
Malianga, Washington, 150
Malinga, L. M., 158
Mandela, Nelson, xx, xxxi, 218, 227,
228; politics of, 159–63
Mangisto, Mariam, xxv
Mangwende, Helen, 122–23 n.47
Manuel I, 7, 8
Margai, Milton, xxix
Marriage, 49–50
Marx, Karl, 135
Mathu, Eliud, 139
Mau Mau uprising, 99, 139–40, 221
Mazzrui, Ali, 175
Mboya, Tom, 132
Mcerwa, Thami, 159
Meany, John, 203, 204
Memmi, Albert, 59, 72, 93, 94–95,
121, 201, 209, 211; *The Colonizer
and the Colonized*, 60–63, 125–
26; on culture of violence, 215–
16; on racism, 207–8
The Merchant of Venice (Shake-
speare), 2, 17
Meredith, Martin, 98, 135, 223
Methodist Church, 70, 112

About the Author

DICKSON A. MUNGAZI is Regents Professor of Education and History
at Northern Arizona University.

ISBN 0-275-95260-6

90000>

9 780275 952600

HARDCOVER BAR CODE